Appo

Recollections of a member of the Sydney Push

Also by Richard Appleton

Poetry:
I am the World (1953)

Reference:
The Cambridge Dictionary of Australian Places
    (1992, with Barbara Appleton)

As editor:
There Was a Crooked Man: The Poems of Lex Banning
    (1987, with Alex Galloway)
'*Brave British Boys*': *Memoirs of Cook Year 1946* (2003)

Appo

Recollections of a member of the Sydney Push

Richard Appleton

DARLINGTON PRESS

First published by Darlington Press 2009
Darlington Press is an imprint of SYDNEY UNIVERSITY PRESS

Fisher Library F03, University of Sydney NSW 2006 Australia
Email: info@sup.usyd.edu.au

National Library of Australia Cataloguing-in-Publication entry
Author: Appleton, Richard, 1932–2005
Title: Appo : recollections of a member of the Sydney Push /
                Richard Appleton
ISBN: 9781921364099 (pbk.)
Notes: Includes index.
Subjects: Appleton, Richard, 1932–2005
                Authors, Australian--20th century--Biography.
                Libertarianism--New South Wales--Sydney.
                Sydney (N.S.W.)--Social conditions--1945–.
Dewey Number: A828.309

Front cover: Portrait of the author by David Perry, 1963–4
        (photo: Peter Arnot)
Back cover: Dick Appleton at *The Australian Encyclopaedia*, 1974
        (photo: Alex Skovron)
Cover design: Miguel Yamin, the University Publishing Service
Typeset in MinionPro 10.5/12.6

Contents

Acknowledgements

Richard, known to some as Dick and to others as Appo, was keen that readers might share his recollections — and smile. His was a life of contrasts, and he knew well that any one person could provide only glimpses of a complex, changing scene. He died in 2005, and thus I am left to thank all those whose help and interest he truly appreciated.

Many people have assisted in the completion of this book. Firstly, I thank Richard's elder daughters, Kirsten and Helen, who had urged him to put on paper some details of experiences which stretched from the Depression of the 1930s to the depressing years of the Howard government.

On receiving the first experimental chapter, A.J. (Jim) Baker asked that more be written, and quickly, for the readers of his magazine *Heraclitus*. Accordingly, these recollections were published in issues 99–114 of the magazine, from August 2002 to April 2004. For his encouragement I thank Jim deeply.

As far as was possible, every individual mentioned in a personal context was consulted before that original publication. For the support and the information freely given, Dick and I were both grateful. Rather than list those individuals, I thank them all. A smaller number provided frequent feedback: Jean Curthoys, André Frankovits, Terry McMullen and Albie Thoms were among these. Others offered criticism, and I thank them: statements from Dorothy Addison-Walsh, Robin Appleton and Mark Weblin led to certain amendments. Others again, from widely divergent periods of Richard's life, came forward after his death offering help to see that the book was published in a unified form. For this loyalty and thoughtfulness, I thank them also.

Thanks are due as well to those who collected and offered photographic and other material, including Ross Free, Geoff Mill and Doug Nicholson. Space did not permit the inclusion of it all. Particular thanks go to Lyn Collingwood for picture research, to David Perry for use of the well-loved portrait on the cover, and to Alan Walker for preparation of the index.

Special acknowledgement is made to Dr Anne Banning for permission to include works by Lex Banning, to Faber & Faber for permission to include the poem by T.S. Eliot, and to Margaret Fink for permission to include poems by Harry Hooton. John Olsen was most gracious in allowing the publication of his personal note and cartoon.

I need, too, to thank our daughter Beth, who has supported me through both my time of grief and my passion to see Richard's story reach a wider readership. To that end, I am indebted to Sydney University Press and its Business Manager, Susan Murray-Smith, for enabling me to attain his goal.

Lastly, I am profoundly grateful to Richard's friend and colleague, Alex Skovron, who read all the copy as it was written and later agreed to edit the manuscript. Alex's patient and meticulous work, as well as his moral support, has been invaluable.

Barbara Appleton
August 2009

Introduction

About halfway through the year 2003 the expatriate Australian cultural commentator Clive James pronounced me dead. In a book of essays published at that time he wrote:

> If you read Ezra Pound early on — and when I was coming of age in Australia in the late 1950s we all did — you can spend a lifetime wondering how he ever got under your skin. He was still alive when my bunch were getting started, and one of us, Richard Appleton, the black-clad glamour boy of Sydney's Downtown Push, was in regular correspondence with him. (Though the Downtown Push was more concerned with gambling than with the arts, the occasional poet was allowed in as long as he showed clear signs of dissipation.) … Appleton, who was born with a formal sense that made his meticulous carpentry poetic in itself, was among the most gifted young Australian poets of his time. But his obsession with Pound was as fatal to his mind as his impression that Benzedrine was a form of food was fatal to his body. Appleton suppressed the natural coherence of his gift in order to sound like the *Cantos*, an aim in which he succeeded all too well. By the time of his premature death, his poems were not only in fragments, he was *calling* them fragments — always a bad sign. His self-induced disintegration as an artist was a *memento mori* that I never forgot …[1]

On 28 June 2003, very shortly before *As of This Writing* was published, James had been broadcast together with Peter Porter on the ABC's national radio series *Book Talk*. The subject was 'Sex and Love in Literature and the Arts', and among such august literary names as Flaubert, Dickens, Evelyn Waugh, Kingsley Amis and Philip Roth, my name was mentioned. James recited, from memory he said, a poem of mine called 'The Red Rose and the Briar', written in the 1950s. (That poem is reproduced in chapter 6 of this book.)

About my poem James used such phrases as 'psychologically subtle' and 'magnificent formal sense'. Consequently when, just after that program was broadcast, he learnt that I was still among the living, and telephoned me to apologise for declaring me dead in his forthcoming book, I was happy to forgive him. After all, not everybody gets to read his own obituary, and a glowing one at that.

Had I, as James assumed, departed this world in the 1950s, one of the main strands of these recollections would no longer be relevant. (Besides which, I obviously couldn't have written them at all.) That strand is my flight from the spectre of respectability; in that flight I fled to another spectre, one said by Karl Marx to be haunting Europe — communism. But communism, at least in Australia, was very respectable indeed, or at least the members of the party advocating it were. It was through that Sydney Push, referred to above by James, that I managed my escape. My experiences with the Push form another strand of this book.

Unlike the pursuit of happiness or of an orgasm, both of which I will argue tend to elude one when pursued, respectability tends to sneak up on one from behind, and subvert one's critical iconoclasm. The price of apostasy is determined dissent, and the Push was prepared to pay that price. Other books, all of dubious quality, have been written about the Push. Mainly, they have focused on its sexual promiscuity. As a matter of course, I too mention some instances of Push sexual behaviour, but if that had been all there was to the Push it would have differed little from other bohemian groups.

My life in the Push is intricately entwined with the remaining major strand of these recollections: my transmogrification into an encyclopaedist. But for my involvement with what there then was of the intellectual life of Sydney (in the 1950s), it is unlikely that I would have gained the literacy and self-confidence to drift into such an arcane profession. Later, several Push academics became contributors to *The Australian Encyclo-paedia* during my editorship of that all-Australia-embracing reference work. The history of the encyclopaedia, outlined in some of the following pages, is interesting in its own right.

Except where it is necessary for the continuity of my own story, I do not in these recollections discuss my children or my former wives or lovers. Their private lives, and mine, remain at least partly so.

1 And Then, to the Lincoln

It was late in 1949 that my elder brother, Harold Appleton, departed these shores for England, supposedly never to return. When he left he abdicated his title, as had the former king, Edward VIII. Like that king's brother, I inherited the title, and like him I was for a time inarticulate in my new role. Harold's friends (Appo's friends) became my friends, though at first they referred to me only as 'Appo's brother'; later, *I* became Appo.

This circle of friends is pivotal to my story. They included, among others, Lex Banning, John Olsen, Beth Doran, Lester Hiatt, Peter Hellier and Lillian Roxon, most of them aspiring to be writers, painters, singers, actors, academics, etc, or at least posing as such. My brother was sailing to England to become a Gielgud or an Olivier, a peak that he felt one could not achieve in Australia. I myself had some claims to being a poet, and later aspired to be as great as Homer or Dante, and certainly greater than Shakespeare. (Ezra Pound once wrote that he named his son Homer Shakespeare Pound, in precise order of importance, but at seventeen I was not burdened by such humility.) When my brother's ship had torn itself free from its myriad of colourful streamers, these friends, or some of them, took me with them to the Lincoln Coffee Lounge.

This Mecca of the Australian arts was in Rowe Street, Sydney, then a narrow lane parallel to and between King Street and Martin Place, and joining Pitt Street to Castlereagh (which it no longer reaches). Opposite the Lincoln's tiny entrance stood the doorway to the Long Bar of the Hotel Australia, then Sydney's most reputable venue for social and formal events. But downstairs in the Lincoln a very different world awaited.

If one of Sydney's then frequent electricity blackouts was afflicting that city, from the top of the Lincoln's stairs one looked down on almost Stygian gloom, punctuated by the gleam of minute kerosene lamps, which sent pungent fumes mingling with those of tobacco smoke and the aroma of coffee to welcome one into the underworld. On the walls hung would-be Satanic paintings by Rosaleen Norton, whose exhibition at Melbourne University in that year had been raided by police because of its alleged obscenity. Around small tables sat groups of mainly young men and women, arguing animatedly about politics and painting, poetry and philosophy, sex and sociology, science fiction and the meaning of life.

Many of them were clad in corduroy, the women wore pony-tails and no make-up, and the men, or many of them, wore beards. As I was to learn later, art students could be identified by the blobs of dried paint decorating their apparel (probably not always left there on purpose); some drama students by still displaying grease-paint on their necks and collars, left over from the previous night's, or week's, rehearsals (definitely left there on purpose); but writers had to make do with a display of fountain-pens, preferably leaking. For my youthful self, recently discharged from the Royal Australian Naval College (of which more later), this was not only a very different world but a wildly exciting one. So I hastened to join it.

To some extent the romantic climate of the Lincoln is summed up by a song written by Martin Haberman, an American then enrolled as a psychology honours student at Sydney University. It was sung to the tune of 'The Streets of Laredo' (though the advice 'if it's too silly to say, then sing it' is perhaps applicable). Until 1999, the philosophy professor David Armstrong thought that I was the author; I wasn't, but it *is* possible that I was at least partly the subject. My memory of the words is as follows:

> As I walked out in the streets of old Sydney
> I met a young artist a-minus one kidney,

His eyes they were bloodshot, his face it was green;
'Twas plain he'd been taking too much Benzedrine.

With an effort I parted his pale lips so thin
And therein inserted my last flask of gin;
In the next thirty minutes, before he grew cold,
His heart-rending, tear-jerking story he told:

'In the days of my youth I used to go drinkin',
'Twas first to the Long Bar and then to the Lincoln.
I thought I had friends, but it happened this way:
They were not my friends 'cause they led me astray.

'I gave a small party for folks who were arty,
I'll tell you what happened, or haven't you guessed?
At five in the morning 'twas going right smartly.
The very next dawning I got dispossessed.

'My friends were all sorry, they bid me not worry,
As kindly sad tears of compassion they shed;
And ever so kindly a place they would find me
— in the clothes closet or under the bed.

'I quickly grew haggard as weakly I staggered,
My face had the look of a man in a dream;
Though I knew that I shouldn't, a medical student
One morning advised me to take Benzedrine.'

His eyes they were sunken, his cheeks they were shrunken,
He smiled the sad smile of a man who's to die;
And, as I leant closer, he said, with a sigh,
'Tell all my kind friends at the Lincoln, Goodbye.'

His eyes then grew glassy, his spirit flew past me,
With a last drunken shout, to its maker it sped.

> The clouds then grew darker, the pale moonlight fled
> From the place where the poor suffering artist lay dead.

This perhaps represents the romantic climate of the Lincoln, but it is at odds with its intellectual climate. Among the Lincoln's regulars, as well as artists, writers, etc, there were students of philosophy at Sydney University who were strongly influenced by the empirical and realist theories of Professor John Anderson. It was in that year, 1949, that the prime minister, Robert Menzies, having resumed office after eight years in opposition, sought to ban the Communist Party of Australia. Though ardently opposed to communism, Anderson argued against the party being banned, but his hatred of Stalinism had expanded to include any form of Marxism, or indeed socialism. It was those students of Anderson who objected to his moving further to the right who began promulgating Libertarianism at the Lincoln.

Until the 1950s the theories that came to be known as Sydney Libertarianism were not fully formulated, but those who were to become its advocates constituted by 1949 an identifiable group with common interests. The literary and artistic groups referred to them as 'The Push' (a label that they themselves had already adopted), and attempted, usually unsuccessfully, to exclude them from their parties. But most of the writers' and painters' groups, of which I had become a member, had no objection to turning up at Push parties, and gradually most of these groups merged. They all came to be known as the wider, or downtown, Push. It was the Libertarians' input, though, that distinguished the Lincoln's bohemia from other bohemian gatherings.

So what is or was Sydney Libertarianism? This is not the place and nor am I the person to write a thesis describing it, but in my view it has at least three main strands. Some would argue that following and betting on horse-racing and playing cards for high stakes make up a fourth strand, but I am competent to discuss only three. The first comes from Wilhelm

Reich via John Anderson. In the *Australasian Journal of Psychology and Philosophy* in 1941 Anderson wrote:

> In fact, it is especially in regard to sexuality that the conception of sin finds application and that 'guilt' is felt; and it may be that, without exercising some command over the sexual life of the lower orders, authorities could never keep them docile.[2]

Reich's theory of the association between sexual and political liberty was accepted by Sydney Libertarians with fewer qualifications than those of Anderson. Libertarians argued that political liberty could be attained only in a society that was sexually libertarian and uninhibited. It seems to me that this theory is inevitably linked with the pursuit of an orgasm. And sometimes I wonder whether the pursuit of an orgasm is not just as futile as the pursuit of happiness, even though the former is not enshrined in the Constitution of the United States of America. Both experiences are presumably desirable, but if pursued too anxiously both also tend to elude their pursuers.

The second strand is 'permanent protest' (a term that surely owes something to Leon Trotsky's 'permanent revolution'). Jim Baker describes it as follows:

> The Libertarian Society was founded at the University of Sydney in 1952 by some of the adherents of the philosophy of Professor John Anderson, partly in reaction to what they saw as Anderson's growing conservatism. The Libertarians asserted anti-authoritarian views at a time when Australian attitudes were generally conventional and conformist. Their influence spread ... especially to a wider 'lumpen-intellectual' group known as The Push.
>
> Sydney Libertarianism criticises traditional political, religious, moral and sexual views ... It agrees with some of Karl Marx's social theory, but criticises Marxism for 'Statism' and illiberalism ... It upholds what it calls

'permanent protest' or 'anarchism without ends' — that is, a permanent struggle to keep alive libertarian values and interests.[3]

While in general agreement with this strand, I fell foul of some Libertarians because of it. Shortly after my accession to the title 'Appo' and my acceptance by the Lincoln underworld, I joined the Communist Party. This, and my later embracing of Trotskyism, and, still later, joining the Australian Labor Party, led to my being labelled a 'meliorist' — a Libertarian term of obloquy similar to the Stalinist term of abuse, 'reformist'.

The third strand, and the one with which I found myself most in agreement, was pluralism. In 1960 David Ivison wrote:

> In brief, this social theory is based on a pluralist view of society, on the recognition that any society is composed of a number of different ways of going on. These different social activities are never completely reconcilable; there is no lowest common denominator among the ways of going on which would give rise to some consensus of which the state (or any other institution) could be the guardian. Different social groups just do pursue different activities, and these activities often conflict. What [do] occur are compromises and limited agreements, concessions in return for the implementation of some parts of a policy, and these compromises, concessions and adjustments are sometimes made through the machinery of the state. However, the state is never an impartial arbiter, but a biased referee, a system of social activities which [has] interests of [its] own.[4]

There were, of course, theories postulated in the Lincoln other than those put forward by Libertarians. The most notable of these were the anarchotechnocrat utopias of Harry Hooton, but there were also Stalinists, Trotskyists, traditional anarchists, socialists, liberals, conservatives and fascists. Many of these are discussed in a subsequent chapter. This chapter concludes with my inability, at first, to live up to the first strand of

Libertarianism — and so, by the theory behind that strand, presumably to my being doomed, at least for a time, to an authoritarian future.

At the time of my discovery of the Lincoln I was rigged out as a respectable middle-class seventeen-year-old was expected to be — grey flannel trousers, tweed sports jacket, shirt and subdued tie, and shiny shoes. Over all of these props I was enveloped in an aura of British-Australian superiority to all foreigners, including what Anderson called 'the lower orders'. I soon put paid to all that, or tried to.

I was until then domiciled at my guardian's Edwardian-style household in Mosman, a suburb deemed by Lincoln regulars to be beyond the black stump. Because I had enlisted in the permanent navy before a peace treaty formally ending World War II had been signed — though long after the last shot had been fired and a second nuclear bomb, of a different type, tried out on Japan to see if it worked — I was paid a Commonwealth Reconstruction Training Scheme (CRTS) allowance while I was furthering my education. So I could afford to cast off the chains of respectability and move out. I packed some books and clothes and did so. After purchasing a corduroy jacket and a beret to signal my adherence to the Lincoln's bohemian code, I rented a bed-sitter in a rooming-house slum in Paddington.

In 1949 Paddington was far from the trendy and elite suburb it has since become. Many, if not most, of its dwellings were rooming houses bursting at the seams with their numerous residents, and it was also the sly-grog capital of Sydney. At that time, alcohol could be purchased legally only from pubs, and only between 10.00 am and 6.00 pm for six days of the week, and not at all on Sundays. I made use of this local amenity only once or twice, because sly-grog prices, like those of any other substance sold illegally, were ridiculously high. First it was necessary to hail a taxi (neither I nor most of my friends then had telephones), even when one lived within walking distance, and order the driver, 'To

Caledonia Street for grog'. When the taxi arrived at the first sly-grog outpost the driver was instructed to douse his lights; at the next, money and one's order were demanded; then, at the scene of the crime, one was handed a sugar-bag full of bottles, and the driver was instructed not to turn on his headlights until he was out of the street.

My Paddington room had a bare 40-watt light globe, a gas ring, a washing basin, a single bed (75 centimetres wide), a table with a single chair — its sole claim to being a bed-sitter — and a wardrobe. The toilet and bathroom were communal. In the latter the landlady had glued a notice to the wall demanding that tenants leave the facilities as they found them. This was difficult to do unless one worked at a dirty job and bathed only once a week — otherwise it was impossible to match the grot already in the bath. A minimal selection of cooking utensils and cutlery was also provided. This sparse living space offered me the same sexual potential as enjoyed by most other habitués of the Lincoln, provided that the landlady chose not to notice. But my one attempt to realise this potential turned into a humiliating farce.

Clad in my new uniform, beret and all, I became a regular at the Lincoln. On one wintry occasion when, as well as my beret, I was wearing an overcoat with its copious collar turned up about my cheeks as I descended the Lincoln's stairs, Lex Banning's voice came spluttering up from below: 'Somebody should inform that young man that the Spanish Civil War is over!'

On my second or third visit a woman called Anne, who had known my brother (probably in the biblical sense as well), insisted that I take her to see my room. Together we boarded a tram and were trundled along Oxford Street to Paddington and nervously (on my part) walked to the terrace and climbed the stairs to my room. What, I asked myself, was the correct next step? To procrastinate, I made us both a pot of tea, and dawdled for some time over my own cup. It was obvious what Anne then wanted me to do, but I was far too unsure of myself to take the first step, and she apparently not sufficiently uninhibited to take it herself. So we left that room, in an awkward silence, and another tram trundled us back to the Lincoln. I don't imagine that Anne was highly motivated by either lust or love — she simply wanted to be the one to 'take the cherry' of Appo's brother.

On another occasion my inhibitions humiliated me even more. One evening after a party, Barry Kennedy (of whom more later), a woman called Joan, another young woman whom I shall call B, and I took ourselves to Joan's small Kings Cross room. There, Barry and Joan had the luxury of sharing Joan's single bed, while B and I made do under a blanket on the floor. I managed some sexual foreplay, but still could not bring myself to touch her genitals, let alone proceed to their conjunction with mine. Despite this, or perhaps because of it, B and I remain warm friends more than fifty years later.

Why was I so inhibited? A little self-pitying excursion into my life before the Lincoln is now in order. And besides, I have yet to get myself born.

2   Three *Was* a Crowd

Anno Domini 1932 continued the Great Depression, an era probably as much dominated by economic hypochondria as is our own; but it also ushered in the opening of the Sydney Harbour Bridge, the establishment of the Australian Broadcasting Company (as the ABC was at first called), and the election of Franklin D. Roosevelt to the presidency of the United States. As well, in mid-January, it ushered in me.

I remember some snatches of my early childhood. I remember recovering from pneumonia (unexpectedly, in those pre-antibiotic days), and the strange feeling of wearing shoes and socks again and trying, not very successfully, to stand up and walk. I remember my calf-love for Suzie, a little German Jewish refugee girl in my infants class at Mosman Public School, and the afternoon there when my older sister and brother failed for some reason to collect me from school, though I don't remember how I got home. I remember my mother admonishing me for shouting 'Heil Hitler', because Hitler was 'not a nice man'. And I remember the last time that I saw my mother, in a private hospital in Mosman.

There, I insisted on arranging the flowers that my grandmother had brought. This angered her so much (or, more likely, she later was so irrational because of her grief at her daughter's death) that she told me my mother had died because I was naughty with the flowers. I was about six at the time, and my mother actually died of kidney disease. But grandmother was adept at allocating blame; she also blamed my father, whom she hated, for his wife's death, asserting that she contracted the disease because he rented a house in Thompson Street, Mosman, which necessitated her climbing a steep hill to go shopping. (If this were the case, kidney disease must have been rife among residents of Katoomba!)

My mother's death catapulted me into learning rapidly how to cope with adults, and I soon developed enough deviousness to contend with theirs. This was largely because of the enmity between my grandmothers. The maternal one, Rita (Sarah Henrietta) Kellner (née Button), was said to be the daughter of a former governor of Bombay. Nobody named Button ever governed Bombay, and Rita's father, who died when she was two or three years old, was a grazier in the Gulgong region. But then, Rita was thought by some to be a Russian princess. Never mind that she had married a Prussian herbalist, (Ernst Heinrich) August Kellner, in Paddington, Sydney, in 1896; she wasn't about to let anybody forget her claims to superiority. She and August had four children, of whom my mother, Valeska Cameroux Kellner, was the third. Valeska was married against the wishes of her mother to Laurence Appleton, an Australian industrial chemist. Rita strongly disapproved of Laurence, seeing him merely as some sort of tradesman. Consequently she refused to see her elder daughter again until Valeska's first child, my sister Betty, was already two years old. My grandfather, August, paid for mother's wedding dress, but that is all that I know of him even now, other than that he was interned during World War I (though his elder son, Oscar, was then fighting against Germans in France) and that he died in 1930. Rita never spoke of him, and nor did her surviving daughter, Mabel. It was an ageing and bitter, but loving, Rita with whom I lived immediately after Valeska died.

Rita's circumstances were relatively penurious; she was dependent, I think, on an allowance from her younger son, (Heinrich) Aubrey Kellner. As the Depression ended and World War II began, we lived in a succession of boarding houses in Cremorne and Neutral Bay. During this time my father enlisted in the AIF, and my sister Betty had been taken into the home of a friend of Valeska's, one of four spinster sisters living together in Mosman. My brother, Harold, had been placed with my father's sister, Eileen, and her husband, Eric Blackwell, who lived on a small cattle station near Tabulam, in north-eastern New South Wales. But there was no way that my father was about to let me stay with Rita, whom he saw as the adversary of both himself and his mother. Their problem was who would have me.

My paternal grandmother, Minnie, was born Helena Minnie Pickering in England. She had been fairly prosperous during her marriage to Joseph Ambrose Appleton, who had ship-owning interests and was a company managing director. But after he died in 1907 she, too, had a lean period during which she owned and presided over a boarding house to maintain herself and her five children, of whom my father (born 1900) was the youngest. Her finances changed for the better in 1910, when she married Harold Whitelaw, a former boarder of hers who was a fairly senior public servant. Minnie Whitelaw, too, disapproved of my parents' marriage: her youngest son had been treacherous enough to marry 'the daughter of a *German*'!

Soon I found myself something of a shuttlecock between these two ladies. On one occasion Rita sent me by taxi, cash on delivery, to stay with my father at Minnie's house in Mosman. When the taxi with its penniless passenger arrived there, nobody was home. Neighbours, I think, paid for the cab. On another occasion I was stupid enough to praise one grandmother's cooking to the other, and consequently was sent to bed without any supper.

At that time my brother, Harold, was boarding during the school term at Hurlstone Agricultural High School, and returning to the Blackwells at Tabulam each school vacation. On one such holiday my father instructed Rita that I was to travel by train to Casino with Harold, to be met there and driven to Tabulam. His purpose was never explained to me, but presumably he hoped that they would keep me there with my brother. They apparently decided, though, that fostering one child was enough.

Shortly before my father sailed overseas with the AIF he arranged (or more likely demanded) that Rita put me on an overnight train to Grafton, to stay there with his brother, Reginald Appleton, and his wife, Dorothy. This Rita unwillingly did, but because of wartime travel restrictions, and aged only about seven, I had to travel on my own. When the train arrived at South Grafton station the following afternoon I was asked by fellow-passengers whether I wanted to get off there or travel on to the smaller Grafton station across the Clarence River. Naturally, I did not know (and nor probably had Rita known), but I decided to get off anyway. As it happened, I chose correctly.

In retrospect, it is clear that my father hoped that Uncle Reg would take me in, at least until the end of the war, and thus thwart his mother-in-law (or, more charitably, that he wanted to provide me with a family environment). While living for just one term with Reg and Dot Appleton, I attended Grafton Public School, but my uncle, with three sons of his own, did not want a fourth, so I was once again sent back to Sydney.

While I was on my way back, Dot Appleton rang Rita, saying 'Oh, Mrs Kellner, he thinks that he is going back to you, but he isn't!' A solution had been found: I was, in fact, bound for a Church of England 'boys' home', less euphemistically known as an orphanage. As a result of the Depression, and later the casualties of World War II, there was no short-age of inmates for such institutions.

Minnie Whitelaw took me to that institution by taxi, and on arrival asked me whether I would like to live there. The building was a run-down Victorian mansion of two storeys, with large but long-neglected grounds, and did not look at all inviting. I was by then devious enough to know that I had to compose my answer so that it was ambiguous, so I said brightly 'Where else *can* I go?', obviously enunciated as a rhetorical question. But when later I was taxed with this reply by Rita Kellner, I protested that what I had said was 'Where *else* can I go?'

Before being left in this repository for unwanted male children I was bribed with a toy of some sort. So when I was sent out to 'play with the other boys' while Minnie and the matron of the establishment came to terms, I, or rather it, became the centre of attention, toys being few and far between in the orphanage. That night I was repeatedly asked whether

I was a bed-wetter. This I vehemently denied, so of course I did wet the bed. Hence I was sentenced to sleep with a layer of thick and smelly rubber between my unbleached calico sheet and me forever and ever, amen, even though I never wet my bed again. In most institutions the purpose of the rubber was to protect the mattress, but there, even the laundering of extra sheets was seen as undesirable.

Food at the orphanage was frequently bloody awful: boiled parsnips were commonly served, and for a time our desserts consisted mainly of sago that had been contaminated by ants and consequently tasted strongly of formic acid. My grandmother Rita had always removed the seeds from grapes (seeds caused appendicitis, she believed) and peeled them (I don't know why) before allowing me to eat them. In my turn, I refused to drink my bedtime egg-flip for her unless it had been sufficiently whipped to have no floating and slimy white-of-egg in it, and no skim from heated cream. Given this spoilt background the meals offered at the orphanage failed to appeal — but eating every last scrap of them was compulsory.

A rather meagre library was provided for the boys, no doubt comprising unwanted books donated by parishioner supporters of the home and culled by the staff for undesirable topics. We were not encouraged to use it. If one was discovered idly reading anything other than tracts, or 'improving' texts such as *The Pilgrim's Progress*, tasks were found for the offender on the grounds that 'Satan finds work for idle hands to do'. Fortunately, in my fifth and sixth classes at Ashfield Public School I was blessed with a teacher who, if he caught me reading a novel under my desk during class, sent me outside to finish the book — provided, of course, that I continued to do well in exams. (In retrospect, it was probably as well that at that time I was not up to reading Tolstoy's *War and Peace*, or my education would have been severely interrupted.)

School had disadvantages as well as advantages. Some of those boys in my class had obviously been instructed by their parents to have nothing to do with 'home boys', otherwise they risked contamination. Others, on occasion, offered me some of their lunches — which definitely were more tasty than what we were supplied with, treacle spread thinly and without butter onto stale bread — so usually I accepted provided that no other 'home boy', who would have definitely reported me to the matron, was watching. We also, at school, had class debates. Because I could write coherently, our teacher at first always chose me to be part of the debating team. But lack of self-confidence had endowed me with a stutter, and after a while I was dropped from the team. The teacher explained to me that he had assumed initially that my stutter was a nervous one, but he now thought it must be congenital. He was right the first time, but the stutter stayed with me until some years after I had become part of the Push.

But before that, while I was still in fifth class, the Imperial Japanese Navy intervened, causing considerable panic (and very low rents) in Sydney. We boys were evacuated from Ashfield to a Barnardo's Home near Picton. I especially remember the frost-covered mornings there, with frost whitening leaves even on tall trees, when (as a presumably reformed bed-wetter) I was deputed to drag a five-year-old bed-wetter out of doors to wash his urine-soaked sheets in icy water. The poor little bastard cried so piteously that I usually ended up washing the things myself. During our time in Picton my father sent back from the Middle East carved camels and donkeys, Italian badges, and other military memorabilia — all items likely to be displayed in the homes of service-men's families at the time.

Within the grounds of the Barnardo's institution, the education de-partment had established a composite primary-school class, which was attended by the Barnardo's children and by us refugees from Ashfield. The boys seemed much tougher than we were, and the big Barnardo's girls, smoothing down their skirts over their ample bums before sitting at their desks, terrified me. But fantasy helped me get by: walking back from school to our quarters with a boy by the name of Alan Fletcher, I discovered that he shared my fantasy that we were really in an English

Greater Public School (GPS, as certain expensive private schools are still called) and that both of us mentally referred to the Barnardo's principal as 'The Doctor'. Evidently our reading patterns had been similar.

Soon, though, the United States entered the war, and we were shunted back to Ashfield. This was probably during the school holidays at the end of my fifth class in primary school, because my father, having been brought home from Tobruk, took me with him for a holiday at a boarding house at The Entrance, near Gosford. He was shortly to be discharged from the army as medically unfit, but he was still in uniform, with marks on his sleeves where sergeant's stripes had been crudely unstitched. In Tobruk he had invented a pattern of camouflage that persuaded German pilots that a well, which was still in use and very necessary, had already been blown up. He was promoted, but before long was demoted again, probably because of drunkenness. (I have often wondered why, with a science degree from Sydney University, he was not commissioned as an officer, as university graduates in that war usually were, but perhaps he preferred to stay in the ranks. This may have altered his fate, for it was then seen, though not officially, as perfectly reasonable for officers to get drunk.)

His demotion certainly didn't deter him from continuing to drink. One evening, a boy with whom I had been playing at The Entrance whispered to me, 'Dick, I don't like to say this, but I think your old man's drunk.' The following morning he was, indeed, hung over, and he asked me to bring him a mug of tea. I did so, but inadvertently stirred into it two teaspoons of salt, rather than sugar. The chundering that followed possibly helped him to recover from his hangover. But it did not help his general medical condition. Only recently have I learnt from his war record that, while at The Entrance, he visited a doctor because he was repeatedly vomiting blood.

At the end of our stay my father said to me, 'I'll bet that this was the best holiday you ever had.' And so it was! For the first time in my life I was free to get up or go to bed when I pleased, to collect soft-drink bottles and cash them in at local shops, to wriggle my toes in the sand of Tuggerah Lake to catch prawns, and above all, free from attending church or reading tracts. Then it was back to the orphanage.

Early in my days there, another boy had taunted me with 'You're an *orphan!*' 'No,' I denied this, 'because my father's still alive.' 'That don't matter,' shouted he, 'We're all *orphans* here!' And orphans we all were. That allowed us privileges of a kind: one task much sought after by the 'big boys' was to be one of the pair who from time to time walked to the Peek Freans biscuit factory on Parramatta Road to carry back for the delectation of all the orphans a tin of broken biscuits donated for that purpose. Sometimes, instead, it was stale cakes from a kindly cake-shop proprietor or slightly-off fruit from a greengrocer.

Then there was the war. 'Big boys', if they had not that day been *bad* 'big boys', were sometimes allowed to stay up longer than the 'medium-size' or 'little' boys and darn the holes in our communal socks while listening on the radio to a serial by the name of *First Light Frazer*. This was a tale about a gallant British spy behind German lines, though what he did or why I can no longer remember. Before or after that thriller we sometimes heard the BBC News, preceded by the sound of the bells of Big Ben. Why, I wondered, if the Germans were bombing Croydon, did we hear no explosions? Croydon was, and still is, the name of a suburb adjoining Ashfield in Sydney's inner west, but it was in the suburb of that name in London that one could hear, and see, and feel, the bombs.

I was also puzzled that a part-Negro boy among us orphans objected with his fists if anybody said to him: 'Nigger! Nigger! Pull the trigger!' At the time it seemed to me an innocuous, if rather meaningless, rhyme. I was puzzled, too, by the accusations against me of being 'spoilt'. In retrospect it is easy to imagine why the other boys should resent my having visitors (usually my grandmother and my sister) on most weekends, and often spending time away from the orphanage during school holidays. At that age though, like the part-Negro boy, I responded with my fists.

A few last memories of my time there. The occasion when I was in charge of a crocodile of boys walking to a cinema in Ashfield: one boy left the crocodile and refused to return, so I punched him on the nose, causing profuse bleeding and his being taken in by a concerned resident. As a result I was beaten, and demoted from being a 'big boy' to the ignominy of being a 'middle-sized boy'. Then there was the appointment of a new matron. We boys all detested her within days of her arrival, so I wrote a note of complaint to the governing church committee. Followed by a gaggle of boys, I knocked on the committee-room door to deliver it. At once all the other boys vanished, but I did so only after handing in the note. For whatever reason, the matron was dismissed, but her replacement was far, far worse.

During the two years that I remained in that matron's charge my grandmother Rita died, and so, a little later, did my father. My sister, I think, told me of the first death, but I learnt of the second from the new matron, who said briskly, 'Dick, I don't want you to be silly about this, but your father's dead.'

And then there was the chicken-pox, or was it measles? Whatever it was, some of the orphanage boys had already been infected when a boy sleeping a bed or so away from mine found red spots on his chest when he awoke one morning. He jumped up with joy, opening his pyjama jacket, rubbing his chest and dancing on his bed; no more domestic duties or school, he thought. I looked hopefully at my own puny chest and found that it, too, had sprouted spots, so even though I usually welcomed school as being far less repressive than the orphanage, I jumped up, rubbing my chest also, to join him in his dance of joy. But alas, the matron looked out through her bedroom's glass doors and sprung us. Both of us were beaten for 'playing with our breasts'.

Shortly after this I rejoined the middle class. I was taken in by the guardian mentioned in the previous chapter, who was one of the four sisters with whom my sister Betty was then living. (No doubt Betty had been pleading my case for several years.) I was accepted, on my sixth-class teacher's recommendation (he was the one who had sent me outside to read), to enrol at North Sydney Boys' High School. The Qualifying Certificate, without which one then received little or no secondary education, had been abolished in the previous year. In 1945, my second year at North Sydney High, I applied for entry to the Royal Australian Naval College and was accepted. The naval college deserves, and gets, a chapter of its own.

My legacies from the orphanage were ingrown toenails (because of wearing hand-me-down shoes that were too short), a talent for deceiving adults, and a profound distaste for low-church Anglicanism. I also learnt how to steal apples from the front of greengrocer shops, but the term 'shoplifting' had not, I think, then yet been coined.

I did go back to the orphanage once, about three years later. Resplendent in my cadet-midshipman's uniform — naval officer's cap badge, eight gold buttons on my jacket, and thin white ribbons under smaller gold buttons on both sides of the front of my collar to indicate my lowly rank — I wanted to confront and dazzle the chicken-pox matron (and possibly to show her that I still had no breasts). At the door, whom should I meet but my fantasiser friend, Alan Fletcher, dressed up in a suit to show that he, too, had come up in the world, and probably there with motives similar to my own. To our mutual disappointment, that matron had been replaced.

3   Only Two Kinds of People in this World

My guardian was one of the Langhorne sisters. There were four of them living in their largish house in Mosman, all of them unmarried. In order of seniority, their names were Eileen (my guardian), Edna, Jean (Betty's guardian), and Ray. Their parents had produced ten children, nine daughters and one son, and to their father it seemed obvious that the son should succeed him on his pastoral property, and equally obvious that he must marry off all of his daughters. He succeeded with only five of them.

To effect this diaspora of daughters he had sold some land and bought the Mosman house and also the dwellings on either side. These latter two he demolished, and extended the double-storeyed home where, late in 1943, I joined the four spinster sisters. In terms of disposable income, they were not wealthy; their father had bequeathed them several properties in the Mosman and northern beaches area, and these were all rented out, but because of rent restrictions under the wartime Labor government, they yielded only a relatively small return. But the Langhornes weren't poor either: they had recently economised by dispensing with the services of a cook, though for a while they retained their full-time gardener. All four sisters were working or had worked, but only in occupations that were considered suitable for 'ladies' rather than working-class women.

At the age of eleven I did not really appreciate how unlikely it was that both my sister and I should be taken in by the Langhornes. Whereas our numerous uncles and aunts had between them adopted only one child (our brother Harold), these sisters, who were not kin to us at all, had adopted two! Apparently Mrs Langhorne had been friendly with our grandmother, Rita Kellner, while Jean Langhorne had been a friend of our mother. They most certainly were under no obligation; they were just very kind and generous women, who had reached middle age in a near-purdah situation, overshadowed by the Edwardian values of a dominating father, and unable or unwilling to discard those values.

To the Langhornes, it was obvious that no boy could grow up to be the right sort of man without first being indoctrinated by the Boy Scouts. So I was. At the Second Mosman Boy Scouts I learnt several new swear-words, I learnt how to cheat my way to win a fire-lighting badge by using methylated spirits, and I learnt how to jump on and off moving trams. But I also learnt a song. When I came home I sang that song to entertain the Langhornes. It was about a wedding at which the groom failed to appear, and its concluding stanza went something like:

> And at the church, no groom turned up,
> But a telegram boy with his nose turned up.
> The telegram read,
> 'I do not wish to wed;
> You'll find me in the river with my toes turned up.'

It was not the most tactful song to sing to four spinsters who had been brought up to believe that, for a woman, success in life was to be meas-ured by the marriage that she had made. One of them responded by saying, 'Well, he was no loss.'

The intrusion of an almost adolescent male into what had been an all-female household must have been just that. My sister had by then finished her schooling and was employed by the Commonwealth Bank, and I too was away at school five days of the week, so they presumably had some relief. As for me, the relief of being freed from the confines of an institution was liberation enough.

The discipline at North Sydney Boys' High School was not onerous, and before catching a tram (fare one penny) to school I could take our dog for a swim at Balmoral Beach. I could go out when I chose to do so; I could climb trees, of which there were plenty within the Langhornes' grounds, and I could read without either admonition or needless interruption. All this I gave up because of my romantic vision of life in a British navy.

The Langhornes still called England, and not Australia, 'home', and in their own home there was no shortage of imperial bric-a-brac, making sombre the various living rooms: ebony and ivory elephants, a small carving of a lion, and numerous framed prints of subjects such as 'A Stag at Bay' and 'Stormy Seas'. To be fair, though, there was also a stuffed kookaburra.

When the end of World War II was approaching, the Langhornes dug out flags they had kept of our allies in the previous world war. These included the Union Flag, of course, the French and Belgian flags, and those of Italy, the (white) Commonwealth countries, and (I think) of the United States. They had also kept the flag of another World War I ally, Japan. This they were not about to fly to celebrate victory, but neither were they about to discard it; they frugally relegated it to the task of polishing shoes. Sometimes, too, their view of the world moved even further back into British history. I remember Edna reciting to me some doggerel about the French flag that went, 'Blue to the mast; False to the last'.

But at that time I too was a British patriot; I thought of myself as being a 'British Australian', and I believed in King and Country and the British Empire. At the age of nine I had published in the *Mosman Daily* a piece of verse entitled 'The *Sydney*'s Last Fight'. It read:

> Face to face with the enemy fleet,
> The *Sydney* made a stand,
> Musket in hand the enemy meet
> A cheery British band.

From the *Sydney* a shot boomed out,
It reached the enemy's deck,
After it followed a British shout,
Though the *Sydney* was nearly a wreck.

The *Sydney* drove the enemy back
Though bullets round her flew,
Several times a gun would crack,
And often groans came too.

But on the *Sydney* they heard no noise,
There was no noise to hear,
There were no more brave British boys,
'Twas the end of their brave career.

Actually I had not written it about the *Sydney*, but about an imaginary eighteenth-century British man-of-war. The newspaper's editor would publish it only if I changed its subject to a real and more recently lost warship, and at that age my 'artistic integrity' was not highly developed, so I agreed. It would have been better though if he had also substituted 'rifle' for 'musket'.

During my two years at North Sydney High I had avidly read Captain Frederick Marryat's *Mr Midshipman Easy* and at least some of C.S. Forester's Hornblower series, so when the school presented me with an advertisement seeking entrants to the Royal Australian Naval College I read it with great interest. To be selected I had to pass an examination set by the navy, and a medical assessment by a naval medical officer, before being interviewed by a selection committee of naval officers. I also had to be 'of substantially European descent'. (Yes, that was then required in Australia, though it presumably did not apply in the Royal Indian Navy!) Why did I apply? Already, I think, the all-pervading respectability of the Langhorne household was beginning to irk me. Life was confined to those things one *must* do and those things that it was all right to do; outside those boundaries there were many sorts of desirable things to do that one *must not* do. The navy, or at least the navy of Midshipman Easy or Horatio Hornblower, seemed not so hog-tied to respectability.

At the age of thirteen I sat for, and passed, the exam, which was easy, and I also proved medically acceptable — though today my fairly poor co-ordination would probably have put paid to my nautical ambitions. At the interview I was asked how the number four was shown on a clock (i.e. IIII not IV), and what colour were Commander Plunkett-Cole's eyes (he had just closed them), and I guessed, correctly, that they were grey. The only other question I remember was whether I liked cricket, and to this I lied shamelessly that I did, though in fact I detested it only slightly less than I did rugby union. In January 1946 I received a letter marked OHMS (On His Majesty's Service). It informed me that I had been selected, and ordered me to report to the Naval Railways Transport Officer (RTO) at Central Railway Station at a given time and date. My guardian then signed the enclosed form. This surrendered to the navy all my rights for the four years at the college and the subsequent twelve years as an officer.

There was a week or so of flurry during which I was measured by a tailor for a uniform (officers-to-be were not to be seen in off-the-hook garments), and immunised rather painfully against smallpox by the family's ancient doctor. At the due time and date I presented myself to the Naval RTO at Central, who after at least three roll-calls was at last convinced that all seven expected 'snotties' (midshipmen and/or cadet midshipmen) were present and ready to be shepherded into the Melbourne Express's first-class carriages.

The naval college was at that time within Flinders Naval Depot (HMAS *Cerberus*) at Crib Point on the shores of Westernport Bay. During the Depression of the 1930s it had been moved there from Jervis Bay to save money, despite the risk of officers-to-be being contaminated by the proximity of ordinary naval ratings. Consequently, on our arrival in Melbourne the following morning, we had to wait around for the little steam engine that every afternoon pulled three or four dog-box carriages, with outward-opening doors, to Crib Point. There, a rather decrepit naval bus awaited us, as did two fierce-looking cadet captains (prefects, to landlubbers), who had been deprived of three days' leave to welcome the new intake. This they did, when the bus reached the college, by shouting 'Smack it about and out of the bus — the last two out get beaten!'

To be a sailor, or a soldier, the first requirement is to wear a funny hat. Conforming to this dictum, and for reasons just possibly known to the navy, of our uniforms only the headgear and footwear were available. The latter were black leather boots and gaiters. We were ordered to our alphabetically allotted four-person cubicles (cabins) to dress ourselves in these, with ill-fitting boiler suits bridging the gap between gaiters and cap to preserve decency. Thus clad, we were assembled on the college's circular drive (known, improbably, as the Quarter Deck) and addressed by Commodore Harold Farncomb. 'Out of eight hundred applicants,' he told us, 'you sixteen have been selected to become officers and gentlemen of His Majesty's Australian Navy. For the next two years your lives will not be worth living.'

And they weren't.

What to say about the college? One former cadet who later became Governor of New South Wales, the late Admiral Sir David Martin, described it as 'a cross between an eighteenth-century British frigate and Borstal', but he was in the Year below ours, and for that Year beatings by senior cadets had been abolished. Our Year was beaten almost every evening by cadet captains, for trivial offences or for no offences at all, and sometimes just to 'smarten us up'. Every so often the term officer (the lieutenant responsible for our Year) inspected our bums, and if they were too badly bruised we were excused beatings for a week. Unfortunately my bum did not bruise easily.

And then there were the more official punishments, ordered by term officers for offences alleged by cadet captains. These punishments, called 'jankers', were numbered from one to ten; and number four, for example, included thirty minutes of drill followed by forty-five minutes of marching for 220 yards and then double-marching (jogging in step) for the same distance, and all the time carrying a simulated .303 rifle held by one arm alternately over one's head and then to one's front. At gym, too, we were often ordered to hang by our arms from wall-bars until at least one of us fell, and all the time we were harangued to the effect that cadets were 'the lowest form of marine life'.

Even in our bunks we were not safe: while we lay at attention, cadet captains pawed over our folded clothing in and on our chests of drawers, and if they were not satisfied that all the folds were at near-perfect right angles then the contents of the drawers were tipped on to the deck (floor) and we were ordered to refold them. While this lengthy process of demolition took place, one particular cadet captain took pleasure in berating us because all sixteen of us had obviously been brought up in brothels.

Our relief from this kind of bastardry was to reply in kind. We could not retaliate against the seniors, so instead we would sometimes bastardise one of our own Year. Peter Arnold, who was to die in 1959 when he crashed because the tail of his recently repaired naval aircraft failed to function, was usually the chosen victim. We would upturn several settees in our gun-room (junior officers' recreation room) to create a cage, and with cries of 'Cage the Ferret!' imprison him and then prod him with a poker that had been heated in the fire there.

As at the orphanage, I found that our time in the classroom was far less repressive than any other of our waking hours. I enjoyed knowing more about French history than did our French teacher, though why we also studied naval French remained a mystery to me. At the Annapolis naval academy in the United States they studied Russian, so perhaps, I thought, nobody had told our defence authorities that the French were no longer our major sea-going enemies. (Nobody had told Edna Langhorne, either.) There were other compensations: I enjoyed sailing and foot-racing, and when on leave and staying with the Langhornes, I found that wearing a naval uniform ensured that I was served liquor in hotels without question, even though I was seventeen or younger during all of my three and a bit naval years.

In my first year at the college I became a mutineer, or at least Commander Plunkett-Cole thought that somebody was a mutineer. We were suddenly informed that our next leave (school vacation) had been truncated to three weeks instead of the four weeks we had been led to expect. A little impetuously, I wrote a short piece of satirical verse about hanging the officers from the Quarter Deck mast (flagpole). This I pinned, unsigned of course, to the official notice board containing the news of our reduced leave. At the following Sunday Divisions (inspection and drill followed by a church service), the commander read to the assembled cadets the Articles of War, in which S.11 stated:

> When a mutiny is not accompanied by violence, the ringleader or ringleaders of such mutiny shall suffer death, or such other punishment [keelhauling perhaps?] as hereinafter mentioned.

I have since been told that it was then compulsory to read aloud these Articles from time to time, but I still firmly believe that this timing was triggered by my poor doggerel.

As well as sailing and pulling (rowing) naval craft on Westernport Bay, we did, on occasion, actually go to sea. Most memorable was the voyage for which we embarked variously on two British destroyers, HMS *Cockade* and HMS *Contest*, and two escort aircraft carriers, HMS *Theseus* and HMS *Glory*. This was in 1946, when the Royal Navy was badly battle-scarred. Lacking money, the British cannibalised damaged aircraft to construct 'new' ones. (The US Navy, I have been told, simply pushed damaged planes overboard.) Probably this was the main cause of the disasters that followed in the exercise that took place in Bass Strait. Two aircraft fell into the sea, and a third, though warned off by the batman, continued its landing, in the process decapitating the batman. One body from a submerged aeroplane was recovered, and the first lieutenant of *Cockade* screamed at his crew not to put 'that thing' on the deck until a canvas tarpaulin was laid down. Our RAN term officer ordered all the nearby cadets to come and look at the body, because we would have to get used to this sort of thing. Indeed, though schoolboys, that was why we were there.

As to the sailing of naval cutters on Westernport Bay, I remember one incident, in retrospect rather ludicrous. In my third year at the college one day I found myself in command of a cutter manned otherwise entirely by thirteen-year-old and fourteen-year-old First Years, all of them seasick. Consequently I ran that boat aground on a mud bank. The force of the impact snapped the mast. Some time later a power boat with a lieutenant aboard pulled alongside. 'What's wrong, Appleton?' hailed the lieutenant. 'The mast's broken, sir,' I replied. Back came the shocked admonition: 'Not "broken", lad. "Carried away" or "sprung". Never "broken".' I was not stupid enough to make the obvious reply: 'Well, it's buggered anyway!'

For my first two years in this Borstal-cum-Bedlam college I had assumed that the agreement signed by my guardian was unbreakable — and that hence I was doomed to serve for a further fourteen or fifteen years. In third year, though, and even more so in fourth year, we were almost gods, whom juniors could not address without a personal suffix after every statement. For instance, a junior might say: 'The red flag is up on the firing range please Appleton [or whoever].' We were privileged to walk where juniors must double, but the juniors must also ensure that the seniors came first. I knew though that this godlike status would not last. As midshipmen in the gun-room of a warship we would be subject to the autocratic whims of the sub-lieutenants, and then as sub-lieutenants we would be godlike again in the gun-room, but outside it at the beck and call of anybody senior in rank; and when we attained the status of junior lieutenants we would still be at the beck and call of any more senior officer in the ward-room (senior officers' recreation room); and then, and then …? So when, late in my third year at college, it got through to my discipline-addled brain that not all the cadets who had by then left the college had been dismissed as 'unsuitable as officer material', I wrote to my guardian, Eileen Langhorne. Could she, I asked, rescue me from the navy without her being compelled to pay an outrageous ransom?

She was obviously unwilling: our end-of-year leave came and went while I stayed with the Langhornes without the subject being raised. Then, early in my fourth year at college, matters came to a head. A cadet captain of my own Year, Julian Barry, marched me in before our term officer and charged me with possession (for the umpteenth time) of the wherewithal for smoking. I pleaded guilty. The term officer adopted his most officerly voice and asked, 'Appleton, don't you want to be a naval officer?' 'No sir,' I replied, 'I have already written to my guardian asking her to try to have me discharged.' There was a stunned silence. Then the hearing was immediately closed and I returned to our gun-room. I was closely followed by Julian, who collapsed on to a settee shaking with laughter.

(During my fourth and final year at the naval college, too, I probably inadvertently made it easier for myself to gain a discharge. During one evening's 'prep', our English master, presumably lacking pedagogic inspiration, gave us the task of writing an essay entitled 'How I won my VC'. By then I was more intent on amusing my fellow-cadets, and impressing them with my world-weariness, than I was on reassuring my superiors. My essay was much in the manner of the Flashman novels, not yet then published. I set it in the Boer War, in which I was an officer playing cards for high stakes one evening, and drinking heavily. Naturally I won. On the following morning one of my card-playing colleagues, who owed me money from the previous evening, fell to enemy fire. Suffering from a hangover but determined to keep the bloke alive until he paid his debt, I rescued him from under a hail of bullets. This was not the kind of morale-boosting heroism expected from officers-to-be.)

From two sides, I was then the target of pleas to reconsider. Eileen Langhorne delegated an army captain, a friend of the family, to visit the college. He pointed out to me the virtues of life in the armed services as opposed to the boredom of life in a commercial or government office. How right he was! But it didn't seem to occur to him that anybody from 'our class' could work anywhere other than in an office or in the services. I was not really surprised. One naval officer had earlier opined that nobody who had served six months on the lower deck was any longer fit to become an officer. This lieutenant had served in the World War II convoys to Russia in the same ship as his rating brother, and had observed naval protocol by speaking to that brother only to give orders. And the Langhornes, though kindly people, would probably have agreed in principle: such terms as 'the great unwashed' and 'the hoi polloi' came readily to their lips, as did 'a touch of the tar-brush'.

Our term officer had what seemed to him the most cogent argument for my remaining in the navy: 'Appleton,' he said, 'do you realise that there are only two kinds of people in this world, those who are pukka officers and those who aren't?' At the time I had no wish to dispute this dichotomy; I was just determined to become one of 'those who aren't'. So eventually I had my way and was discharged from the navy, without, as far as I know, the Langhornes paying any large ransom.

Ironically, as I then became an ex-serviceman I was allotted a ration of cigarettes — a commodity very much in short supply in those post-war years. Earlier, too, I had been provided with cigarettes. On one of my leaves in Sydney I had injured my knee, and, rather than let me convalesce at home, the navy saw fit to admit me to Concord Repatriation Hospital. At that establishment, unlike at the naval hospitals of the period, patients were not segregated by rank. There, I was issued with a card that entitled me to a fixed number of cigarette packets each week.

My fellow-patients quickly showed me how that card could be manipulated. All one had to do was to spit on the hole which had been punched in the card to indicate that a week's ration had been dispensed, and then rub the card until the hole was obliterated. No doubt the service personnel undergoing treatment at Concord gallantly saved some civilian smokers from lung cancer by fraudulently obtaining more than their equitable share of the available cigarettes.

4 And Back to the Lincoln

After eluding the navy's claim to owning my life for a further thirteen years, I returned to living full-time with the Langhornes. Once the euphoria of escaping from naval discipline had evaporated, I found that life there was not as liberating as it had been immediately after my leaving the orphanage. For them too it must have been a trial. By then I was well into adolescence, and soon after returning to Mosman I had manifested my generalised lust by vulgarising the walls of my room with magazine clippings depicting scantily clad young women. This provoked Eileen to present me with a booklet outlining the sexual habits and genital anatomy of rabbits. And just when I least needed further sexual stimulation, the Langhornes took in a niece of theirs from the country. She was about a year older than I was, and she exuded a compelling aura of nubility. One evening when all four of the Langhornes were out she suggested that we play strip-poker. I laughed, pretending that she was just joking, but I don't think that she was.

I had no problem in coping with the Langhornes' insistence that I wear to the dinner table, even in high summer, a jacket and tie — at the naval college even the sports uniform included a blazer and tie — but their 'What will the neighbours think?' syndrome began increasingly to irk me. One evening, at about eleven o'clock, when the sisters had all retired to their respective rooms, my brother and a friend of his rang the front-door bell. I invited them in and plied them with port wine and fruit cake, which pleased them but not the Langhornes. Apparently I had offended against suburban respectability. What I really needed to do was to flee from it.

A little before my brother's departure and my consequent induction into the Lincoln (Harold, apparently, did not want to expose his seventeen-year-old sibling to the dangers of bohemia) the Langhornes were visited by a relative of theirs, Sir Charles Belcher.[5] He had been in Kenya helping to administer the empire on which the sun was about to set. Obviously baffled by my moodiness, Eileen Langhorne asked him to talk to me. She thought, presumably, that I lacked 'male guidance'. Unfortunately, perhaps, she also told him that I wrote poetry. So Sir Charles began his male guidance by trying to gain my confidence, to this end extolling the virtues of Rupert Brooke, and quoting Brooke's well-known lines:

> If I should die, think only this of me:
> That there's some corner of a foreign field
> That is forever England.

Unthinkingly I responded by quoting from the only poem of Brooke's that I really liked, 'The Old Vicarage, Grantchester':

> And when they get to feeling old
> They up and shoot themselves, I'm told.

I had intended no malice, but as soon as I stopped reciting I realised that a sexagenarian might well take this as an insult. He later told the Langhornes, 'That boy has something on his mind.' Fortunately the Lincoln rescued both me and the Langhornes from what was becoming an impossible situation. It was then, as related in an earlier chapter, that I escaped to a rooming house in Paddington.

My Paddington period did not last very long. When a tiny room near Musgrave Street Wharf at Mosman became available I surrendered the Paddington one to Peter Hellier, after first nearly poisoning him by making a pot of tea in a teapot containing month-old tea-leaves festooned with green mould. The Musgrave Street room was in the same tenement that included the larger upstairs room recently vacated by my brother. It was now occupied by Barry Kennedy, who was to introduce me to the local branch of the Communist Party. My little room below Barry's was the scene for my first, and far from successful, foray into sexual initiation.

Wendy, whom I took home one night from the Lincoln, was obviously sexually experienced, while I wasn't. (At that time I was of the view, as many of my contemporaries, male and female, still are, that sex in itself was enough, without any affection, or even liking, for one's sexual partner.) After our brief and unsatisfactory coupling in or on my single bed, we both went to sleep. In the morning I arranged, or thought I arranged, for Wendy to return the following evening and wait for me there. So I gave her my sole and hugely cumbersome key to the room. But she presumably was unimpressed by my lack of sexual prowess, and I didn't see her for nearly a week, so other ways of entry into my room had to be found. Consequently, on one of my keyless homecomings I found a note from my landlady reading: 'Dear Mr Appleton, when climbing into your room through the fanlight, would you kindly not stand on my sewing machine.'

This sexual fiasco presented an opportunity for verbal vitriol from Sope (Neil C. Hope), another habitué of the Lincoln, who was sitting there with Wendy when next I saw her and who was not one to neglect such openings. He said as loudly as he could: 'Don't worry, Wendy, Appo's balls will drop soon.' I was not really surprised, for Sope was apt to exclaim loudly, when he encountered me on trams or trains, 'Ladies and gentlemen, this is Australia's greatest poet!'

Sope's main verbal opponent was Lillian Roxon, though their adversarial wit did not flower fully until the days of the Tudor Hotel, which are described in a later chapter. Lillian befriended me for a while, as she was wont to do with young men. In 1950 we met accidentally at Sydney University, and she immediately led me to the office of *Honi Soit*, the students' weekly newspaper, and asked 'Can I bring a Fresher in?' The question was rhetorical, as most of the newspaper's staff also patronised the Lincoln and hence were acquaintances of mine.

Opposite the Lincoln's Rowe Street entrance there stood, as noted earlier, an entrance to the Long Bar of the Hotel Australia. At that bar, suits, collars and ties were the norm, but not compulsory. Women, of course, were not admitted — unless they were barmaids and thus sufficiently degraded so that the obscene language of the patrons could do them no further harm. To drink with a female friend it was necessary to sit at a table in the hotel's lounge, and there collars and ties *were* compulsory. My friend Jane (of whom more later) and I disdained respectability, but had no objection to enjoying its privileges, so we ordered drinks in the Australia's lounge. To conceal my lack of a tie I wore a scarf, and my lack of a jacket was disguised by an overcoat. But the waiter was not deceived. He demanded that I remove my scarf. At the sight of my naked neck he expelled us into the outer darkness.

During the Lincoln days, too, there was the episode of the John Olsen mural. A German Jewish refugee called Fred, a Lincoln habitué who lived in a Bondi flat, was in the habit, whenever his wife was away, of throwing a party. At one such party an exuberant Olly painted a cartoon-type mural on one of the flat's walls. When Fred's wife returned she insisted on having the mural removed.

Omnipresent at the Lincoln, when he was present there at all, was Harry Hooton. He described himself as an anarcho-technocrat, and argued that man should have power only over things such as machines, but never over other men. But Hooton also presented himself as an inveterate opponent of the past, in all of its manifestations, and in this sense he was a precursor of the post-modernists. In his last book, published after his death, he wrote:

Ulysses. A human being, a proper noun, an ancient Greek. Who could turn to this exhausted soil without overpowering disgust, save the crawlers who putrefy in the universities! Ulysses. Seven letters wasted, ten seconds sacrificed ... To occupy our minds with Ulysses, St Joan, Thomas à Becket, Ned Kelly, or anything that has happened in the last 10,000 years is cannibalism. Leave the human necrophagites to crawl ...[6]

As most Libertarians, like their mentor John Anderson, saw James Joyce's *Ulysses* as the greatest and most important of modern novels, there was ample room for argument here. Lex Banning, too, was less than enthusiastic about Hooton's reference to T.S. Eliot's *Murder in the Cathedral*. (I don't know which writers were the targets for the references to St Joan and Ned Kelly.)

Hooton held that polemic was an art form and that all poetry should be didactic. Yet on those rare occasions when he briefly abandoned both of these doctrines he could write good verse. An example is 'The Cart', republished in *It Is Great to Be Alive*:

> We buried him at last:
> A hundred monks in file,
> With heads and eyes downcast,
> Had followed without guile,
> With neither smirk nor smile
> Until, the crossroads passed,
> They found out their mistake —
> But we buried him at last.

> It was his wife's idea
> To have a hundred monks
> March along behind
> The hearse.
> To put it terse:
> There weren't any monks —
> But we got a hundred drunks

(With promises of beer)
Who said they wouldn't mind
Dressing for the part
And bringing up the rear —
It was his wife's idea.

It nearly broke her heart …
With downcast eyes and head,
They lost the hearse
And, which was worse,
They followed instead
With slow and measured tread
The night-cart.
       (They should have looked ahead
       For it nearly broke her heart.)

Still, we buried him at last.
(It was not his wife's idea —
Her instructions were quite clear —
They were not to raise their heads.)
The hearse went on ahead.
At the crossroads we instead
Followed the cart.
       We should have looked ahead
       For it nearly broke her heart.
       But … we buried him at last.

Terry McMullen aptly summed up Hooton's impact when he wrote: 'One can recognise that there is nothing above examination, but one can still feel uneasy to criticise the ideas and style of someone who can argue with Hooton's facility that 'I am infallible but so are you'.[7]

It is difficult to imagine two people less alike than Harry Hooton and Lex Banning. The latter suffered from cerebral palsy; this caused involuntary movements and incoordination, mainly of the arms, neck and face, though his legs too were mildly affected. Banning spoke with difficulty, and grimaced, spluttered and spat as he spoke, but he had an acute and well-furnished mind. His circle at the Lincoln comprised not only poets and/or writers such as Derek Hoste, Sylvia Lawson, Mari Kuttna and myself, but also some aficionados of science fiction, including Vol Molesworth, Doug Nicholson and Graham Stone. Whereas Hooton sought to bury the past, Banning frequently preferred to live in it. An example is a fairly immature (and untitled) piece of verse he wrote shortly after having been enrolled, though unmatriculated, at Sydney University (Banning's baptismal names were Arthur Alexander):

> Through this gate the great Agamemnon
> Passed, and was Troy's despair.
> Now through this gate comes Alexander
> Advancing on Australia fair.[8]

The past also recurs from time to time in Banning's mature, highly polished and beautiful poems, such as 'A Memorandum for the Prince Hamlet':

> I would you mark this well, my lord,
> how could I with a little anger
> crack this shell of straight mortality,
> and, as you say, perhaps win freedom:
> perchance to hurl myself into
> the angry sun, or dance among
> the concourse of the weeping planets,
> or even, as I've heard your lordship say,
> to go a progress through the guts of a beggar.
> And if from stars to stomachs seem
> fantastical I pray you think on this,
> that all the figures of our proud astronomy
> are, maybe, nothing but our poor perceptions
> of the peritoneum of some cosmic fishmonger.

Thus may a man attain to be
a sort of universal indigestion,
and so engender in the aching firmament
discharge of meteors and bad comets.

A pretty thought, my lord, with which
to go to bed.[9]

As might be expected, the Lincoln had its Stalinists as well. One of them was Eric Parker, who worked as a coalminer near Newcastle but rode his motorbike to Sydney when not on roster, and another was Harry Reade. Both of them addressed individuals as though haranguing a crowd at the Domain. Despite our frequent arguments, Harry Reade remained a friend of mine until his death in 1998. His obituary in the *Sydney Morning Herald* on 16 May of that year described him, accurately enough, as:

> wharfie, artist, cartoonist, maker of award-winning animated films, seaman, fruit picker, journalist, sugarcane cutter, street photographer, shark fisherman, playwright, rabbit shooter, sailor, boat-builder, communist, rainbow-chaser …

But Harry was, as well as all those things, a dedicated and wholly convinced dialectical materialist, which many communists weren't. In 1960 he went to Cuba, where he made animated films for the Castro regime, and in the following year he fought for Castro at the Bay of Pigs. Returning to Australia by way of the United States was out of the question for him after that, so he went to the Soviet Union. In 1970 Harry did return to Australia, disillusioned with communist rulers but still a Marxist, at least in most respects. He had decided that Marxism was wrong in seeing progress in the growing size of the capitalist economies, but still believed in the 'dialectical' process by which 'the quantitative becomes the qualitative'. That the size of those capitalist economies was the necessary trigger, in Marx's view, for their evolution into socialism, did not deter Harry's heresy. Still, it is not uncommon for leftists to accept some or most of Marx's economic theories, and to reject dialectical materialism, but the reverse is extremely rare.

Another major Lincoln group with which both Harry Reade and I were associated comprised mainly art students (as opposed to arts students). It included, among others, John Olsen, Brian Mooney, Peter Lake, Reg Schurr, Barry Kennedy and Dan Russell. The Norton paintings mentioned in an earlier chapter did not grace the Lincoln's walls for very long, and among the many other paintings, photographs, cartoons and caricatures that replaced them I especially remember a cartoon of John Olsen's. It depicted a group of painters, all recognisable as denizens of the Lincoln, with easels set up on the George Street tramlines. A tram-driver was shaking his fist at them, and the balloon emanating from Olly's mouth read: 'Let's move on to Pitt Street, it's too crowded here.' (At that time Pitt Street, too, was a busy tram route.)

It was with this group that I took part in my first protest demonstration, an activity not common in the 1950s. In 1952 William Dargie won the Archibald Prize for portraiture, while we felt strongly that the award should have gone to William Dobell. We stormed the Archibald exhibition at the Art Gallery of New South Wales, probably bewildering or amusing the onlookers, but certainly alarming the aged attendants. And we achieved what most demonstrators seek — recognition, and our photos in the newspapers.

As well as patronising the Lincoln, the art students' group also on most afternoons drank, until it closed at six o'clock, at the Royal Hotel, which stood at the intersection of King and Castlereagh streets. But that hotel's days were nearly done, as were the Lincoln's, and the Libertarians began to cultivate the licensee of the Tudor Hotel in Phillip Street. There, they pioneered the right of entry for women to drink in public bars; until then women had been confined largely to dark and dingy 'ladies' parlours' and 'ladies' lounges'. Inner Sydney's smaller pubs were desperate by then for patrons, and as Roelof Smilde remarked at about that time, 'If we'd told [the publican] that one of our companions had two heads, he would have just seen that as double drinks.'

As the Lincoln's days drew to a close, most of the Lincoln groups began to see the Tudor as their main meeting place for the foreseeable future. Those who didn't seem to have merged back into the suburbia from which they had so briefly escaped.

5   My Time in the Communist Party

Shortly after joining what became the Sydney Push, I joined (or thought I joined) the Communist Party of Australia. Barry Kennedy was my mentor, as he was for Dan Russell, who joined the Mosman branch with me in 1949. Barry was a devout communist in that he conformed religiously with whatever was the 'party line' at that time, but not so devout as to prevent him spending his leisure time in Prince's and/or Romano's, then Sydney's most prestigious nightclubs. Though shortly to study law, Barry was then a student at Julian Ashton's Art School; and he wore suede shoes to prove it.

At that time Australian communists regarded their English comrades with some disdain, as being mainly intellectuals. This was epitomised by a joke, then current, about an English communist trying to persuade a worker to join the party. The worker replies: 'Well chum, I'd like to join your party, but I can't afford them suede shoes you all wear.' Well, if an Australian worker who lived in Mosman (which even then was unlikely) had been asked to join Mosman Branch, he might well have said that he couldn't afford the shiny shoes that the male members all wore.

For Mosman Branch was far from being a radical cell of horny-handed proletarians. Its dominant personality was Russel Ward, then principal of Mosman Intermediate High School and later a professor of history at the University of New England. Other members included a bank manager, a barrister, a shopkeeper, and Rupert Lockwood, then editor of the Communist Party weekly, the *Tribune*. The female members appeared to be all very respectable middle-class housewives. The branch had, I was told, once boasted a working-class member, but he had proved to be politically unreliable and they had to get rid of him.

Into this august group came the teenagers Dan Russell, who was another art student, and myself, a would-be poet. I was wearing the obligatory corduroy jacket and desert boots (the nearest things to suede shoes that I could afford), and Dan was probably dressed in much the same way. We became the only young members of that branch.

As such, we were warmly welcomed, and promptly given all, or nearly all, of the legwork to do: putting up posters, letter-boxing what was euphemistically called literature, and selling the *Tribune*. This was at the beginning of the Cold War, and we thought of ourselves as rather brave. I remember that on one occasion I was selling, or trying to sell, the *Tribune* at Milsons Point railway (and tram) station; I was wearing a green safari jacket, mustard-coloured corduroy trousers and a French beret, and my hair was long for that era. I was trembling a little, expecting hostility from the commuters, but what I got was ridicule. 'Look,' said one bloke to his mate, 'a Cornell Wilde boy selling Tribs!'

On another occasion, with some trepidation because of our belief in (probably imaginary) Mosman vigilantes, Dan and I were pasting up communist posters on Musgrave Street ferry wharf. We finished un-scathed, with posters on every upright post, and repaired to my nearby room to drink red wine. The next morning, though, when we walked to the wharf on our way to the city, the tide had risen, and with it the pon-toon which formed the wharf; and all our seditious posters were either submerged or at least below eye-level.

My most curious task came about because the shopkeeper member of Mosman Branch leased his shop at Clifton Gardens, and claimed to have the franchise for all of the covered seating areas in the beachside park there. To raise funds for the branch (there was no 'Moscow Gold' in Mosman) he authorised me to patrol these areas and to charge those using the facilities sixpence or some such sum. The family picnickers would have been more than a little shocked, I think, had they known that their coins were being de-laundered (as it were) to subsidise the dreaded Reds!

In the political climate then developing in Australia, to join the Communist Party was probably at the apex of all the possible methods of rejecting respectability. Communists were depicted, especially in newspapers and by their cartoonists, as 'red rats' or 'red-raggers', and held in contempt by all right-thinking (and I use those words advisedly) citizens. They were despised, though, not mainly because of Stalin's horrendous and murderous regime in the Soviet Union (which not long before had been 'our gallant ally') and the Eastern Bloc, but because of their leading role in the radical policies of many Australian trade unions.

When I joined Mosman Branch I was at first very much in awe of the other members, and especially of Russel Ward, whose name I initially misheard as 'Russia', which I took to be a revolutionary alias like Lenin, Trotsky or Stalin. He encouraged my study of the party gospel, and I very much enjoyed reading the *Communist Manifesto*, Engels's *Origins of the Family*, and *The ABC of Communism*, in my edition attributed solely to the authorship of Bukharin (already a non-person by the time I read it), ignoring entirely the contribution of Preobrazhensky, who had become a non-person rather earlier. Lenin I found didactic and turgid, and Stalin unreadable. Marx's historical works I read with pleasure, though I managed only the first volume of *Capital*. At that time I had not read any of Trotsky's works.

But Rupert Lockwood had. Rupert rarely, if ever, came to branch meetings, but I attended a party (the other kind of party) at his home one evening. On his shelves were the Moscow Foreign Languages Publishing House editions of Trotsky's (pre-expulsion) works; so I asked Russel why, if Rupert could read Trotsky, I couldn't? He replied that Rupert was an experienced Marxist who would not be seduced by Trotsky's arguments (and I, presumably, wasn't). His further comment was more interesting: he said that Trotsky's advocacy of world revolution had been putting at risk the survival of the Soviet Union. Maybe so; but this was a far cry from the official 'party line', which was that Trotsky was in league with

Roosevelt, then later with Hitler, to overthrow communism in Russia! I resolved then and there to find and read the writings of this man whom Winston Churchill had stigmatised as 'a bladder of malice'.

On most Sunday afternoons, if we had nothing more interesting to do, Barry, Dan and I would 'go to church' in Sydney's Domain. There, we joined the faithful who always assembled around the Communist Party soapbox to hear Big Jim Healy, a leader of the wharfies, lambast the bosses and anybody else who had attracted the party's ire. Rupert Lockwood was frequently also a speaker, and a distinctly more menacing one than Big Jim. It almost seemed that at any moment he might sool the NKVD on to those who were the target of his wrath. (I think it was the NKVD at that date — during the Communist Party's domination of the Russian empire they changed the name of their secret police just as frequently as Australia's principal conservative party changed *its* name.) Those days are gone. But it was not the Cold War that killed off the Sunday 'Church of the Domain': it was the pubs being allowed to open on Sunday afternoons.

Russel's position was altered by the defeat of Chifley's Labor government in the elections of 1949. Mosman was in the Warringah electorate, a blue-ribbon Liberal seat then held by Percy (later Sir Percy) Spender. The Australian Labor Party (ALP) decided not to endorse a candidate, as there was no hope of unseating Spender. But like many ALP branches in unwinnable seats, Mosman Branch was a left-wing body; one of its members, Bill Fisher, decided to stand as an Independent Labor candidate. (Fisher was later to become a judge in the New South Wales industrial court.) The Mosman branch of the Communist Party delegated Dan Russell and myself to assist Fisher's campaign. On election day Spender shouted at us that we would know better when we grew up, and after the poll was declared he refused to shake hands with Fisher. And Menzies became prime minister, vowing to ban the Communist Party. Russel decided that he would try to save his wife and children from once again being subjected to intrusive raids by the security services. He indicated that he would resign from the party.

At about this time the general secretary of the Communist Party, Lance Sharkey, was ensnared and imprisoned. Stupidly, when pressed by an eager reporter, he had asserted that if Soviet forces, in pursuit of an aggressor, were to enter Australia, Australian workers would welcome them. They wouldn't have, of course, but Sharkey was found guilty of whatever he was charged with (not treason, I think). The Communist Party immediately began a 'release Sharkey' campaign. (Even in the 1970s, when I was commuting daily from Katoomba to Sydney, this slogan was still decipherable on the railway workshop walls near Central Station.) Civil libertarians also supported the campaign, and a meeting was held in Mosman which included, among others, left-wing members of the ALP. In the chair was Bill Wood, Rhodes Scholar and communist, and when I moved 'that this meeting endorses Sharkey's words', Bill knew how to deal with troublesome radicals. Somehow the motion was never put.

Libertarians of the Sydney Push were less sympathetic to Sharkey. A song then sung by several of them and probably written by one of them, and, like 'The Red Flag', sung to the tune of 'O Tannenbaum', went:

> The working class can kiss my arse
> I've found a bludger's job at last.
> No need to work, no need to toil,
> I sit around and do fuck-all.
>
> The judge, he said three years I've got,
> I wouldn't care if I'd copped the lot;
> I wouldn't leave if they gave me bail,
> I'm Commissar of Long Bay Gaol.

Early in 1950 I was subjected, as a 'Fresher', to Orientation Week at Sydney University. At a political meeting there, a Liberal Club spokesman denounced both Hitler's revolution and that of the Russian Bolsheviks. I rose to my feet and spouted the 'party line' that Hitler staged only a *coup d'état* not a revolution, as capitalist economic domination was still in place. It is probably as well that I had not at the time read Deutscher's account of Trotsky's *coup* that triggered the October Revolution.[10] On my way out of the meeting I was accosted by members of the university's Labor Club, then dominated by communists, obviously eager to recruit me. When I explained that I was already a member of the Mosman branch of the Communist Party, they looked at me askance, possibly because they relished their own clandestine role in politics, but more likely because they thought I must be an *agent provocateur*. Either way, I did not join the university branch of the party, but remained in the Mosman branch for a little longer.

The final duty asked of me by that branch was to represent youth at a 'Peace Conference' to be held in Melbourne, at which the Red Dean of Canterbury was to be the star speaker.[11] Russel Ward gave me, for expenses, a twenty-pound note (a huge sum for me at that time), and if there was an attendance fee, the branch or Russel must have paid it. I cannot remember whether I hitch-hiked south or took the train, probably the former, but either on the way to or in Melbourne I teamed up with Geoff Mill, another Sydney University student who, like me, belonged to the Sydney Push.

Both of us stayed at a university hostel in Brunswick Street, Fitzroy. This was a dilapidated three-storey building entirely managed (or mismanaged) by the students themselves, nearly all of whom were members of the Melbourne University Labor Club. Hygiene was not a priority, and in one of the first-floor bathrooms there was a sign warning inmates not to flush the toilet because it would flood the kitchen below.

The conference was staged at Melbourne's Exhibition Building, itself as much a relic of Queen Victoria's reign as was the Red Dean. Resplendent with fluffy white side-whiskers, black clerical garb and gaiters, his presence far outshone those of the other two speakers, American clerics of one persuasion or another. They looked drab in conventional lounge suits. All three, though, were equally long-winded and boring. As a diversion on the first day Geoff suggested that we enliven proceedings by throwing ourselves from one of the building's many indoor balconies, shouting 'Peace!' as we plummeted floorwards. Deciding that this might be unwise, we spent much of the three-day conference at nearby pubs, making good use of Russel's twenty pounds.

Shortly after my return to Sydney, Dan Russell and I decided to resign from the Communist Party. We composed a joint letter complaining that the party was too politically conservative, too authoritarian, and without any real input from rank-and-file workers, and promptly dispatched it to the Central Committee. For some weeks or months we heard nothing about our resignations.

Then, at a party (the other kind again) we encountered an aunt of Dan's who was also a party member. She informed us that the party had decided that we were guilty of a syndicalist deviation (though neither of us had then read Georges Sorel), and she also pointed out that one could not resign from the Communist Party.

'Well, so what?' I countered. 'So we are expelled.'

'You are both too cynical to believe in anything, and in any case you were never proper members of the party,' she said, and (to me) 'Stop stroking that bloody moustache!'

Thinking back, I suspect that she may have been right about our never having been 'proper members'. It seems likely that, because of our relatively tender years, Russel Ward had never formally enrolled us, thus hoping to save us from security attention should the party be banned. At any rate, I did not ever receive a party card, certainly not the notorious and flamboyant red one embossed with a yellow hammer and sickle. But surely the Australian Security and Intelligence Organization (ASIO) must at least have recognised my subversive status by rewarding me with a security file. I have never, though, exercised my right to demand to see a copy of it, presuming that it exists.

Regardless of all this, I doubt if Russel's legalisms, if that is what they were, would have saved us from the wrath of the security police, any more than would his own resignation have saved his family from intrusions, had Menzies succeeded in having communism banned.

6   At the Golden Cabbage

The move from the Lincoln to the Tudor accelerated dramatically when the lease of the former's premises was sold by its proprietor, John Barry. The new owners sought patrons with far fatter wallets than ours, and preferably not given to dressing in bohemian garb. Banning and some others continued to drink at the Royal, but they also drank at the Tudor, while I don't recollect ever seeing Hooton there.

But why 'The Golden Cabbage'? Peter Hellier, the bloke that I nearly poisoned with mouldy tea, coined the phrase: he Franco-phoneticised 'the Tudor' into *le chou d'or*; hence 'The Golden Cabbage'. I pirated the phrase when I parodied the life-style of the Push both at the Tudor during the hours in which the law allowed it to sell alcohol and after its six o'clock closing time. I called my poem 'At the Sign of the Golden Cabbage'. It reads:

> I'll tell you, she was as willing as me,
> As warm as the sand and as soft as the sea;
> But things just happened differently.
>
> I'll tell you, only the Push that we knew
> Put paid to the two of us seeing it through;
> I doubt had Penelope kept faith with ease
> Squired by distracting bastards like these:
>
> One was pink, like a beer-blotched Cupid,
> And said nothing true, nor yet appeared stupid,
> But teetered word-pictures on the ears of the mob;
> He made discrediting motives his job.

Yet others 'had talent', were mystic, were fey,
And spoke of their souls while they probed for a lay;
But we all were so frightened by Sigmund Freud's warning
That we seldom identified bedmates till morning,

And then those so coupled would pledge to be true
(At least till the next night's drinking was through)
And she and I, well it can't really matter,
But we wakened, confused by the wine-sprung chatter

And bedded, separate, contentedly,
Amazed at our new partner's adequacy;
But I'll tell you, she was as willing as me.

The third stanza was my reprisal against Sope's 'sending me up' whenever he found the opportunity. Apparently it hit home, because when he got around to reading it he thrust his face within a bristle-length of mine and hissed: 'I'm *not* like a beer-blotched Cupid!' Earlier, Eris Walsh had observed that the poem was 'a bit close to the bone'.[12]

The end of Phillip Street where the Tudor stood was, then as now, the domain of lawyers, mainly barristers, but there were also journalists, because the Journalists' Club was then in Phillip Street and all four daily newspapers still retained premises in the city centre. (There were at that time four dailies, each of them with a different proprietor.) People of these two professions sometimes drank at the Tudor. The hotel itself had two bars. One was at street-level and the other, the saloon bar, was on the first floor, and also boasted a few tables and chairs. The lounge was on the second floor, and this occasioned disputes between Push people and a succession of waiters. Push people preferred to buy drinks in the saloon bar and, if they decided to drink in the lounge, to themselves carry their drinks there. The waiters were determined to carry the drinks upstairs and charge higher prices accordingly. They hoped (usually vainly) to receive a tip as well. These contests were almost always won by the Push.

Fairly early in the Tudor days there began the Great Argentine Ant (would-be genocidal) War. These ants hailed originally from Brazil, though first identified in Argentina, and were thought to have arrived in Sydney in shiploads of timber. They produced no formic acid and hence had no sting, but they would eat almost anything in their path — ants, other insects, pet birds in their cages, and the sweat of the odd feverish invalid who was confined to bed; they proliferated, sensibly I suppose, at Rookwood Cemetery. In a suburb near that cemetery, after we sprayed it, dead ants clogged the gutters to a depth of up to some seventy-five millimetres. The New South Wales Department of Agriculture was allotted the task of seeking out infestations of this omnivorous illegal immigrant, but the responsibility for annihilating it was given to the Commonwealth Scientific and Industrial Research Organization (CSIRO). This they did, or attempted to do, by spraying infestations with chlordane at first, but when this poison seemed insufficiently lethal, they switched to dieldrin. As in any search-and-destroy operation, though, manpower had first to be recruited to undertake the search.

And what better source for such manpower could there be than university students in need of casual work? Or so thought the Agriculture Department officer responsible for conducting the campaign. He placed advertisements for job-seekers at Sydney University, probably at first in the science and medical faculties, since these students formed a majority of the team when first I joined it. But the news quickly percolated through to the arts faculty and hence to the Tudor, and to me.

In those days, when one Push member discovered reasonably congenial casual work, other members sought to join him (or her) almost immediately. This occurred very soon in the Argentine Ant War; within weeks the medical and science searchers had returned to their studies, and by then, those working with me comprised almost entirely members of the Push. We were equipped with swordlike instruments that had rubber hand-grips and a long metal blade with a forked tip to enable us to turn over debris on the ground and look for brown ants about three millimetres long. When we came upon some, one of us licked his finger to pick up an ant, and then crushed it. If the crushed insect emitted no odour of formic acid it was probably Argentine, so one preserved it in a phial of alcohol for further examination, duly dating the phial and noting the location where the ant had been found. Among those who worked with me as a bold ant-hunter (shades of Hemingway?) were Darcy Waters, Roelof Smilde, John Olsen and Derek Hoste, and quite frequently our searches deteriorated into farce. On one occasion Darcy and Roelof tried to provoke a strike, but I cannot remember why.

The dual control of the search-and-destroy campaign generated its own farcical scenarios, far surpassing anything that we Push members could stage. When the limits of any infestation had been determined, the CSIRO took control and we traded in our swords, not for plowshares but for little two-stroke engines on wheels which drove the pumps with which we sprayed poison on to the ant-plagued areas. Two employees were allocated to each engine, one to operate the spray and the other to keep the engine chugging along and to refill its insecticide tank with diluted chlordane (or later, dieldrin). Briefly, John Olsen and I operated an engine together. One morning we ant-hunters returned to a paddock that we had sprayed on the previous day to find sheep lying dead or dying. The Agriculture Department officer, his department having financial responsibility, was explaining to the sheep-owner why chlordane could not possibly harm sheep, while the CSIRO officer (whose department hadn't) strolled by, muttering 'That's interesting. We wondered what chlordane would do to mammals.'

In my last days as an ant-killer I was promoted to working at our local base preparing the dieldrin solution for spraying. The dieldrin was delivered to us in huge drums in the form of a yellow powder, which I dissolved in some kind of petroleum. I then added solvent so that the spray-engine operators could dilute the noisome fluid with water before using it as a spray. For this task I was instructed to wear a mask and gloves, but on hot summer days I rarely did so. On one such day I knocked off and, as usual, took myself, unshowered after a sweaty day's work, to the Tudor, where I sat with a group that included Black Judy (Judy Hellier, née Bodkin). She looked at me with alarm and said, 'Dick! What have you done to your hair?' Apparently it was powdered with yellow and standing up in tufts glued together by the dieldrin solution. By then I had reached the conclusion that I could damage my liver sufficiently just by drinking enough alcohol, without resorting to dieldrin as a booster, so I gave up being a bold ant-hunter. After all, I was a mammal, too.

In 1953, having by then reached the magical age of twenty-one, I dropped in at the office of my late father's solicitor to claim my long-awaited inheritance. This consisted of government war-saving bonds plus a cheque, amounting in all to about three hundred and seventy pounds. My sister and brother, being older, had already received similar sums, my brother using his to transport himself to England. But at that office I learnt that I, and I alone, was to benefit from an additional inheritance.

My paternal grandmother, Minnie Whitelaw, had bequeathed me some two hundred pounds. (An apology of sorts for incarcerating me in an orphanage?) This was in the care of her widower, Harold Whitelaw. Obviously he did not approve. He arranged to meet me at a set time at Strathfield railway station, on a platform nominated by him. There, he slow-marched up to me, said not a word, handed me a cheque, and marched away again, still without a word. He was doing his duty, but in no way would he conceal the fact that he hated doing so. My pride was not sufficiently damaged to make me hesitate a moment about making use of all those nice green pound notes once the cheque was cashed.

At both the Lincoln and the Tudor I had a close, but sexually unconsummated, friendship with a young woman by the name of Jane, mentioned in a previous chapter. We discussed books together; we watched movies together (usually at the Savoy, then Sydney's sole 'art cinema'); we drank together at the Tudor and other pubs during daylight hours. But we rarely attended parties together — and it was at parties that most new couplings occurred — because Jane had a strict Roman Catholic father who allowed her out in the daytime to attend (as he thought) university, but confined her to the family home after dark.

On one occasion she came into the Tudor shortly after a rather attractive red-headed girl had draped herself over my knees. 'What are you doing all covered with female?' Jane demanded of me, and the redhead jumped up and disappeared, no doubt to seek a less contested lap. On another occasion I met Jane soon after I had been in bed with Dagmar Carboch (who was given to using exotic perfumes), and Jane complained that I 'stank of female'. Despite these and similar comments of hers, and despite Jane's ready availability at almost any time, I did not twig that she was not averse to a sexual relationship with me. The Langhornes, I think, must have imbued me with their father's Edwardian middle-class and male-dominant view that there were some women with whom one went to bed, and others with whom one didn't (at least outside the bonds of Holy Matrimony). It was mainly about Jane and the B mentioned earlier that I wrote 'The Red Rose and the Briar', a piece of verse probably incomprehensible to those unfamiliar with the folk song 'Barb'ree Allen':

> Feverish, Barb'ree Allen lies
> With wreaths of mist a-twist her eyes;
> It shan't be long before she dies.
>
> Before she dies as William did
> (Whose love for her grew old unsaid)
> Consider why she'll soon be dead:
>
> She'll soon be dead, as dead as he,
> But one might argue reasonably
> Blame can't be laid on Barbaree

Who liked Sweet William very well.
He hastened to his self-made hell
Because he lacked the wit to tell

Her, take her, bed her down;
He slept with wenches round the town
And found his wit — when *she* was gone.

When she was gone *death* sidled in;
Friends planted him where *she* will lie, when
Dead. They'll rise as roses then.

As roses, then, they'll bloom on trees
Enjoying, kindly fate decrees,
Impassioned intercourse — through bees.

By this time I was not completely obtuse sexually. I was then living in an attic at Dawes Point, which was no doubt beneficial to my self-image as a starving poet. One evening a young art student who lived in a room below climbed up to my attic wearing only a dressing-gown, which she had left open at the front, and then threw herself onto my bed, moaning that she was 'so-o-o tired'. This time I did twig. Similarly, when Dagmar directly propositioned me, I was happy to oblige. I cannot remember where this coupling took place but, given my performance, it was definitely not in an orgone box. Neither was it soundproof: for some months afterwards I had friends of both sexes greeting me in an attempted strong East German accent with: 'You are *vairy* affectionate'. Dagmar had thus rebuked me when I kissed her, thinking it only polite to do so before copulation.

Dagmar at that time was in a non-monogamous relationship with Alan Blum, another friend of mine. Blum, a German Jew, was labelled as an enemy alien during World War II, and either joined or was conscripted into a labour battalion of the army. He later studied philosophy under John Anderson, and subsequently became a Libertarian. In an earlier chapter I outlined what I saw as the three main strands of Libertarianism, but omitted to point out that Anderson's realism, logic and empiricism were essential ingredients. But Anderson himself strongly disapproved of Libertarian Andersonians, and when Blum, after gaining first-class honours, was selected by a university committee for appointment as a teaching fellow in philosophy, 'because the post was a junior one Anderson managed to evade giving him the job'.[13] When I first met Blum he was living on the proceeds of a small wholesale import business, which did not at all suit either his intellect or his interests.

After my flop ('fling' is too strong a word) with Dagmar I was sitting with her and Alan Blum one evening at a table in the Tudor. (Six o'clock closing had by then ended.) Alan, who was bisexual, decided to hold my hand. I gently disengaged it, and remained at that table for as long as politeness required, before moving to another table, where Lex Banning and others were sitting. 'Trying to keep it in the family, was he?' spluttered Lex.

And the Push itself *was* a family, though a rather vituperative one, and for me for a long time it was the only family I had. There is more to say about the Push in the Tudor, but that is done in a later chapter. To conclude this one, quoting Lillian Roxon says a little about the atmosphere then prevailing in the Push. In her book *Sex and Anarchy*, Anne Coombs quotes Dottie Addison as recalling, at one of the many parties she and Eris Walsh held in a house they rented in Kensington, that:

> Lillian stood in the middle of the room, naked except for briefs, her arms raised above her head, trying to attract the attention of some man she was interested in. When Dottie asked her why she was standing with her arms up like the Statue of Liberty, Lillian replied that her breasts looked better that way. [14]

In general, Coombs relies too much on oral 'herstory' and not enough on painstaking research, but to me this story rings true both for Lillian and for Dottie.

I also recollect Lillian, in the Tudor, singing a parody that she had adapted from a then popular swing song:

> I'll be seeing you
> In all the old familiar places,
> At the pub and at the races ...

But other Push members have attributed this parody to Germaine Greer, which would place it in the Royal George rather than the Tudor and also in another decade. Germaine and the George are dealt with later, but I certainly remember a nonsense definitely created by Lillian, and vintage Lillian at that. About some woman that she presumably disliked at the time, she recited:

> Mirror, mirror, on the wall,
> Who's the greatest fuck of all?
> With you around, old funnel cunt,
> No other bitch is in the hunt.

When I quoted these lines to Lillian's biographer, Robert Milliken, he replied to the effect that this was surely out of character for a middle-class Polish Jewish girl of those days. But then, Milliken had never enjoyed the privilege of drinking at the Tudor.

Lillian, of course, did not confine her social life to the Tudor. For all I know, her interest in rock music, which was later to bring her fame in the United States, had already begun — but if so, she fortunately did not inflict that music on those in the pub. Certainly she continued to associate with her former socialite friends from Sydney's eastern suburbs.

On one occasion, during her brief liaison with Brian Mooney, she introduced that then rather inarticulate young art student to those friends with: 'This is Brian Mooney. You know, one of the Mooneys of Moonee Ponds.'

7 From the Push to the Bush

While I have no wish to compete with Henry Lawson either as a bush yarn-spinner or a bush-balladist, in both the Lincoln days and those of the Tudor I did make several excursions into the bush. This was partly because of my highly erroneous belief that bush life made one healthy, and partly because of my only sometimes erroneous view that when both lodging and food were provided as well as wages, as they then were for bush workers, it was easy to save money. The money was intended to bankroll a period in Sydney of writing, conversing and drinking without the need, for a while, to work at all.

My first such excursion was with a bloke called Willie, who would probably prefer that I omit his surname. Both of us being veteran hitch-hikers, we did not attempt to thumb a lift out of metropolitan Sydney. Instead we travelled by train to Parramatta, which in the early 1950s was on the outer western fringes of Sydney's suburbia. From the crossroads out of Parramatta we hitch-hiked to Dubbo and presented ourselves at the local office of the Commonwealth Employment Service. There we were offered, and accepted, work as rabbiters on a farm outside Narromine, a small town about forty kilometres west of Dubbo. We were then issued with travel warrants so that we could travel, free, by train to Narromine.

On the farm we were equipped with sharp-pointed and long-handled shovels, as well as crowbars, and told that it was to be our job to dig out all the rabbit warrens in one large paddock. In 1950 myxomatosis had not yet been introduced, and over most of Australia rabbits were present in plague proportions. On the farm we slept in the shearers' shed but ate with the family. Willie, once we were established there, drew on his profound knowledge of agriculture gleaned during his childhood spent in a first-storey flat in the vicinity of Bondi Junction, to lay down the law to the farming family on such subjects as contour ploughing. This they took in good part, at least while we were present.

We were obliged to take weekends off, so usually we headed for the fleshpots of Narromine. There we were spared the expense of sleeping in hotels because one of the Langhorne sisters, Marge, was married to a local dentist, and that couple took us in. Sometimes though, Willie kept me on edge with his far from subtle passes at their teenage daughter. I had no occasion to test the dental skills of Marge's husband, but I hope they were superior to his views on optic hygiene; his recipe for avoiding styes in one's eyes was to wash them daily with Lifebuoy soap, a strong carbolic-acid concoction then popular with males as a remedy for body odour. I failed to inquire whether blindness was more prevalent in Narromine than elsewhere in the bush.

The theory behind excavating all the rabbit warrens was that when they were gone a funnel-shaped rabbit-proof fence could be constructed and the rabbits, with nowhere to hide, could be driven there and bludgeoned to death. But this theory was postulated on the assumption that the rabbits would not have the time to dig new warrens. At the rate that Willie and I were digging, they could probably have emulated the Viet Cong of later years and dug out a maze of tunnels before we had finished. After inspecting our work at the end of our efforts over three weeks the farmer had therefore reluctantly to 'let us go'. Part of our contract had been that we could keep, and sell, the skins of all the rabbits we killed, but we weren't much good at stretching and curing skins, either, so maggots had feasted on them, rendering them valueless.

After being sacked from the farm, and still stinking of rabbit despite several showers, it was back to the Commonwealth Employment Service office at Dubbo for us. This time we were allotted work with a fencing contractor on a sheep station some considerable distance out of Warren, a town itself some ninety kilometres north-west of Dubbo. Again we were issued with travel warrants and we boarded a train bound for Warren. At Nevertire, a tiny hamlet to the south-west of Warren, we expected to change trains, and join a small motor-train which would ferry us over the final twenty kilometres. But it couldn't: the line between Nevertire and Warren had been washed away by floods. That year, all the rivers of the Murray-Darling system were in flood. A truck that was short, but had huge wheels, was substituted for the motor-train, and on this vehicle, known for some reason as a 'blitz-wagon', we were rattled and squelched for the rest of the way into Warren.

There we were welcomed by the fencing contractor, who shouted us lunch in a pub, but in lieu of his paying for us to sleep there, he extolled the virtues of sleeping under the stars and 'getting an early start'. So that is what we did, though as far as I was concerned there was more star-gazing than sleeping; the mosquitoes couldn't sleep either. Because of the floods, the dirt road from Warren to the sheep station was passable only by blitz-wagon, by riding a horse, or by a horse-drawn cart. The contractor had brought with him only the last two of these, so in the morning he asked, a little shyly, whether either or both of us could ride a horse. We both said that we could, but when Willie tried to mount the horse from its right side the horse knew that he couldn't, so Willie was relegated to the cart. I was no horseman, but I had ridden a little on my Uncle Eric's cattle station near Tabulam, so I was able, reins in hand, to mount the nag. The horse-drawn cart carrying Willie and the contractor then set off at a trot. There was no way that my citified and unpractised bum would bear trotting all the way, so I cantered the horse until the cart was on the horizon behind me, and then walked it until the cart was on the horizon ahead. This pattern I repeated again and again throughout the day. We had one rest on the way, but did not reach the sheep station until dusk. When I dismounted my legs would not hold me up. I sank gracefully as well as gratefully to the ground.

Even then, our journey was not over. The shearers' shed where we were to sleep and eat lay some considerable distance from the homestead across paddocks, most of which were covered by floodwater. It was almost like being in the navy again! After lighting hurricane lamps and loading the cart with supplies, we had to steer the draught horse from low water to low water so that the horse (whose name was Ongie, but I cannot remember the contractor's name) always had firm ground rather than inland sea under his hooves. We finally made it to the shed, fed ourselves, and collapsed into exhausted sleep.

Our evening meal that day had consisted of baked beans on toast. In the morning too we were fed with baked beans on toast, and at lunch our diet remained the same. That evening I proposed to the fencing contractor, who had contracted to feed us as well as pay us, that I should take over as cook and have time off from post-hole digging to ply my new trade, and he agreed. I had attempted very little cooking before this, and at first the skills I had acquired by playing darts in pubs stood me in good stead. To avoid scalding myself when opening an over-boiled can of food, I would stand back, old-style tin-opener poised in my right hand while I sighted on the can, and then throw the opener. The steam that then erupted turned to water vapour in the air, then back to steam again when it landed on the hot fuel stove. But at least the contents of these cans were not usually baked beans. Gradually my culinary skills improved as I learnt to cook eggs, mutton or beef, potatoes, and even damper, but all vegetables other than potatoes, as well as milk (powdered), had still to come out of a can, as we had no refrigeration.

The mechanical post-hole digger, if then manufactured, had not yet made its way to outback New South Wales. So crowbars and long-handled shovels were our main tools, just as they had been on the Narromine farm. This time, though, it was the crowbar that was most in demand. With it one dug the post-hole as deeply as necessary, shovelling out the soil as one went along. One then inserted the post, shovelled back the soil in layers, and rammed each layer down with the reversed crowbar.

Because of the floods, only about a quarter of the ground around our shed was above water, and snakes, mainly brown snakes, had congregated in the relatively dry areas. The contractor used to chase them, catch them by the tail, and then break their backs by cracking them as he would a whip. Since the only time that I had attempted to crack a whip it had wound itself, rather painfully, around my face, I had no wish to practise the technique with live brown snakes. But as the gang's cook I had to cope with snakes when I needed to capture and harness Ongie and have him pull the cart to the homestead to bring back supplies.

Ongie was an obstinate beast. Between our shed and where he usually chose to graze was a creek, running a banker in that year of floods. To cross it one moved one's feet sideways on a taut wire stretched just above water-level while leaning on and clinging to a similar wire stretched at about chest height. To harness Ongie to the cart I would cross the creek, drive him into it, and throw stones at him to make him swim to the other side. On more than one occasion, after Ongie had been driven to the side of the creek where I wanted him to be, once I had inched my way back on those wires almost to dry land I found that a snake was basking in the sun just where I needed to step up on to the bank. Back across the creek I would go to collect a handful of stones. With these, I would make my way back halfway across the creek, with some difficulty because I had only one hand free to hang on to the upper wire. I would then throw stones at the snake to drive it away, by which time, of course, Ongie would have swum back to his preferred side of the creek and the whole process had to be repeated.

After we had built fences for about four weeks the flood worsened, and soon there was no dry land left on which to build more. So the contractor rode back to the homestead to ask the squatter what he wanted us to do. While he was away I let off their chains a pack of dogs (beagles and others) that the squatter kept for those occasions when he saw fit to pretend that he was an English squire, and needed a pack of hounds to go hunting. The pack had not been fed for at least a week, and the floodwaters had reached it and were still rising. There was a bloated green carcass of a sheep drifting slowly by, and I realised that the dogs, when set loose, would fight over it because they were starving, so I first attacked the carcass with an axe, releasing noxious fumes that made me vomit, and hacked the sheep into relatively small portions before slipping the dogs from their chains. Where they went and whether they survived I never found out.

When the contractor returned it was with instructions for us to move to a shed near the homestead and to continue fencing, but this time in the home paddock. By then the floodwaters had risen far enough to completely cut the sheep station off from Warren, so neither bread nor any other commercially produced foodstuffs were available. We were reduced, like the early European settlers, to living on meat and damper. I was still cook, but also had to build fences all day, so by trial and error I learnt how to cook dampers *in absentia*. For a while we subsisted sometimes on soggy dough and sometimes on ashes. Soon though, I became proficient at kneading flour and water into a dough, putting it into an already hot oven, and then adding just enough wood to the oven's firebox to cook the damper without burning it. This job done, I would hurry off to work.

Fencing near the homestead did not last long, because the floodwaters continued to rise. But while it did last, one morning the squatter, whom I had never seen before, rode up 'mounted on his thoroughbred' (though probably it was just a very ordinary nag), stopped, and pointing his whip at a fence-post that we had finished ramming firm, announced: 'That cove is crooked.'

Crooked or not, it didn't really matter, for the next day the floodwaters took the post, for all I know, to the mouth of the Murray River, and we were laid off.

When the flood had subsided sufficiently to open again the road to Warren, and we were about to leave the station, Willie, not being one to contain his curiosity for fear of offending, asked the contractor what he did about his sex-life. 'Oh well,' he responded (with remarkable aplomb, I thought), 'I just visit Mrs Hand and her five daughters.'

I went bush again about a year later. This time my companion was a well-spoken young Englishman. He may or may not have been a remittance man, but if he was his remittances from England must have been small and unreliable, because he was always broke. I didn't get to know him very well; when we had hitch-hiked to about forty kilometres west of Orange he developed an acute phobia about the always distant horizon, and returned to Sydney. I never saw him again.

Again I thumbed my way to Dubbo, because that was where the wheat-and-sheep belt blended into the western plains, where squatters grazed sheep for wool and cattle for meat. Jobs were usually readily available there in the 1950s. This time the Dubbo office of the Commonwealth Employment Service dispatched me to a job as a farm-hand on a property just out of Eumungerie, a township about seventy kilometres north of Dubbo. When I presented my travel warrant to the stationmaster at Dubbo I perplexed him by asking for a rail ticket to U-mun-*jerry* instead of what I learnt on the spot was the correct pronunciation, U-*mung*-j'rie. It was probably as well that I learnt that before I arrived there.

My new employers were an oldish and very Scottish couple. The husband, Jock, had taken over the farm and its homestead after serving in some military capacity during World War II. Because they intended to live and farm there for only about three years, they had decided that it would be profligate to pay for furnishing their home with more than rudimentary necessities. This traditionally Scottish parsimony also extended to meals: at lunch one day Jock admonished his wife as she was preparing to serve roast mutton, with 'Och, you're making gravy; if I had known that, I wouldna have brought in vegetables.' Despite this frugality, they were not really mean.

My tasks were many and varied. I fed the guinea-fowls and chooks; I helped mend fences; I helped in harvesting and bagging the wheat. And when the shearing began, I rode out to round up the sheep and herd them into the yards, before turning into a tar-boy and fleece picker-up in the shearing shed. I also pressed the wool into bails, on one occasion committing the Sydneysider's much-laughed-at solecism of pressing the wool without first lining the press with a hessian bail. Early in my time there Jock asked me if I could drive a tractor, and I foolishly told him that I could, though I couldn't even yet drive a car. The plough was duly coupled to the tractor and, after a jerky start because of my lack of clutch-control, I completed what I thought was a perfect ploughing circuit, only to find when I returned to my starting point that my bronco-bucking start had jerked free the plough, and all that I had done was to take the tractor for a joy-ride.

About once a fortnight I would help Jock to string up a sheep by its hind legs so that when he cut its throat its blood would gush out. No refrigeration being available, the meat would then be stored in a mesh safe covered with a wet hessian bag and hung in a breeze-way. Despite the relative coolness of this Coolgardie safe, the portions of the beast most prone to stink needed to be consumed first. So the sequence of meals was always the same: first the innards, including the tripe, then the brains and the various cuts of chops, and last the fore- and hind-quarters, roasted if the sheep had been young and tender, but stewed and/or curried if it had been old and stringy.

At Eumungerie, too, we were beset by floods, though relatively minor ones. For a week or two during which the road to town was under water to a dangerous depth, I was without tobacco. I twitched and I bitched and I snapped at Jock whenever he gave me a job to do. Unfortunately it was during this period of my drug-withdrawal symptoms that Jock decided to assemble a header that had come to him crated more or less in the form of a giant meccano set. (A header was or is an agricultural contraption used for harvesting the heads of wheat and carrying the grain to the bagging site.) Jock wrestled with its various parts for hours and at one point I was trapped in the wheat box just as he was about to screw it down. While he was using his crowbar in an attempt to free me, a nearby shearer drawled to his mate, 'You know, give old Jock a crowbar and a sledge-hammer and he's not a bad mechanic.'

When the flood had receded enough, I borrowed a horse from Jock and rode into Eumungerie for a beer. For almost fifteen days I had smoked nothing, because I had nothing to smoke, so I told myself that I would give it up for good. Still, I thought, it would do no harm to purchase a small packet of ten cigarettes just to smoke while I was drinking. After a couple of hours I had finished that packet, and still thinking I might quit smoking I bought eight packets of tobacco and a hundred cigarettes, just in case, before riding back to the farm. I didn't give up smoking.

While working for Jock I suffered a horrendously painful abscessed tooth. (Bad teeth were probably another legacy from the orphanage.) Jock offered to use his pliers to extract the offending molar, but I preferred to take Bex powders by the baker's dozen until I could ache my way to the nearest dentist, in Dubbo. The 'good lie down' recommended after the Bex could not take place until after the dentist had prised out that tooth — then I collapsed for three days at the Dubbo home of Willie's father, a communist barber.

In that year, 1951, Robert Menzies, the first conservative prime minister since early in World War II, had passed in Federal Parliament legislation to ban the Communist Party, only to be stymied by the High Court, which ruled that he did not have the constitutional power to do so. To gain that power, he put a referendum to the people on the question. Two years earlier, in 1949, the then Labor prime minister, Ben Chifley, had held, unsuccessfully, a referendum seeking power to nationalise Australian banks. With the Menzies referendum in the offing, Jock's wife asked him whether she should vote 'yes' or 'no'. 'Well,' he replied, 'it'll be bad if you vote "yes" and bad if you vote "no", but I think that you should vote "yes".' 'But Jock,' she objected, 'are you sure that they don't want to seize the banks?' In that referendum I voted for the first time, and my vote was 'no'. My action was illegal, since I was only nineteen and the voting age then was twenty-one, but I voted absentee and in my brother's name, he being already in England by then.

Not long after the anti-communist referendum was rejected, a Sydney friend sent me a letter. On the envelope he appended to my name DLit, PhD, and numerous other degrees to which I had no claim. The Scottish couple asked me if I really did hold all these qualifications, and though I firmly denied it, they didn't really believe me. They began looking at me askance, probably wondering what I was *really* doing on their farm. Living in such an atmosphere quickly became intolerable to me, and besides that it seemed to me time that I returned to the Tudor and my real world, rather than rusticating on in this Scottish-cum-Ocker fantasy land. So I 'snatched it' (packed in the job and picked up my pay) and fled back to Sydney.

8   To the Tudor Again

If one knew nothing about the post-war demographic history of Sydney it might well appear that a malign fate stalked every Push pub, striking and killing it as soon as its respite from bourgeois repression had reached its apogee. This was not the case. Inner-city hotels, other than those catering for the very rich, were doomed to extinction. Those few that tolerated the Push did so only because they could attract few other drinkers. In truth, many of these publicans detested serving any such unconventional group, and one that, to boot, insisted on the right of women to drink in their public bar. They served us only as a forlorn attempt to survive financially in the face of an onslaught by property developers. This detestation was possibly not the case with the Tudor but was with all or most of the subsequent Push pubs except, perhaps, the Royal George and certainly except the Criterion. At this last Push hotel the publican, Fred Cooksey, actually liked the Push and sometimes even attended our parties.

For most of the older Push members, including myself, the Tudor days saw the definitive flowering of the Push, though for many others a rather later blossoming time would be argued: the days of the Royal George. This is as appropriate as any other place in these recollections to raise the question of Push seniority. In her analysis of the 'hierarchy' of the Push, Anne Coombs wrote: '... Darcy [Waters] and Roelof [Smilde] were there from the beginning to the end, and this longevity is one of the reasons for their pre-eminence. They shaped its style and preoccupations. But longevity is only one reason. Jim Baker, too, was around for the duration, but Baker never acquired the stature of Darcy and Roelof.'[15] Well, I myself had a fair share of Push longevity, and this was not my experience. At the Tudor, Alan Blum, Jim Baker, Dagmar Carboch, Elwyn

Morris, David Ivison, and sometimes June Wilson were the dominant theoreticians, and hence dominant in conversations. But Coombs also wrote: '[The Libertarian academics] held to a realist, empirical, anti-relativist position while around them the shifting sands of post-modernism grew into dunes. Holding to their rock-like "facts", they were left stranded by the deconstructionists. Abandoned in an academic wasteland, they remained unrepentant, unmoved by philosophic fashions.'[16] And this was meant as a *criticism*, not as a paean of praise!

It was almost compulsory for the more indigent male Push members to work, for a while, as tram conductors. Sydney's trams at that time catered for illiterate travellers, as well as those with poor vision, by displaying on their destination rolls different patterns and colours to identify their routes. The proverbial Bondi trams, for instance, displayed the word BONDI in white letters on a black background above a red ball on a white rectangular background; Coogee Beach trams bravely wore a solid green rectangle above a black rectangle on which the destination was printed in white letters; and trams on their way to Abbotsford had a rectangle of black with the destination printed in white above a white rectangle displaying a red saltire. The exceptions were those trams leaving Wynyard Station for the inner-northern suburbs and those leaving Erskine Street Wharf to travel through the city up King Street on their way, via Kings Cross, to Watsons Bay. Travellers on those were, one assumes, taken for granted as being literate and with clear vision, since they had to make do with just a printed destination.

I did my stint from Dowling Street tram depot, shuttling between either Circular Quay or Central Station and the farther southern beaches — Maroubra, La Perouse and destinations in between. Nearly always I was assigned to an old toast-rack tram, on which I must move myself sideways and apelike along its foot-board, letting go with one hand only after securing a firm hold with the other. But my main job was to collect fares, and this necessitated the use of both hands to dole out tickets to the passengers in return for their coins. While doing so, one held on by the use of one's right elbow. On these outboard trams we were paid three-pence an hour (or was it threepence a day?) danger money. Only once was I in serious danger: my tram was travelling through heavy traffic at Taylor Square and I was relying on my elbow being behind a curve of smooth metal to keep me on board, when a drunk fell heavily against me. My elbow-hold was not drunk-proof; had not a passenger grabbed my arm as I fell I would most probably have been severely squashed by a large truck.

Another who did his stint on the trams was Sope, who claimed (or was it boasted?) that he cowered in the rear driver's cabin rather than collect fares while his tram rattled at high speed across Sydney Harbour Bridge and through the tunnel to Wynyard Station. There were many other Push people who worked on the trams, but I can remember only Grahame Harrison and, I think, Bob Cumming.

During the Tudor era I did not venture only into jobs that were fash-ionable with the Push. Among the myriad of manual and/or clerical workplaces that had the ill-fortune to employ me, a few stand out as memorable. One such job was in a lolly factory, where it was my task, day after day, to put sugar on jubes. These jubes, all either red or green, came to me on a pallet drawn by a storeman-and-packer (a class much superior to a process-worker). I would shovel them into a wire basket that served as a vibrator, pour sugar on them, and turn the vibrator on. While the jubes vibrated until I judged them sufficiently sugared, every so often I would spot what seemed to be either a purple or a yellow one. I would turn off the vibrator and search for this interloper, but it was never there. After lunch (usually eaten on the footpath outside the factory) work was more relaxed, but it had its problems. If I processed fewer than a set quantity of jubes, my employer would sack me; but if I exceeded the 'darg' set by my trade union, that union would black-list me. So once I had sugared my way to the union's darg, I would lean on the still vibrating basket until the knocking-off siren sounded, composing verses that inevitably were too jerky for publication.

The clerical jobs were usually even more boring. All of them were preceded by a portentous set-piece sermon by the personnel officer (who for some inscrutable reason is now always referred to as a 'human resources manager'), who informed one of what the job allegedly offered as great opportunities to 'better' one's self. Dressed in the obligatory suit and a tie of a suitably modest hue, I would then record orders on an appropriate form and pass them on to another clerk whose task was to arrange their delivery. Worse, though, was a job with a legal firm. There, I had to browbeat debtors into agreeing to pay their debt according to the terms of some formula that both they and I knew perfectly well would be impossible to meet. That job did nothing for my self-esteem.

A job with rather less prestige but more interest was one I shared, for a time, with Reg Schurr. We both were employed as some type of nursing attendants at a sanatorium (or tuberculosis hospital) at Waterfall, then just to the south of Sydney's suburbia. There, the patients were segregated: first according to sex, then according to the severity of their suffering. Wards for both men and women were divided into three. Those for whom the infection had been diagnosed early and who would probably recover were in the first. In the second were those in whom the disease was more advanced; these patients, if they failed to show signs of recovery, would in time be moved to the third wards. To borrow from Dante, this third circle housed the death wards: here, females with far-from-pneumatic drooping dugs and males with readily countable protruding ribs sweated out, in summer, the last weeks of their lives. Menial jobs at this hospital were the task of a bunch of aged alcoholics, who lived, when they chose to do so, in an adjoining but isolated building. They did not appear to be patients, but men (there were no women) who were fed and housed in return for their labour. We were cautioned against leaving around such fluids as lemon essence or methylated spirits, which contain alcohol, and told never, ever to venture into their sleeping quarters after dark.

Some considerable time after I left this Waterfall death-house job, both Paddy McGuinness and I applied for work as Santa Clauses in the now defunct Flemings Fabulous Food Stores. Oddly, I was accepted, but Paddy was knocked back. Even then, Paddy looked far more like a Santa Claus than I ever will.

It was during the Tudor era that the laws compelling hotels to close their doors at 6.00 pm were amended. The closing time was moved to 10.00 pm, though a compulsory meal break between 6.00 and 7.00 pm remained in force for a while. At about that time I vanity-published a slim volume of verse with the modest title *I Am the World* (1953). A piece about six o'clock closing is the only work from it that I would now choose to perpetuate. Entitled 'surrealism at 6 pm', it read:

> the reeking bar reached out and dragged me in and
> drank me
> while my salamander seethed and steamed in outside
> mist
> and as the sluts and phallic reptiles thanked me
>   i clawed the slobbering barman
>   and bit his hairy wrist

The title of my book, making it seem like a religious tract, probably put off potential buyers even if the verse didn't, but a young woman in a city bookshop delighted me by trying to sell me a copy. Stupidly, I didn't think to ask her to meet me after work. The book did help me in its own way: it earned me the sack from one of the most boring clerical jobs I ever had.

That job was with the Royal Agricultural Society. I had to record the butter-fat content of the milk of bovine kindness of various breeds of cows. In those days, though not now, the more cream there was, the better the product. Later I was promoted (?) to recording the progeny that resulted from the sex-lives of various elite breeds of dogs. At the Society's Sydney office the news that this new clerk called Appleton had published a slim book of verse erupted across the desks with the speed of a scandal. First, though, there was praise. The chief clerk invited me into his (almost) private cubicle and informed me that he had once bought a book. Because that book had been purchased second-hand, he took it home and sterilised it to ensure that it was clean enough to read (how the devil does one sterilise a book?), but he neglected to tell me what this supposedly sterile tome was about. Shortly afterwards I was told that my services were no longer required; publishing verse, or at least my kind of verse, did not have the Society's approval.

Like working as a tram conductor, attending a racecourse and betting on horses was in the Tudor days almost compulsory. This duty I usually evaded, but not always. When I did go to the races at all, it was mostly only to Randwick, the closest course to the Tudor. Unlike racing devotees such as Darcy Waters and Roelof Smilde, who spent much of their time when not at the races or playing 'boards' (cards) poring over the fine details of each horse's pedigree and form, I read only the brief summaries of the horses running that day, and read them only on my way to the races. I circled the names of all those nags that the sporting journalist had seen as 'having a chance' and then bet on whichever of them had the most favourable odds. On one Saturday this method of selection gave me a win of about twenty-five pounds, so I hired a taxi to take me back to the Tudor. Darcy, having lost on that day, asked me for a lift, and for all of the (mercifully short) journey from Randwick to the city he enlightened me on the myriad of reasons why my horse shouldn't have won.

At this time, too, there were the Kenso parties. Dottie Addison and Eris Walsh had rented a largish house in the suburb of Kensington, and both of them liked parties. Dottie, though, would sometimes sit at a table in the midst of the noise composing and typing a 'whodunnit'. Dottie was a formidable woman, but so were several others of the Melbourne sorority with whom I had first encountered her. One of them lived in an old loft on one door of which there was a sign saying 'Gents'; but if one were foolish enough to step through it one would fall one storey to the ground at risk of life, or at least limb. At one Kenso party, while jazz was playing and Lois Maze was regaling us with hilarious anecdotes, Dottie, while dancing with Johnny Earls, stripped him in time with the music. At the end of that party, all the bedrooms being occupied by (presumably) copulating couples, Johnny and I, lacking the money for a taxi to wherever we were living at the time, looked for somewhere relatively warm to sleep. Fortunately, wall-to-wall carpets were not then compulsory, and Johnny solved his sleeping problem by lifting the room's carpet-square and crawling under it. Thinking that if an asthmatic could brave the dust-mites then so could I, I followed suit.

Another Push house at that time was one rented by Roelof Smilde and Marion Hallwood in Mosman. It was there that I first publicly manifested what I now realise was my obsessive-compulsive disorder. Armed with a bottle of brandy, a jar of amphetamines (then legally and readily available), large quantities of high-quality white paper and a fountain-pen filled with black ink, I would go there uninvited and sit at their dining-room table trying to write poetry. Sometimes I would sit there day and night for two or three days, oblivious of the household while they played cards, slept, or went away. They assumed — quite correctly I suppose — that I was mad, because I rarely wrote more than one word. This I would scrutinise carefully. Invariably I would find some imperfection in my penmanship; so I would hurl that sheet of paper into a corner and select another sheet to begin again … and again.

One evening in the Tudor, close to the by-then closing time of ten o'clock, Elwyn Morris suggested that she and I should, the next afternoon, hitch-hike together to Canberra to see Sope. Full of alcoholic enthusiasm, I agreed, and promptly forgot about it as I made my way home to Dawes Point. At lunchtime the following day I had joined Peter Hellier and a bloke who preferred to be known as Cassius at the Tudor for a beer, as was then my custom, when Elwyn walked in. Why, I wondered, was she wearing shorts, and why was there a huge ruck-sack on her back? She soon told me. Another time, I argued, next week perhaps; but Elwyn when determined was hard to gainsay. So shortly the Hume Highway was graced by an incongruous couple: one an obvious hitch-hiker, and the other wearing a corduroy jacket and carrying a leather briefcase.

We made it to Goulburn by about midnight. By then, if sex was in either of our minds, winter had frozen it out. Hitch-hiking, too, was for us frozen out, and we boarded a decrepit train for the nation's capital. (Nobody who *was* anybody then travelled by train to Canberra.) Arriving there at about 5.00 am, we at first decided that we had better wait until a more acceptable hour before awakening Sope and his parents, but the cold of a winter morning in Canberra soon dissuaded us. These parents of Sope were Christian Scientists — which led him later, when his appendix burst, to thank the god he didn't believe in that he wasn't at home at the time — and they were unimpressed by having to breakfast with an unshaven man who sipped brandy from a flask and smoked incessantly. After I left, Sope told me, they referred to me only as 'that silly man', a mild enough comment in the circumstances.

During this visit to Canberra, Sope took us to a party attended mainly by student diplomats from a college recently established to train university graduates for the diplomatic corps. Somehow, during drinks, conversation led to one of these (not very diplomatic) aspiring diplomats disparaging some bloke not there. 'And he actually wore *Stamina* trousers,' he concluded. As I had only recently inherited sufficient money not to continue wearing these cheapest of the cheap nether garments, I blushed and carefully stared at my new suede shoes. Sope, to his credit, strongly defended the virtue of Stamina strides.

Around that time Sope was teaching English at a high school in the western New South Wales town of West Wyalong. There he introduced me to a fellow-teacher by the name of Marcia. His motive was most certainly either matchmaking or seduction by proxy, but I was happy to go along with it. Seduction in a country town in those days, I discovered, required more ingenuity than I could muster; I made something of a pass one evening in the grandstand of the local showground, but that setting somehow did nothing for the libido. No doubt if I had taken Marcia to my hotel room the publican would have winked at it, but Marcia's life as a teacher in that town would have become unlivable. My hopes were renewed when we were both invited to a party at 'Tom's flat', but Toms Flat turned out not to be what the Americans call an apartment, but a dusty patch of cleared paddock surrounded by abandoned goldmine shafts. Though it *was* flat.

It was while courting in West Wyalong that I met for the last time my uncle, Aubrey Kellner. One of Sope's local friends was the son of the proprietor of the town's cinema. He, Sope, myself and others were drinking in the bar of my hotel when Aubrey came in with the cinema's proprietor himself. Aubrey was there in his capacity as head in Australia of the Metro-Goldwyn-Mayer (MGM) film distribution network — some years earlier he had been given gratuitously a sea trip to the United States, where he had posed for the obligatory photograph with the studio's then stars, Jeanette MacDonald and Nelson Eddy (who happened to be his mother Rita's favourite actors). Everybody in West Wyalong was impressed by my having such an illustrious relative, though little did any of us then realise that Aubrey's job would soon become extinct. Even the social elevation that my uncle's celebrity had given me did not much impress Marcia, so I abandoned my seduction attempts and returned to Sydney and the Tudor Hotel.

Arguments, or perhaps debates, were the common currency of many conversations at the Tudor. I remember one argument I myself had with Cassius, who was an admirer of Harry Hooton. Hooton's poetry, insisted Cassius, was 'alive', whereas Lex Banning's poetry was 'dead'. I cannot remember who scored a win in this wrangle, but I have subsequently grown to realise that any debate in which one or more of the terms used is indefinable is completely pointless. There was another argument in which I was involved with a young Andersonian, probably either Alwyn Karpin or David Ivison, about the nature of 'red': is it a quality or a relationship? The Andersonian view, of course, was that colour is a quality. I argued at the time that it was a relationship between the (human) eye and the light rays reflected from the red object. My argument was fallacious because it confused the objective characteristics of 'redness' with one method of perceiving them.

One argument at the Tudor, which I overheard but in which I refrained from participating, was about a character by the name, it seemed, of 'May-uh'. The two participants could agree on almost nothing about this person. This did not surprise me at all: soon after the argument began I became aware that while one participant was speaking of Mao Tse-tung, the other had in mind the academic, Henry Mayer.

My book, *I Am the World*, having been reviewed fairly kindly by Ken Slessor in the Sydney *Sun* (I had met him earlier in the Journalists' Club), I decided during the Tudor days to appeal to a higher authority. So I sent a poem to Ezra Pound, still at that time, I think, a prisoner of the United States army for broadcasting fascist propaganda for Mussolini during World War II. I heard nothing for some months, and then there arrived by mail a magazine entitled *The European*, subtitled 'The Journal of Opposition', with my poem published in it.[17] The main contributor, and probably the editor, was Sir Oswald Mosley, the former leader of the British Union of Fascists. At the time I was a Trotskyist, and found the incident rather embarrassing, as now I find the poem. Entitled 'Daybreak in Drought', it reads:

> The moon, a pale-faced convict,
> Exhales a wisp of cloud, and
> Spins his meteor butt to earth.
> A black head-shroud chokes back
>   last pleas of innocence,

And stars dim out in sympathy
While sullen day awakes to drought.

The red-jowled sun, bon vivant
following aesthete,
Lurches on view, his cue missed twice,
Uncertain feet kicking horizon dust,
The parched tongue of his hangover
Licking on yellowed bones
in dry creek beds.

The earth has fever; with withered skin
and cracked, dry lips
She gasps out futile dust to blind
the sun.
She grips dead stumps with crumbling grasp,
Fearing to lose the last corpse of her last child
for the wind's dissection.

The clouds charge drought with memories
of the mating of earth with rain,
And of lush paddocks of grass
once suckled.
They wipe earth's face with sterile shades,
The horizon swallows them ...
And the day moves on with the slow inevitability
of a steam-roller.

During the Tudor period, I also edited *Arna*, journal of the Sydney University Arts Society. This, Lex Banning organised. He persuaded Marjory Davison, then a final-year honours student in English, to stand for election with me since, as only a nominal student that year, I could not have been elected if standing on my own. Marjory, in turn, agreed to continue her studies and let me, in effect, act as the sole editor. This was in 1955, when the origin of the name 'Arna' was a mystery. It remains so, despite my claiming in my editorial to have solved it. Quoting from the first issue bearing this title, the 1938 edition, I wrote that Arna was 'the name of a Sun God who figures in the myths of certain aboriginal tribes as the donor of laws and culture to mankind'. Subsequent research has failed to unearth the word 'arna' in any known Aboriginal language.

The most innovative aspect of the 1955 edition was my introduction of the works of Australian artists to this Arts journal. As well as a cover design by the then unknown John Olsen, reproductions (in black and white, unfortunately) of his work and that of Lorraine Trebilcock, Roy Fluke and John Coburn were included. Olsen's cover depicted the sun behind a foreground of coastal shrubbery, and in the shrubbery lurked the impostor god Arna. Contributors of verse and/or prose included John Rybak, Lex Banning, Charles Higham, Bruce Beaver, Vincent Buckley, Dagmar Carboch, Sylvia Lawson, John Croyston and George Clarke.

I had then been devoting all my time for some months to chasing contributions and advertisements for *Arna* and then seeing it through the press at Edwards and Shaw. And in that time I had not only earned no money, but had lived on some of the proceeds of the advertisements in that journal. I was penniless and in debt, and was shortly to flee to Melbourne. During the Lincoln and Tudor period, though, I made two other onslaughts into rural Australia, neither enjoyable, so Melbourne must wait until after the chapter recalling them.

9 Hot Work — If You Can Get It

In Sydney in the 1950s, Broken Hill was seen by many as a city of legend. There, we believed, the union, not the State government or the police, was in control. With their lead bonus, the workers were the best-paid in Australia. (Never mind that they were probably destined to die of lead poisoning.) So when Willie suggested that we go there to make our fortunes, after some hesitation I agreed.

The hesitation was warranted, because Willie by this time had acquired a car. Of what make the car was, I cannot remember, but it was an open vehicle, and because of this lack of a solid roof it was elevated to the status of being labelled a 'sports car'. Already he had once managed to completely capsize it, preserving his cranium uncrushed only by dint of clinging to the stem of the car's steering-wheel. Broken Hill was far enough away to provide ample opportunities for accidents, and the front-seat passenger had no such stem to cling to for support.

We began our marathon motoring effort, I am fairly sure, with only the two of us in the car, but somewhere along the way we acquired a young woman. West of Orange, the highway diminished to a single bitumen track for traffic moving in either direction. In those days cars had no indicator lights for turning left or right, and certainly no hazard or reversing lights. Drivers relied on hand-signals to indicate their intentions — an outstretched right arm and hand to turn right or overtake, and a right arm bent so that forearm and hand pointed skywards to turn left or come to a halt. This did not help much when an oncoming vehicle seemed bent on 'playing chicken', and when there were then no speed limits in the far west, nor, for that matter, any breathalysers, anywhere.

What we really needed was a hand-signal indicating 'Yes, we *are* chicken! We *will* pull over for you.'

After Dubbo there was no bitumen at all, other than in towns, and the road was a narrow strip of corrugated red dirt, stretching to the distant horizon. The corrugations, much to my relief, kept Willie's little car to a relatively low speed — at that time I could not yet drive — and the west-bound traffic, mainly high-powered station vehicles or trucks, swept past us in a cloud of dust, their speed lifting them from the top of one corrugation to that of the next. We, on the other hand, jolted up and down over and into every one of them.

The first night we slept beside the road somewhere in the vicinity of Dubbo, the young woman with Willie. The second night, though, a little to the west of Nyngan, she came, uninvited, to sleep with me. In retrospect it seems likely that Willie had put the 'hard word' on her — sex in return for a lift. Outside the Push circle, most young women then were not prepared to appear openly promiscuous.

At Wilcannia, and in need of a beer, the three of us went into the wrong pub. All the other drinkers were Aborigines, who looked at us askance but made no comment. The (white) barman served us all right, though not in any friendly way. Had we been black and ventured into the *other* pub, our reception no doubt would have been even less welcoming.

The cost of petrol and running repairs to the car had eroded our cash substantially, well before we reached Broken Hill. I had suggested that we stop at some other and closer town and find work for a while, but Willie replied to the effect that Peter Hellier, then working as a journalist in Broken Hill, would not let us starve. In the event, he did.

Lacking fuel, we coasted for the last mile or so into Broken Hill, parked as best we could, and asked a couple of policemen where we could buy a meal. At that hour (about midnight), they replied, the only place was the (theoretically illegal) two-up school. So there we went. That night we slept rough once more, and the girl vanished, never to be seen again, at least by me. The following morning we fronted Peter at his work.

Peter did agree to guarantee us for a week's sleeping quarters at an hotel, but further than that he would not go. With our remaining coins we bought a loaf of bread and, yes, we did find work. We lived on that loaf and the precious water from the hotel's taps for a week — at that time water still arrived in Broken Hill by steam train. Where Willie worked I cannot remember, but I worked at a gas plant. Shovelling coal into a furnace in the heat of summer (usually more than forty degrees Celsius) on a diet of bread and water, I found debilitating.

And for us, high wages at Broken Hill proved a myth. It was true enough that workers at the lead mines were paid a hefty bonus, but that work was confined, by union decree, to those born and bred in the sovereign State of Broken Hill. Outsiders such as we were, when engaged in menial work, were paid at a lower rate than workers in Sydney, though rent and food prices were geared to cater for those blessed with a regular bonus. So, after a week at the furnace, I was paid, I ate, and I left the 'Silver City'.

With Willie and his car remaining in Broken Hill, I hitch-hiked down the Silver City Highway, crossing the Murray River into Victoria near Mildura, and hitching farther south to the town of Ouyen (pronounced *oh*-y'n). There, drought provided me with work. In normal seasons a machine for grading wheat according to the size of grain was used to select the biggest and best grain for replanting. In drought-stricken north-western Victoria that year it was used for a different purpose: to select any grains that were large enough to be acceptable at all at the wheat silos. I worked as assistant to a bloke who operated one of these machines.

I remained there for three to four weeks — long enough to earn some money with which to return to Sydney, but also long enough to reward me with abraded arms and knees from hefting hessian bags of wheat, each weighing about thirty-two kilograms. The just-large-enough grain was dispatched to the silos, for human consumption, while the much more numerous bags of tiny and shrunken grain were reserved for animal fodder.

My next, and last, foray seeking work in rural Australia was in the company of the artist and folk-singer Brian Mooney. We had hoped to find work near Cairns, but only Brian made it to that northern outpost. It was winter, so Brian lent me his father's overcoat. On either the first or second evening we reached a bitterly cold Woodenbong, where we were fortunate enough to find, beside a timber mill, smouldering sawdust on which we could sleep warmly. In the small hours of that night Brian was awakened by shouting and wheels of sparks dancing against the black sky and its stars. It was his father's overcoat, with me inside it; the heat had impelled me, unwisely, to jump and dance and shout. This had the effect of fanning the flames of the burning wool.

The following morning we shouldered our belongings and began hitching towards the Queensland border, but our sooty appearance and my scorched and tattered overcoat provoked the local brats to greet us with shouts of 'Bagmen! Bagmen!' until our first lift rescued us from them.

By the time we reached Gympie we were running out of cash, so Brian withdrew most of his savings from the local branch of the Commonwealth Bank. At the Commonwealth Employment Service office we were told that jobs were scarce — Australia was then suffering a recession — but if we back-tracked to Kingaroy we would probably find jobs harvesting peanuts. This we decided to do, but as we were trying to thumb a lift out of town a station-wagon carrying what I first took to be khaki-clad soldiers screeched to a stop. 'How far are you going?' I asked the driver.

At that, what seemed to be a whole posse of khaki-clad figures jumped from the car and surrounded us, and I then saw their police badges. 'It's a matter of how far *you're* going,' their sergeant rasped. '*Southerners* aren't you? We've had a lot of trouble with *Southerners* round here.' After thirty to forty minutes of interrogation we were instructed to be out of town by sundown. I thought it prudent to refrain from pointing out to them that getting out of town was just what we had been trying to do when they so rudely detained us.

Neither Brian nor I knew what harvesting peanuts might involve, but the next day we were to find out. The peanut-farmer harnessed his tractor to a plough to which was hitched a braced oblong of hessian. As the plough unearthed the peanuts, Brian and I, almost on all fours, scrambled after it, picking up the peanuts, roots and all, and throwing them on to the hessian. Eight hours, and probably more, of this under a hot Queensland sun was, to say the least, trying. And the pay was lousy. After the first day we decided to work there only another three days to build up a 'bank', and then to try our luck farther north. Unfortunately, not much luck was available.

We had been advised that lifts were more likely on the inland route to Rockhampton, via Gayndah, Biloela, etc, rather than on the coastal route, where rivers had to be either forded or crossed by vehicular ferry. If that advice was sound, then the coastal route must have been bloody awful. Because of the recession, quite a few job-seekers were on the road looking for a lift, our numbers considerably in excess of those of the sparse traffic heading north. More than once we saw people boiling sugar-cane leaves in discarded tins, in the hope that this would result in something edible. But there, at least, water was available; at another place on that long road Brian and I stood for some six hours in the sun, with no lift in sight and no water to ease our increasing thirst. At last, one rattle-trap lorry that could have come straight out of the pages of *The Grapes of Wrath* did stop. It was too full of family to pick us up, but the driver drained a little rusty hot water from the lorry's radiator and gave each of us a small, and rather too tasty, but nonetheless very welcome drink.

Eventually we were given not only a lift but also the offer of jobs, by the manager of a boxing troupe, which rested between bouts while travelling in a largish van. This job Brian accepted. But I could not see myself in that (no doubt thespian) role, so I accepted the lift but declined the job. I cannot remember to which township this van carried me, but from there on I continued north alone, eventually reaching Rockhampton.

It is hard to recollect the sequence of my misadventures after I left Brian. I remember Rockhampton beer as being rather good — at that time all major rural centres (and some not so major) had their own breweries. Some brewed very fine beer, others awful; Mudgee 'Mud' was the worst that I tasted. On one summer day in Dubbo I had opened an unchilled bottle of this brew, and poured it directly and without any tilting into a glass. One solitary bubble erupted.

North of Rockhampton I decided to try the coastal route through Sarina to Mackay (pronounced M'*kye*). By the time I reached that city I was almost broke and feeling rather desperate. At a pub there, I met a North American Negro (probably a deserter from the United States army during World War II) who befriended me. He took me home to his Aboriginal partner and their children, living in an Aboriginal riverside slum, fed me, gave me a bed for the night and, in the morning, breakfast.

While eating that breakfast I remembered that one of my fellow-unfortunates at the Royal Australian Naval College, Julian Barry, lived with his parents in Mackay, where his father had a legal practice. So, after obtaining directions from my overnight benefactor, I set out to visit him. I was warmly welcomed, and Julian's mother lamented that he, unlike me, had never been adventurous enough to move freely around Australia, working wherever was convenient. To her credit, she looked askance for only a moment after I told her where I had slept the previous night.

Either before or after Mackay, despairing of a lift, I briefly 'jumped the rattler'. My illicit use of the railway system was less dangerous and more comfortable than that of the American hoboes. These, I have read, usually travelled in unoccupied cargo spaces on flat-bed rolling stock: I slept, reasonably well, on a freight train, in the compartment usually reserved for drovers who were supervising livestock carried on that train. But I was frightened — of arrest, or I don't know what. When, while it still was dark, the train came to a halt at a tiny station, I debarked, and spent the remainder of the night in its waiting room. That morning, I was shaving with cold water from the station's water tank when the stationmaster turned up. With some trepidation I watched him approaching, but he simply bade me 'Good morning' and went about his railway business.

It was almost certainly north of Mackay that I accepted two jobs, I cannot remember in which order. Both were connected with sugar, but unlike my earlier Sydney job, they had nothing at all to do with lollies.

One of them was working for an obviously recent immigrant from Italy. Presumably he had been a peasant in his home country, for we ate from a common bowl. His dog subsisted on what we failed to eat, devouring it from the same bowl. At that time, when sugar was mostly harvested by slashing with a hand-held long knife, it was customary to burn the cane before the cane-cutters moved in. This was partly to make it easier to cut, and partly to minimise the risk the cane-cutters took of treading on taipans, cane-toads and suchlike creatures. My employer, though, thought that his small crop would sell at a better price if it remained unburnt, and so more juicy. My job was to grasp each sugar plant with both hands, and then to move them sharply downwards to defoliate the plant. That was the theory of it, but in practice I got rid of more of the skin from my hands and arms than I removed leaves from the cane.

I lasted in that job for just two days. Then I grabbed my pay, hitch-hiked to a pub in the nearest northward township, and ordered a beer. When I tried to pick up the glass with my right hand, as I normally do, I found that I could not close my hand sufficiently to safely lift the glass. Two hands were needed. Another drinker noticed my plight. He, too, was of Italian descent, but born in Australia and with an accent to prove it. He invited me to his farm, which he told me he had already sold, and was living on the proceeds before joining the North Australian Workers' Union and taking a paid job. Having to drink Brandivino (an obnoxious concoction of sweet sherry and brandy) with my breakfast of steak and eggs, was a small price to pay for his hospitality.

The other job was in a sugar mill. There, after I had demonstrated my ineptitude at coupling or uncoupling the rolling stock of a sugar train, I was relegated to working in the 'gas loft'. This 'gas' consisted of the leaves and other waste products of the sugar cane, all of which were used to fuel the furnace that began to brew the stems of cane into a dark and sugary molasses. High above that furnace, in the loft, I breathed in the dust as I shovelled what I could of the 'gas' to fire the furnace. This was the second furnace to which I had been sentenced during my travels, and while the near-fundamentalist Church of England clergy at the Ashfield orphanage may have considered such a sentence suitable for someone of my ilk, I didn't. So I hitch-hiked north again, eventually reaching Townsville.

In that city I learnt that there was a glut of casual workers around Cairns, to the north, but also that the Commonwealth Employment Service could offer me a job as a railway fettler in the west of the State. I decided to take that job. The steam-driven railway locomotive pulled my dog-box carriage south, and then west, through Charters Towers to Hughenden, a distance of almost three hundred kilometres, and then, on a branch line, to Stamford, about a hundred kilometres farther to the south-west.

Stamford consisted of a pub, a general store, a stationmaster's cottage, and a village of tents housing the fettlers. On the eastern horizon there was a solitary tree, and on the western, none. As there had been no rain in the area for at least two years, precious little other vegetation survived between these very distant places on that parched infinity of plain.

The railway gang that I joined there was not just any mundane mob of maintenance fettlers. Dignified by the title 'Flying Gang', we were to rush to anywhere at all where the transport system threatened to break down — anywhere, that is, within pumper distance of Stamford. (A pumper is/was a small flat-bed trolley about two metres long and less than that wide. It was propelled along railway lines by its occupants 'pumping' the two handles that drove the trolley's wheels.)

When I joined this Flying Gang, my period of enforced unemployment had returned my hands to their normal soft state. Our main implements were crowbars and sledge-hammers, so I excused my ineptitude with them by explaining that I had done no 'manual labour' for some time. This was a mistake. My choice of language, along with the curly-brimmed straw hat that I had come by on my travels and the dark drooping moustache that I then wore, led to my being dubbed 'Manuel Labor, the Mexican bandit' for the duration of my time with that gang. Another nickname bestowed on me was 'The Squire'. This was not only because of my accent, but also because of my jacket. Like my borrowed overcoat, it too had suffered in the Woodenbong fire: burns at its back had created two tails, which fluttered behind me as I worked the pumper in the cold of an inland morning.

Because of that cold, warm clothes were desirable for going to work, but by midday we had stripped to shorts and boots. On the whole, my two new names were indications of friendly acceptance on the part of the gang. This increased when I tried to instruct in his duties a non-English-speaking Latvian by using my extremely limited French — I had learnt at school the French word for 'hammer', but was flummoxed by 'crowbar'. My eccentricities paled when compared with those of another fettler: fancying himself as a cowboy, he dressed for the part, complete with high-heeled riding-boots and spurs, that tripped him several times each day as we walked along wooden railway sleepers.

The occasional crisis enlivened our working days. One was when a train, only two days late rather than the three that we had expected, appeared on the western horizon after we had dismantled rails for sleeper replacement. Nobody, it transpired, had remembered to bring either a red flag or detonators with which to warn the driver. Frantically we drove spikes into rails and sleepers as the engine drew closer and closer, lurching to the left and then to the right as locomotives did on those narrow-gauge lines. 'Mutton for dinner,' muttered one fettler, but surprisingly the train with its woolly cargo rattled over rails held together only by single spikes, and loose ones at that, without mishap, and receded towards the eastern horizon.

Another crisis occurred when Stamford's water-pump broke down. Steam trains, of course, can go nowhere without water and coal, and the coal was regularly dumped in the township from special supply trains. In western Queensland's then waterless plains, that essential liquid was available only from sub-artesian bores, and horrid-tasting stuff it was. So when the pump ceased functioning, so did all transport — either for livestock out of the region or for food supplies, including beer, into it. We worked on that water-pump for three days and nights, hauling up the cables and pipes from deep underground and repairing them, before trains could run again.

When first I arrived at Stamford, I was allotted a tent to share with another fettler, an old seaman, who tried to seduce me. ('Any port in a storm,' he advised me when I rejected his advances.) I was also supplied with cooking utensils, and some sort of stove was communally available. I lived in that tent only until the first payday, then — partly to get away from my would-be seducer, but partly out of laziness — I moved into the pub. There, I was provided with a bed, breakfast and dinner, and given a packed lunch to take to work. Also available, though, was credit, both for food and lodging, *and* for beer.

At the end of about three months it hit home to me that I was getting nowhere financially, and that if I continued on this path I would go grey while still wielding a crowbar and sledge-hammer. So I was relatively abstemious for two pay-fortnights and built up a very small bank. With this, I set out for Sydney.

Like Bonaparte's retreat from Moscow, my retreat was beset by hunger. My companion, for a while, was another Stamford fettler, also bound for Sydney, but with a bank rather larger than mine because he had lived in a tent while there. So when at a pub still well to the north of Mackay he elected to stay at its bar for the rest of the day, I left him and resumed my hitch-hiking. My lift from that roadside bar was with a couple of desperadoes in a far-from-reliable old car. On the muddy road southward it broke down several times, and I stood uselessly by while they crawled under its rusty chassis to repair it. When we reached Rockhampton, all three of us squelched into a café seeking a meal, but because my companions were so liberally coated with mud they were refused entry until they washed. While we were eating they then asked me to lend them, until the morning, my last paper money, a ten-pound note. Though I knew that it was highly unlikely they would repay me, I felt obliged to lend it to them. I never saw them again.

Somehow, with only a few shillings in my pocket, I contrived to reach Grafton. Hoping at least for a meal, I made my way to the home of my uncle, Reg Appleton — the one who had declined to foster me. All went well for a while, despite my travel-stained appearance, but when Uncle Reg asked me where I had parked my car, I told him that I had no car, and that I was hitch-hiking. My welcome then wilted. As the ever-so-respectable local manager of an Australia-wide insurance company, Reg believed that his reputation would be forever tarnished if a vagrant nephew — and one bearing the same surname to boot — were to be identified by the sober citizens of Grafton. He drove me to Grafton railway station, rather than to the much larger, and closer to Sydney, South Grafton station, where he might be recognised, and bought me a second-class one-way ticket to Sydney.

I arrived there penniless, but to a fond welcome, food and lodging. The wives of two of my friends commented on my bulging forearms — wielding crowbars and sledge-hammers does produce these. But then came *Arna*, financial desperation, and soon, Melbourne.

One last Tudor recollection, though. I was hitch-hiking from an overnight party back to central Sydney with Harry Hooton's most faithful disciple, Bob Cumming. Bob was also known as 'Shortcomings', not only because of his height, or lack of it, but also because of his frequent, but unpredictable, stupidities. Once we managed to win a lift, he proved true to form. He confided to our driver that both of us were farmers, driven from our properties by the recent and drastic flooding in the Hunter Valley. Clearly he was looking for a handout, but whether because the driver could see me in his rear-view mirror as I cringed in the back seat beside Bob, or because neither of us looked even remotely like farmers, he didn't get one. The nearest Bob had ever come to being flooded was when, during World War II, he was arrested by the naval police — known, not very fondly, as 'The Crushers'. Charged with being absent from the navy without leave, he was awaiting trial on board the ferry *Kuttabul* when it was sunk in Sydney Harbour by a Japanese midget submarine.

10   Melbourne Interludes — I

As a confidence man, Bob Cumming had little success; but like other bohemian gatherings, the Sydney Push did have its share of petty and not-so-petty criminals. The most flamboyant was Ashleigh Sellars, a con-man with some flair. Ashleigh's exploits were numerous; one of them involved selling (or, in the case of friends, giving) cut-price air tickets, almost perfectly forged, to several distant and desirable destinations. Ashleigh could never resist the temptation to boast about his successful conmanship, and, probably as a result, had done time in various prisons. It was from Ashleigh that I learnt that homosexuality, and homosexual rape, were the norm within the prison system; previously I had assumed that such practices were largely confined to the more expensive Greater Public Schools, and of course to the acting profession. As well, from my own experiences at the Lincoln, men wearing brown pork-pie hats were to be suspected of sodomy until they proved otherwise. Bisexual intellectuals, like Alan Blum, I did not classify as homosexuals, which simply indicated that I was incapable, then, of logical conclusions. Obviously I was then what now would be called, with dubious etymological basis, a 'homophobe'.

There were also blundering criminals associated with the Push, like Brian Raven. Brian probably thought of himself as an 'enforcer', and certainly claimed to be a Hitlerite. He is said to have once driven his rust-bucket of a vehicle to the bush to expropriate a bootful of illegally culti-vated marijuana; when his car was pulled over by police at Kings Cross and his boot was opened, he escaped arrest because what he had stolen proved to be some other, and quite innocuous, variety of plant. But when I was, as it were, seconded to Melbourne's bohemia, I found the proportion of crims to be far greater there. To be fair, though, there was also a much higher proportion of artists.

The decrepit students' hostel where I had slept on previous visits no longer existed. The only meeting places that I was aware of when I arrived in Melbourne were Raffles Coffee Lounge and the Swanston Family Hotel. The former, much grander than the Lincoln had been, was patronised by, among others, a group of male homosexuals, presided over by the heterosexual Dottie Addison and, later, Patti Dixon. At the latter one might rub shoulders — literally, because six o'clock closing and the resultant crush were still in force in Victoria — with such luminaries as Brian Fitzpatrick, David Boyd, John Perceval, Leonard French and, later, my fellow-exile, John Olsen.

Where, or for that matter whether, I slept on that first night in Melbourne I cannot remember. Soon, though, I moved into a loft near the old Queen Victoria Markets. This I shared with an Englishman whose name eludes me and an engineering (I think) student. Life became a little complicated when I encountered Pam Wilkinson, whom I had known at the Lincoln, where she sat on the periphery of Harry Hooton's circle. She was married to the nameless Englishman, but by then was living with John Cafarella, an artist of sorts, who shared a house (shed?) with Doug Stubbs, another painter.

When first I met him, Cafarella, on learning that I had lobbed in a loft shared with his lover's husband, looked fierce — much as many Australians then expected knife-wielding Italians to look — but when Pam told him that I was 'all right' he became quite friendly. This friendly acquaintanceship soon soured my relations with the English husband. A further disrupting feature of the loft we shared was that it had a toilet and a kind of kitchen, but it had no bathing facilities. A weekly visit to the nearby public bathing establishment was, in the circumstances, the only solution for us to de-stink ourselves during Melbourne's summer. These were two good reasons why I should not lodge in that loft for long, but while still living there I took a job as a porter with the Victorian Railways.

In suburban railway stations, porters then did no 'porting'. Instead, they stood at the exit gates collecting from passengers coloured scraps of cardboard that purported to prove that these passengers had paid for the privilege of commuting to work. Every time I stopped a passenger whose cardboard ticket was invalid, the offender seemed so stricken that I felt obliged to let him or her continue on with impunity. (Conversely, while a tram conductor in Sydney, I had been far too cowardly to attempt to extract a fare from the notorious Bea Miles.) My uniform, including as it did another funny hat, struck fear, as well, into one of the more shady drinkers at the Swanston Family. When I pushed my way to the bar and stood behind him, he darted towards the toilet to make an exit, but stopped when he realised that the cap I was wearing was *not* part of a police uniform.

Standing at railway-station exits and reading scraps of cardboard would have been unpleasant when winter came to Melbourne, but well before it did, one railway official discovered that I actually spoke English. He promoted me to be trained as a van-stower. But van-stowing, like ticket-collecting, was regarded as menial work, and in those days menial work attracted only, or almost only, recent immigrants, who consequently had limited English. Our training consisted of learning by rote the names of all the stations on every line out of Melbourne. These, of course, had to be learnt in the correct sequence. By dint of remembering historical associations, and by other mnemonic methods, I got by, at least for a while, until overwhelmed by boredom. But my poor classmates found great difficulty in pronouncing, let alone memorising, such town names as Corio (pronounced k'-*rye*-oh), Fyansford (*fye*-'ns-f'd) and Traralgon (tr'-*ral*-g'n). I did not last long enough to experience actually loading a train.

At about that time David Boyd threw a party at his pottery studio. One of those drinking there was 'Sydney Bill', a name with which this bloke had been dubbed shortly after arriving, not long after me, in Melbourne. (Decades later he still retained that name, though few in the

Sydney Push would have been eager to reclaim him.) When Sydney Bill did not feel obliged to be seen as macho enough to open a bottle of beer with his teeth (there were then no twist-tops), which often he did, he resorted to placing a penny at the edge of a shelf. He then set the crown-seal of the bottle on the edge of the penny, and hit it sharply with the heel of his hand to jolt off the bottle-top. At this party, Bill chose to demonstrate his method on the edge of a free-standing bookcase on which were displayed numerous examples of David Boyd's priceless pottery. The top of the beer bottle shot off all right, but so did all the pottery on the shelves of the bookcase, crashing to the floor in a scattering of shards. Ever the gentleman, David picked one shard up, looked at it sadly, and muttered: 'Pity. I rather liked that one.'

I did not work directly for the Victorian Railways again, but did so indirectly. In the 1950s, at the railway stockyards, an infamous employment system which trade unionists called 'the bull-ring' was operating. There, those wanting an evening's work lined up hopefully. The stockyards foreman, standing on a platform above them, pointed, one by one, to select those on whom he was willing to bestow work. One wet evening he chose me.

So there I was, shoving and dragging daggy-tailed sheep into cruelly crowded railway rolling stock, in heavy rain, until midnight or later. And daggy *means* daggy! By the time I knocked off, the front of everything that I was wearing was thickly coated with sheep shit. At that time I must have still been living in the loft, because I walked home, of necessity wearing those now noisome garments — it was that or risk arrest for indecent exposure — and then consigned them to the communal garbage bin.

Contrary to what I wrote earlier, I did have another contact in Melbourne, and contact him I did; let us call him S. He lived in Clifton Hill, and was a disciple — far more committed than I was — of Ezra Pound. When I phoned him, he was ecstatic about Pound having forwarded my poem for publication in Sir Oswald Mosley's journal, *The European*, in which Mosley promoted his recommendations for the future of that continent. S urged me to visit him in his flat. There, he lent me Pound's *Pisan Cantos*, which I admired, but then went on, and on, about the perniciousness of Jews and how they were responsible for Pound's incarceration at Pisa. He then accompanied me on a tram back to the city centre, on the way pointing at any fellow-passengers who looked even slightly Semitic and hissing, 'She's one of *those*, isn't she?' I did not wish to associate further with a bloke who accepted me only because of his egregious error in assuming that I, too, was a fascist and racist poet, so I kept the *Cantos* and never saw him again.

Not long after that, a fellow named Peter, who had once visited the Sydney Push on their home ground, offered me his shed to live in, mainly because he saw me as a minor luminary of the Push. The shed, and his partly built house, were in Boronia, then not so much an outer eastern suburb of Melbourne, but rather the foetus of one, waiting to be born. Mud was everywhere. The roads were muddy ditches, and the dwellings, mostly unfinished and owner-built — obviously without consultation with architects — were surrounded by quagmires. A neighbour of Peter's, not an arty type but a collector of vintage La Salle cars, was highly amused to see, at Peter's frequent parties, dozens of real and would-be artists and writers squelching through the mud in their suede shoes.

For me, these parties had consequences. Marion Lucas, then an art student at (I think) the Melbourne art gallery, had met me at the Swanston Family Hotel, just down the road from that gallery. She was one of those who attended Peter's parties, and she began to take an interest in me. As a middle-class Melbourne girl of the 1950s, Marion was at first hesitant about a full sexual relationship; but Peter, who was married but wanted to prove his Sydney Libertarian credentials (or so he thought), insisted that other males, including me, went to bed with his wife. Jealousy overcame Marion's inhibitions.

Boronia, I thought, was unlikely to provide employment opportunities, so I registered with the nearest Commonwealth Employment

Service office, and settled down to live on the dole — though the obnoxious term 'dole-bludger', like 'shoplifter', had yet to be coined. So for a time I lived in my shed and slept in my (usually lonely) bed, and tried to write. After a while, though, the CES did offer me a job, a clerical one, and in Melbourne's central business district. For the first time in my life I had an intelligent employer, for whom I worked as a clerical assistant and/or personal secretary and composer of correspondence. During my still-broke early days as a commuter, the knowledge, from having worked there, of the labyrinthine internal passages of Flinders Street Station stood me in good stead: when I couldn't afford to buy a railway ticket, I could easily debark from a train and make my way into the city without risking the attention of porters more punctilious in their duties than I had been in that role.

After work I frequently met Marion. By then, the Swanston Family had gone the inevitable way of inner-city pubs and shut its doors. For us, being as we were among the less prestigious Swanston Family patrons, the new meeting place was a pub named Tattersalls, near the 'Watch House', as Melbournites quaintly called their central police station. Tattersalls was a seedy pub, its reddish carpet stained with grease, grime, and many other sorts of unseemly grot. The more prestigious of the Swanston patrons, wisely, had moved elsewhere, probably to Carlton.

Marion and I would have drinks at Tattersalls, followed by a meal in a cheap Greek or Italian restaurant; sometimes it was too late, by then, for me to catch a train back to Boronia, and Marion was often reluctant to return to her parents' home in Richmond, so we bedded down on the floor of some friend's room.

Then there was another party, not this time at Boronia but at a fully mature and very bourgeois Melbourne suburb. Melbourne's bohemians did not adhere to the Libertarian ethic that any grog taken to a party became common property. Instead, one always stood with one's source of drinks clearly within view, and preferably within reach. At this party I was minding my own grog, if not my own business, when Doug Stubbs offered to refill my glass with Scotch. Doug? Scotch! I should have taken warning, because Doug rarely had enough money to buy even a glass of beer, and certainly not a bottle of Scotch. But I accepted the drink, and within minutes a bloke wearing a suit (of all things to wear to a party!) stood over me exclaiming, 'So you're the bastard who stole my Scotch!' Whereupon he hit me.

Until then I had been of the view, as I still am, that fist-fighting, or any other kind of fighting for that matter, was something that one put away, like other childish things, on attaining adulthood. But I hit back. Presumably I was winning that fight, because when we both fell through a closed plate-glass door, he fell backwards, and I forwards. He appeared uninjured, but the broken glass cut deeply into the bone behind my right eyebrow, slashed through my beard and the skin behind it, and severed the tendons and a vein of my right wrist. While our hosts were screaming at me to take my profuse bleeding away from their carpet, Marion rang an ambulance.

The ambulance crew first staunched the blood gushing from my vein and then ferried me to the Alfred Hospital. There, I spent what seemed a very long night lying on a stretcher in the casualty waiting area, suffering from increasing thirst from the Scotch-induced dehydration, though possibly also because of shock. For that long night I tried, with very little success, to roll cigarettes with only my left hand obeying my brain's instructions. I was operated on in the morning.

No general anaesthetic was thought necessary, and when, after my wrist was cobbled together, the surgeon had told me that my fingers should work quite well as long as I had no wish to shine as a violinist, I was trundled to a bed in a hospital ward. Very soon afterwards, a bevy of friends visited me. They included Marion, Peter, Patti Dixon, Doug Stubbs and four or five others. With them they carried balloons and streamers, with which they festooned my bed, a flask of brandy and, thank God, tailor-made cigarettes.

For some time after my discharge from hospital my right hand was of little use, so I resigned from my clerical job. Melbourne's emotionally demanding bohemia was becoming irksome to me, and I hankered for the less emotionally demanding but more intellectually stimulating world of Sydney. So Marion and I soon set out to hitch-hike there. My signalling our need of a lift had to be different from the conventional thumb gesture, because I could neither straighten my thumb nor close my fist. What motorists made of my petitions by means of a partly open hand with its thumb bent upwards and pointing towards the sky, I cannot know, but at least some of them did stop and offer us lifts. Eventually, after about two days, we arrived, around midnight, at Sydney's Central Railway Station.

11   Melbourne Interludes — II

Why, after hitch-hiking from Melbourne, Marion and I found ourselves at a city *railway* station in Sydney, I can only surmise. Presumably our final lift had left us in some southern suburb, and from there we travelled by train. No matter how we came to be there, though, Central Station at around midnight was not at all welcoming.

First, we needed somewhere to sleep. Marion, I should think, had never before been in a situation where a bed was not readily available. I had no addresses for Push people, and at that time, anyway, most of them were peripatetic with regard to their places of residence, so we decided to seek an hotel. To this end we hired a taxi. The driver let us out of his cab at several inner-city pubs, all of which claimed that they had no vacancies, though probably our travel-stained appearance together with the fact, in that ultra-puritanical era, that we did not 'look married', militated against us. So it was a case of 'Thank God for the Salvos': our driver took us to their 'People's Palace'. Welcome though it was, that establishment was far from palatial. Sleeping places were divided only by head-high and flimsy plywood partitions, so through the night we were lulled to wakefulness by the snores, farts, fucks and nightmares of our fellow-unfortunates.

In the morning, the question was, how to find the Push? I assumed (correctly, as it happened) that the afternoon and evening meeting place was still the Assembly, a pub to which it had moved, mainly because of its proximity to the Tudor, when that pub met its demise. The Assembly's interior was a yellow-tiled monstrosity with all the old-world charm of a public urinal, its malodorous disinfectant reinforcing that image. Nobody in their right mind would spend daylight hours there when harsh sunlight revealed every crack and stain on the tiles of such a place. So we tried the upstairs Repin's Coffee Lounge in King Street, and there succeeded in rejoining the Push.

Where, in Sydney, we first found a Push bed, I can no longer remember, but soon we were sharing, with two other Push couples, a squalidly modern little brick house in oh-so-respectable Artarmon. There, Marion discovered that she was pregnant. My aim, initially, was to borrow enough money to pay for an abortion, which operation, as it was then illegal, cost about two hundred pounds if it was to be performed by a qualified medical practitioner. I needed work, and found it with the unscrupulous principal of a shady coaching college. My pupils all lived in different suburbs, often several miles from one another, so to cover the distance from one to another within the time demanded by my schedule, I needed wheels. I acquired only two of them. They came in the form of a pushbike-cum-motorbike, which I had to pedal to gain speed before engaging its tiny two-stroke motor. Uphill, I needed both sources of energy. Mounted on this hybrid contraption, I wobbled and wove my way through often heavy traffic from suburb to suburb, but to little avail. My dismal reputation as a wage-earner was such that nobody in the Push would lend me anything like two hundred pounds within the couple of months that abortion remained an option.

In despair, one day I collected the rent for all six of us in that horrible house and, instead of lodging it with our landlord's estate agent, I used it to get miserably and totally drunk, in the process forgetting, temporarily, who I was and where I lived. For Marion, this was enough. She phoned her mother in Melbourne and was sent her train fare to return home, which she promptly did. Obviously my philoprogenitive instincts were sadly lacking, because I panicked and fled north. But by the time I had hitch-hiked almost to the Queensland border, I asked myself, 'Can I really do this to Marion?' It seemed that I couldn't, so I turned around and hitch-hiked back to Melbourne. I must have passed through Sydney on the way, but I cannot recollect doing so.

In Melbourne, I phoned Marion at her parents' home in Richmond. She was overjoyed to the point of incoherence to learn that I was already in her home city, and she ran to tell her parents. I could hear happy shouting in the background before she returned to the phone to invite me to come immediately to Richmond. This, with some trepidation, I did. On my arrival, her parents seemed to be of the kind, then probably rare, who acknowledged that some co-operation had been necessary for me to have got their only daughter with child.

Marriage was at once in the air, though not in the bed until the Church had made it legal. We were married on 21 May 1957 behind the altar of a High Anglican church in St Kilda, with Marion's parents as the only witnesses. But Marion, despite marriage, was unwilling to set wagging the tongues of her numerous relatives by the usual pretence that our child had been born prematurely. She insisted on having him adopted. I was not fully convinced that adoption was necessary, but gave way to her wishes. Probably both of us were too immature to have coped well with the vicissitudes of parenthood. Until our son was born, we lived with the Lucases. Over these months, I introduced Marion's younger brother, Trevor, to my collection, on 78-rpm discs, of Leadbelly, Ewan MacColl, Josh White and other folk-singers. I can therefore claim some credit for igniting the spark that led to his acclaimed, but unfortunately brief, career as a musician.[18]

Once our child had been relinquished, it was as if he had never existed. As a young and outwardly respectable married couple, Marion and I rented a flat in the Melbourne suburb of South Yarra. That suburb then did not yet seek to vie with Toorak as a prestigious place to live, and our flat had been brought into being by the erection of partitions to divide a relatively small house into two. The adjoining flat was already occupied by an Australian actor, Les (who was 'resting' during all the time I knew him) and his young English wife, Wendy. They became, for a while, friends of ours.

So far we were, to some extent, still resisting respectability, and still drinking at the increasingly tatty Tattersalls Hotel. There, an amiable petty-criminal by the name of Bill Collins assured me that he could, and would, 'win' Marion. At that time I was working as a clerk at a shop specialising in women's shoes, handbags and the like, and it was my daily task to walk with the shop's takings to deposit this money in the bank. Bill offered to hold me up, take the cash, and later share it with me. This kind offer I politely refused, but shortly afterwards Bill did win Marion.

This seemingly improbable coupling must have been widely publicised before it took place, because the following morning, while I was still lying in my lonely bed, two women walked in. One was, I think, in her honours year at Melbourne University, but regardless of her academic status, she offered me the chance to revenge myself on Marion. She was willing to join me in bed. I preferred, though, to wallow in self-pity rather than to wallow with her, and so declined.

Doug Nicholson later told me that the scurrilous verses I cobbled together and pinned up on the pub's walls in revenge for this coupling of Marion and Bill Collins got through to Collins and hurt his self-esteem. 'But what can I do?' he complained. 'You can't thump Appo.' Had I known of my immunity from 'thumping' I would probably have versified even more viciously. Not long after this episode I met, for the first time, Little Dark Jan.

Her full name was Jan Millar, and she *was* small and dark. She came to our South Yarra flat with a bloke whose face I remember, but not his name. For me it was lust at first sight, though not only lust. With Marion and those two I strolled out to our backyard; I don't know why, since nothing was growing there except a kelpie pup. Then, Marion and the bloke returned to the house, and I could not resist immediately kissing Jan, and that kiss she returned. She was the first woman to inspire in me such immediate and strong desire. We did not become lovers at once. During that period I was working through a crash course of only one year to become a qualified teacher. That same year Marion and I abandoned our South Yarra flat and, with Les and Wendy, moved into a rather bourgeois but quite pleasant rented house in the suburb of Gardiner. Later, Sydney Bill moved in with us there.

Decades later, Bill was to boast at a Sydney party that he had slept with every woman with whom I had lived. (What this says about Bill and his relationship with me, I shall leave to psychologists.) But if Bill on that later occasion was not lying, his bedding with Marion may have taken place not long after Chester (Philip Graham) had arrived at our Gardiner house with a young and beautiful woman by the name of Eva. One morning, after a party, I found our nuptial bed empty of Marion, but occupied by Eva, looking even more beautiful because she was naked. Unfortunately nothing came of it.

At that party, Chester, before flaking on our lounge, had carefully placed his corneal lenses in an otherwise empty matchbox. Cleaning up the next morning, before I discovered Eva, I threw away the matchbox. I cannot remember whether he succeeded in retrieving these eye-pieces, or was compelled to revert to his spectacles. That was just one of the several parties we had at Gardiner, many of which were attended by more Sydney Push members than Melburnian locals, but none of these parties did much good to the house. There were lawns that by then needed mowing, but we lacked a mower, and none of us realised that refrigerators, then, needed periodic defrosting. While frost of the kind that fridges accrue is more easily compressed than ice, it is so only within limits. Eventually, using force to close the fridge door would no longer work. All in all, by the time our lease expired we had to borrow money from Marion's parents to restore the Gardiner house to even a semblance of order.

Until the demise of the Gardiner house, Marion and I had led an independent, or largely independent, life together; after it, we did not. Frank Lucas, who was a painter and decorator, decided, quite correctly, that we were financially incompetent, and took over our affairs. Had he left us to learn, by trial and error, how to manage financially, we would probably have done so in the end. Instead, he and his wife sold their Richmond home and bought another, and larger, one in the suburb of Canterbury, and persuaded us to join them there.

We would, they told us, be able to live our lives separately from theirs, having a bedroom and a sitting room (well, a veranda) entirely to ourselves. But the myth of separate lives was exploded early in the piece. One night, while pulling a pillow from under Marion's head, intending to place it under her bottom, I accidentally also pulled her long red hair. The scream that she then let go brought her mother, father and brother, the latter two brandishing clenched fists, bursting into our bedroom.

Canterbury, like its neighbouring suburb Camberwell, was what was called a 'local option' area. That meant that there were no pubs, and if one wanted a drink one had no option but to go to another suburb. As is usually the case, the nearest pub to this publess desert was an unsavoury blood-house. I still patronised Tattersalls Hotel, but not every evening. I would have liked, after a day's teaching, to find a tolerable pub somewhere near where I was deposited, on my way to what unfortunately was my home, so that I could cushion my homecoming with alcohol.

I was able, though, to take some refuge from the tediousness of Melbourne life by keeping up a tenuous link with Sydney's literary scene. In June 1959 Lex Banning published in the *Observer*, then edited by Peter Coleman, two poems, one of which was entitled, in its published version, 'John Croyston'. It read:

> Poor Poetry, they said,
> poor Poetry is fled
> and gone to his death-bed.
>
> They said, and I concurred
> until your voice I heard
> and knew that I had erred,

> reading in your eyes
> those words unto the wise
> that 'beauty never dies'.
>
> How vain had been our weeping,
> for safely in your keeping
> had Poetry been sleeping.

But the title Banning had given the poem was 'Being a Variation on a Theme by John Croyston', so he wrote to the *Observer* complaining that the editorial truncating of his title had distorted the meaning of his poem, the subject of which had been the theme in one of Croyston's verses about his 'lights-o'-love'.

It seems that Banning's complaint was justified. The editorial change in his poem's title did distort its meaning. For in the next issue of the *Observer*, along with Banning's letter and the editor's apology, Croyston published a piece of verse entitled 'Variation on a Theme by Lex Banning'. It read:

> Oh, thou art food for poets,
> Brave Poetry,
> On which the poets feed,
> But poorly.
>
> Truly, not thou,
> But the Poet sleeps,
> And not the Poet
> But the Public weeps.
>
> And cruel justice,
> In reverse,
> Puts the thinness
> In their verse.

This exchange of seeming insults provided me with the opportunity to join the resultant convocation of catty rhymes. My title, I decided, had better be longer than my text, so under the heading 'Being a Variation on a Theme by John Croyston, by Lex Banning, and A Variation on a Theme by Lex Banning, by John Croyston, A Variation', I published the following four lines in the 11 July issue of the *Observer*.

> Ring thy change for charity,
> A brace of muses passeth by
> Bedevilled by their bards' dispute;
> Thus unemployed — and destitute.

Croyston wrote yet another response, concluding, aptly enough, with the lines:

> But let me practise charity,
> And force 'An Instant's Clarity',
> Knowing all are overdosed,
> Declare the correspondence closed.

His preceding lines, though, were marred by his being unable to find a rhyme for 'Appletons' other than 'simpletons'.

Banning, too, wrote another response, but only to Croyston's first effort. He did not publish it, possibly because he considered it more acerbic than was then acceptable between friends. But in 1987 Alex Galloway and I did publish it, in the collection of Banning's verse we called *There Was a Crooked Man*. It read:

> Poor John Croyston
> being terse
> imputes a thinness
> to my verse.
> I wonder

could it elsewise seem,
considering whence
I took my theme?

While all this backbiting was taking place, I was becoming an experienced, though not very competent, schoolteacher, working for my first year in an outer suburb, but for my second, mercifully, in an inner-city school. Each morning, looking respectable in the then obligatory jacket, slacks and collar-and-tie, I would be driven by Frank Lucas to the appropriate railway station or tram-stop. This return to the stultifying suburban smugness that I had fled from the Langhornes to escape, increasingly irked me.

I took to 'wagging it', not from school but *after* school. Instead of returning to Canterbury at the end of the school day, I would drink at Tattersalls with Jan and then go home with her. By then, Jan and I were seen by most of our friends as what would now be called 'an item'. I was again frequently taking amphetamines, and because of the resultant nervous twitch, Bill Collins, who was not without wit, labelled us 'Twitchy and Bitchy'.

Marion, for a while, did not know or pretended not to know of our affair, but things could not last like this for long, and I had no wish for them to do so. Eventually, at the end of my second school-teaching year, Jan and I boarded a train and sought solace in Sydney.

12 Of Divorce, Copulation and Death

The Royal George Era Begins

Because we had travelled by train, Jan and I arrived in Sydney in the mid-morning. The express train in which we had fled from Melbourne was then scheduled to arrive at that time and (nearly) always did so. This meant that my home city presented us with no immediate problems as to where to sleep. But like Marion and I on the previous occasion, we were eager, though not as urgently so, to contact the Push, and again, it was the upstairs Repin's Coffee Lounge in King Street that led us to them. This time, at Repin's, our informant was Ley Wolfe, who told us that the main Push drinking place was now the Royal George Hotel, at the corner of King and Sussex streets. Later, I was to learn, Ley told other Push people, 'Appo's changed. He's now the sort of person to whom one would lend money.' How, after only a brief conversation, Ley could have reached such a conclusion, remains a mystery to me, but certainly I was accepted at the George, not only as a 'responsible person' but also as a minor Push celebrity returned from exile.

Thus, for me, a colourful era began. Varied recollections come crowding back, and I will make little attempt to recount them in a strictly chronological order. Friends that I met for the first time at the George included Terry McMullen, Peter Groenewegen and David Ferraro. Lex Banning, having returned from England, was a regular there, as was Jim Baker, and shortly after Jan's and my arrival, John Cafarella arrived there too, as did Germaine Greer. If it was she, rather than Lillian Roxon, who composed the parody of the song 'I'll Be Seeing You' (as mentioned earlier), it must have been then. I saw little of Germaine in the George era: she was not one of the few who saw me as a leading figure of the Push, and it was mainly with leading figures that she chose to associate.

For the next few weeks Jan and I lived mostly together, and sometimes separately, but where, I cannot remember. Jan obviously found the climate surrounding the Sydney Push at that time very much to her taste, though she showed little or no interest in its Libertarian philosophical theories, which were then frequently debated in Push circles. Certainly I did not expect to be her only sexual partner, and neither *was* I, nor she mine.

Soon, and quite reasonably, Marion decided to divorce me, so I asked Barry Kennedy, by then qualified as a solicitor, to act for me, instructing him not to oppose but to facilitate the divorce. Lionel Murphy had not yet enacted the Family Law Act, nor yet even become a senator, though probably he had already thought of both. Divorce was available only if at least one partner in a marriage supposedly *didn't* want it. Among the possible grounds were adultery, violence, lunacy, and desertion. This last required so long a period of separation that most divorcing couples eschewed asserting that it had occurred. In practice, all this meant that without proven evidence, real or contrived, of one of these infringements of the state of Holy Matrimony, divorce could be refused. Usually, adultery was the preferred infringement, but if both partners agreed on the evidence of this transgression, collusion could be taken for granted and divorce refused.

While we were still together, Jan had agreed to be cited as co-respondent when Marion initiated proceedings to divorce me, but this agreement gave rise to moralistic objections by a few Push members who should have known better. Earlier, some character at the Royal George had said to me, pointing to Jan, 'Why did you bring *her* here?' but this I was able to ignore because almost everyone liked her. And it was from among those who *did* that objections were voiced. One Push member by the name of John berated me to the effect that I should not involve Jan in my sordid domestic problems. I replied, with some asperity, that he was demonstrating only his own middle-class moralism by depicting divorce as a sordid domestic problem. Since then, John has been through at least one divorce, but his views have remained unchanged. Paddy McGuinness held similar views. Perhaps I should have made it more clear to them that not only had Jan agreed to be named as co-respondent, but in terms of the law then operating she was so in fact. Marion, had she so wished, could, and probably would, have cited Jan as co-respondent without Jan's or my or, for that matter, anyone's consent. Regardless of all this, though, the divorce turned out to be a farce preceded by a tragedy.

Even after Jan and I drifted apart, I was concerned for her well-being and contrived to see her fairly frequently. By then she was living in a Push house with John and another bloke, but not, I think, cohabiting (a quaint word) with either of them. She confided to me, on one such occasion, that John had led her to recognise that she had been 'doing a Marilyn Monroe'. She admitted that all her manifestations of ecstatic orgasms, as well as her pleas for 'just a quicky' before I set off to work, were a pretence that she played out to make herself more desirable to men. During this period we had no sex together, but like John, I still worried about her.

Her well-being, if that is what it was, came to an abrupt and cruel end when Paddy McGuinness sailed for England and the London School of Economics. As was the custom then, Push people, Jan among them, gathered at Circular Quay to see him off. Those waving farewell were crowded on to a platform perched high above the concrete pier to which the ship was moored. A 'safety fence' was there to keep them in check, but Jan, characteristically enthusiastic and probably drunk, thrust herself too far forward. She fell — and crushed her skull. Mercifully, I was not there, but John, who was by then, I believe, an intern at a Sydney hospital, told me that even if she lived she would remain a vegetable. She didn't live.

In the Lincoln days another young woman had died, in her case by suicide. Of her, Lex Banning wrote the following lines:

Epitaph for Tania

Who was not altogether unlike
the Duchess of Malfi

Remember her;
she had a quality of beauty.

Lament for her;
Time used her poorly.

Speak truly of her;
she was not wholly honest.

Be glad for her;
she died young.

That epitaph might well have been written for Little Dark Jan.

The Law, as Dickens observed, is an Ass, but it is also a Sluggard. Months were to pass after Jan's death before Marion's divorce petition was heard. That farcical hearing was preceded by a lesser farce involving David Ferraro and a young woman, called Patsy, with whom he was having an on-and-off affair. The two had managed by some words or actions to attract the hostile attention of 'Sydney's Finest' — the New South Wales Police Force. These bold enforcers of the law of the land raided and searched Patsy's flat, seeking, one can only suppose, something with which they could charge David and/or Patsy herself. All they could come up with was an hotel schooner glass, labelled ULVA (standing for the then United Licensed Victuallers' Association). So they charged Patsy with 'possession of goods reasonably suspected of being stolen'. Barry Kennedy defended her and, hardly surprisingly, she was acquitted. Had almost any Push household at that time been similarly searched, schooner glasses would have been found, just as they would have been, too, in many non-Push homes.

Christmas came, as it is wont to do, and as always for Push people who had retained no family ties in Sydney, it posed problems. Not only did many Push people reject and resent the Christ Mass aspects of Christmas; they also objected to being subjected, when taking their main meal of the day in a restaurant, to the tawdry tinsel all around and the often inane jollity. Terry McMullen had an additional problem: he detested eating any form of poultry. On Christmas Day it was almost impossible to order, in a restaurant, a main course that did not feature poultry — in those days usually chicken rather than turkey.

Terry then lived in a rented flat in Glenmore Road, Paddington, which until her recent death he had shared with his sister Kathie and her husband, Myles Coman. He invited me, well in advance, to join him there on Christmas Day, and I accepted. What we ate I cannot remember, but certainly we ingested no birds. We did, though, consume quantities of beer, and later, wine. The flat had only a tiny fridge, and that day I introduced Terry to the practice of adding salt to ice. Terry was already in the habit, when lacking enough refrigerated storing space, of making use of a bath with a generous supply of crushed ice. When I arrived at his flat he had half-filled his bath with bottles of beer and covered them with ice, but my 'salt of the bath' solution was new to him. After we poured bags of cooking salt over the ice it solidified, sealing in the beer more efficiently. Terry remembers this as taking place during Easter, and it may have done so again then; but compulsory poultry was definitely confined to Christmas. Easter was *not* 'for the birds', only for their unhatched progeny.

New Year, too, is wont to come round, and the new year of 1963 brought with it two deaths that shook Sydney to the core. This unsolved crime, if it was a crime, had considerable impact on the Push.

On the New Year's Eve heralding that year two parties were held that became relevant to the case: Gilbert Bogle and Margaret Chandler attended one in Chatswood; Geoffrey Chandler and his then lover, Pam Logan, were present at a Push party in Balmain. The Chatswood party had little to do with the Push, but early on the morning of the first of January the bodies of Gil and Margaret, who had left that party together, were found near the Lane Cove River.

Gilbert Bogle was a distinguished research scientist and a former Rhodes Scholar. He was engaged in highly secret work, and in the following month he was planning to fly to the United States to continue his secret research. This led to a number of bizarre theories as to why the couple had been killed. Could it have been the KGB or the CIA or even ASIO? But to the public at large, and to many journalists, the motive seemed obvious. The couple's bodies had been partly naked; they were in a park at night and obviously, it seemed, sex was involved. Margaret's husband, Geoff Chandler, had to be the murderer.

The 1960s have been labelled 'the swinging sixties', but by 1963 Sydney had not 'swung' very far. Those who attended the Push party at Balmain would have considered that sex between Gil and Margaret, or Geoff and Pam, provided little more than a titbit for gossip, and certainly not a motive for murder. This was *not* the view of the Press, nor of the public. Geoff Chandler was hounded by reporters wherever he went, and eventually the publican of the Royal George opened a room in the basement of his pub so that Chandler and his Push friends could have some respite from Press surveillance during their normal evening drinks. The first time I visited that basement room I was not admitted until my Push status had been verified by somebody already inside. Pam Logan, at that time a friend of mine, was not as fortunate as Geoff.

The Annandale house that she shared with other Push people was staked out by the Press, making life miserable for all who lived there. One of them, Mike Walsh, was photographed, and the newspaper responsible captioned the photo as being of Chandler. To enable Pam to leave the house or return again without being hounded daily, the other residents resorted to a series of diversions. Then Pam took ill and was admitted to hospital. There she had a private room, but every time she left it to use a toilet or bathe she was confronted by a lynch mob of the more mobile patients and their visitors. They hissed at her, 'Chandler's woman' and 'murderess' — some of them hitting at her with their handbags. When Pam was discharged from hospital she fled to Canada.

The Royal George over this period was patronised by, among others, Ashleigh Sellars, mentioned earlier, and his henchmen. Then there was Roger Cox, who drove a car, the body of which he had constructed with weatherboard on a vintage car's chassis. To make it more eye-catching, he had painted the boards a post-box red. Roger played Eliza Doolittle's father in a local stage production of *My Fair Lady* and for a while sang ditties from that musical almost incessantly. At the time, several people were recruited to the Push's poker-playing and punting regulars. Of these, only Terry McMullen, along with those listed with him earlier, became close friends of mine.

Marion's divorcing me was a much more protracted affair than was Patsy's legal charade, and much more farcical. Marion's petition was not heard until well into the new year and, because the alleged adultery (or much of it) took place in Victoria, the hearing was to be in Melbourne. I flew there to be Marion's sole witness against myself, Jan by then being long dead. In Melbourne, I took myself to the chambers of whoever Barry Kennedy had briefed to represent me, to find Marion's legal representative also there. Since I was now the only witness, both told me, it was highly likely that the judge would refuse divorce on the grounds of collusion. Would I mind, they asked, if instead of alleging that I committed adultery, they changed Marion's plea to read that I came home drunk every night and beat up the family? 'Yes,' I responded, 'I would mind very much indeed.' So, looking pessimistic about the chances of success, they let the case go ahead on the original grounds.

After that no-doubt legally improper consultation, I sought company at Tattersalls Hotel for the remainder of the day and all of that night. Arriving there, I looked around and thought to myself, 'At last they have put down a new floor-covering.' But no. On closer inspection, I realised that the bitumen-like substance on the floor was almost solid grot, with ruby-like specks of the old red carpet still glowing through in places. Soon afterwards, I believe, health authorities closed down the pub.

That night, I sat up with Sydney Bill, Doug Stubbs, Bill Collins and other friends from Tattersalls Hotel. We drank; we talked; we popped amphetamines to stay awake; and then we drank and talked some more until interrupted by dawn. The next day, when I stood in the dock (yes, one *did* stand in a dock in those days), my resultant laryngitis rendered me almost inarticulate. The judge hearing the case seemed a kindly old gentleman, and he proved both our legal eagles wrong. Attributing my husky voice to my grief at Jan's death, he expressed his sympathy, then granted Marion her divorce.

Outside the court-room, I heard Marion say to her father, 'Richard is looking very old.' 'He's no spring chicken,' responded Frank. But that was fair enough; I felt extremely old. Jan's death, tension arising from the wait for a court hearing, and a night's drinking and talking, had all taken their toll.

The following evening I flew back to Sydney.

13   Under the Bridge

Well before Jan's death, along with those Libertarians, male and female, who discussed such topics as ideology, the Industrial Workers of the World (IWW), Freud, Reich and his orgasm theory, etc, I had become friendly with a group of young women who were Push regulars at the Royal George, though not especially interested in social or political theory. Robin Clode was one of them. Within weeks of my return to Sydney, Robin, Patsy (she of the schooner glass), and another young woman called Liz, I think, would so often turn up at the Royal George together, with me making a fourth, that Darcy Waters took to calling out 'Appo, you beast' to greet our every arrival. The Push being what it was, it did not take too long before Robin (but not Patsy or Liz) and I fell into bed together.

I was, by then, teaching at Newtown Public School and sharing a tenement room with David Ferraro, also in that suburb. Robin, having left Sydney University without graduating, as I too had done, was supervising the welfare of 'difficult' children, while still living with her parents at Bellevue Hill. Most afternoons or evenings, and also on Saturdays, we would get together at the Royal George. One evening after we left the George, she came home with me.

Not long after that episode, I persuaded Robin to leave her parents' house and live with me. When we rented a flat at Milsons Point, we had in common with Johnny Earls and Janie Iliff the same landlady, a Miss Tattersall (that name does recur!), their flat being at the back of the next-door building, ours at the back of ours. (They were not purpose-built flats, but partitioned-off segments of two old two-storey buildings.) Robin's pretence, for the sake of the very respectable views of her parents, was that she was sharing the flat with Janie; Janie's pretence with her parents was the same. Both Johnny and I had dispensed with pretences, other than with the parents of our partners.

Miss Tattersall, whom we came to call Tatty, was a very tolerant woman — once, we were informed, she had been, in England, the equivalent of a 'Miss Australia'. Tolerant she was, but certainly not unobservant as far as her property was concerned. One evening, drunk and not very 'with it', I accidentally knocked over the rather decrepit fence separating her two properties. By the time I had fumbled myself back to my feet, Tatty was there. While I was pointing out to her the folly of erecting a fence to separate the two backyards, she agreed. 'Yes, Mr Appleton,' she mumbled, possibly not having heard what I had said. But, deaf or not, she continued, and completed, re-erecting that inefficient barrier. On another occasion, Robin and I were bonking, too vigorously it would seem for our decrepit bed, and the bed crashed resoundingly to the floor. Within seconds Tatty appeared. I cannot remember what words passed among us, but the bed, too, she promptly re-erected. The passionate moment, though, she could not.

A hiccup in our Milsons Point idyll came soon after Paddy McGuinness, Sue Robertson and Ian Parker moved into the flat above the one rented by John and Janie. Tatty's tolerance was stretched too far: she might perhaps, for a little while, have lived with the almost non-stop parties, though we ourselves came to realise that there was such a thing as too much Push, but party-goers vomiting out of an upstairs window did not amuse her at all. Paddy and Parker departed their flat (Sue had already left) just before what otherwise would inevitably have been their eviction. Tatty then advertised the flat 'to let' in the *Sydney Morning Herald*, the advertisement concluding with the words, 'No Irish need apply'. Those words, now, would constitute an offence, but I felt some sympathy for Tatty's predicament. She might well have added bankers as those who need not apply: when two young bank-clerks turned up to rent the flat, Tatty — remembering that both Paddy and Parker had worked for the Reserve Bank — sent them packing, pursued by epithets.

As well as being beset by parties, our Milsons Point flat was beset by bees. On its outside wall there were two ventilators, one leading to the space between our ceiling and the floor of the flat above, and the other to our bathroom. The former led also to a colony of bees. Most of the bees, most of the time, found their way home to their hive, but the odd bee — presumably one whose co-ordination was as bad as mine — found its way to our bathroom and, unable to locate an exit, remained in angry and solitary confinement. Robin was allergic to bee-stings, so showering was not as relaxing for her as it could have been, and I, though not allergic, suffered some inconvenience. One morning, after showering and dressing, I felt a sharp pain in my groin. Through that day the pain persisted, but I attributed it to psychosomatic causes, until evening came and I undressed. In my underpants I found a dead bee, and in my groin, its sting.

It was around this period that Johnny Earls served time at Long Bay Gaol. He had travelled by train to Wynyard railway station without first buying a ticket. When he was apprehended by railway officials he claimed to have boarded his train at Milsons Point, but intimidated by his interrogators (We have ways of finding out where you got on the train!), he confessed that he had actually boarded at Artarmon. Johnny did have enough coins to pay his fare from that station, but was fivepence short of the sixpence surcharge then levied for paying at one's destination. The railway police held him and called the real police. These worthies arrested him and, almost immediately, arraigned him before a magistrate. Johnny pleaded guilty to fare evasion and was fined five pounds. Despite his request for time to pay, the magistrate, pronouncing 'I know your type', sentenced him to six days in jail. It was a day or more before we in the Push learnt of Johnny's plight. When we did, I hustled around the Newcastle Hotel on a Friday afternoon collecting enough cash to pay Johnny's fine (even then, few of us had phones), but by the time I had done so it was 5.00 pm, hence I was unable to free him until the following Monday morning. That morning was the first time I had ever passed through the portals of that fearsome prison. But Johnny managed to lighten my mood by telling me how his warders had insisted on calling him their most dangerous criminal. And, since he had already served half of his sentence, I had needed to pay only half of his five-pound fine. The balance of two pounds and ten shillings kept us in drinking money for the rest of that day.

Sometimes, after the Royal George closed at 10.00 pm (as it was compelled to do by the law in the 1960s), Robin and I would walk home together, arm in arm, across the Sydney Harbour Bridge. The views at night, then as now, were magnificent, and there was a choice of views, as walkways existed on both sides of the bridge — today the western side is reserved for cyclists.

During our Milsons Point days, Harry Hooton, diagnosed as having inoperable cancer, was in the process of dying, so Margaret Elliott (later Fink) and others were determined to collect and publish his writings before his death. (The writings *were* published under the title *It Is Great to Be Alive*, which book I quoted from previously.) For this, money was needed, and Terry McMullen approached me with a suggestion that together we organise a concert to help fund the publication. Terry undertook to sell tickets in advance and control all the financial aspects, while I agreed to direct the concert itself. Those to take part included Terry Driscoll, Beth Schurr and Don Ayrton. (The handbill for that concert is reproduced opposite.)

I held meetings at our flat with these and others, also inviting Jim McGuire, an old friend of Hooton's; but he declined to attend, so I wrote him out of the script. The purpose of the meetings was partly rehearsal, but also to enable me to estimate the time taken by each poem, song and speech so that the concert would be neither too long nor too short. Don Ayrton was difficult at rehearsals, on one occasion stomping out after shouting: 'Appleton, I cannot stand your methedrined voice any longer.' But he did front up, and sing, on the night of the concert.

...THE MAN I AM

... to blow the bloody gaff ...

An evening of

Poetry Readings, Rhetoric, Folk Songs, Films and Music

at

THE MACQUARIE AUDITORIUM, 136 PHILLIP ST., SYDNEY

Commencing at 7.45 p.m. on FRIDAY, 26th MAY

Come early; music will be played from 7.30, when the doors open

The Programme will include:

- Readings and recordings from the works of Harry Hooton.
- Three Australian films—
    - Wattle Ballad — "The Gold Diggers", produced by Peter Hamilton.
    - "Waltzing Matilda", produced and acted by Geoffrey Mill; camera, Gunna Isakson; sung by Beth Schurr.
    - "Land of Australia", produced by Link Films, drawings by Reade and Clem Millwood.
- Readings of poems and prose from—Oscar Wilde, Carl Sandburg, E. E. Cummings, Wyndham Lewis, Louis MacNeice, W. Carlos Williams, Leslie Woolf Hedley, and Henry Reed.
- Folk songs and guitar music presented by—Beth Schurr, John Earls, Don Ayrton, Brian Mooney, and Ian Macdougall.
- Readings of poems by Australian writers—Lex Banning, J. McGuire, John Rybak, Geoffrey Mill, Robert Cumming, Don Everingham, Jane Iliffe, Ian MacDougall, Richard Appleton and Richard Preston. (A programme—available at the door—will contain texts of Australian poems.)

The Readers will be: Harry Hooton (recorded voice only); on stage— James McGuire, Geoffrey Mill, Robert Cumming and Richard Appleton.

Programme arranged by Richard Appleton.

TICKETS 6/- EACH. AVAILABLE FROM: Morgan's Bookshop, 8 Castlereagh Street; Appolyon Coffee Lounge, Darlinghurst Rd., Kings X; Sheppard's Bookshop, M.L.C. Building, N. Sydney; Royal George Hotel, King and Sussex Streets; T. McMullen, Psychology Dept., Sydney University; AND AT THE DOOR from 7.30 P.M.

PROCEEDS FOR HARRY HOOTON.

Authorized by Terrence McMullen, 36 Glenmore Rd., Paddington, N.S.W.

Printed by HERZL PRESS PTY. LTD., 175 George Street, Sydney

Handbill for the 1961 concert to fund publication of Harry Hooton's writings.

Unfortunately Jim McGuire did too, though not to sing. The concert was moderately successful in its juxtapositions of verse and song, punctuated by some orations praising Hooton, at least until Jim arrived. I had paired together Don Ayrton singing the folk song 'This train is bound for Glory' with a recital of Lex Banning's poem 'This Train', which contradicted the song with:

> This train
> doesn't go to paradise.
>
> This train
> doesn't go to hell.
>
> This train
> doesn't go anywhere interesting.
>
> This train
> doesn't go anywhere in particular.
>
> This train
> consists of eight steel carriages,
> and draws its power from overhead cables.
>
> This train
> is not symbolical.
>
> This train
> is not metaphorical.
>
> This train
> is merely suburban,
> and should never be regarded
> as anything but
>
> this train.

I had similarly paired Beth Schurr singing 'Barb'ree Allen' with my recital of 'The Red Rose and the Briar' (the words are quoted in full in an earlier chapter). Other songs and poems I had paired similarly. But during several of the concluding items, I was pushing, with the help of others, against the frail stage door to prevent a red-faced, drunk and furious McGuire from storming on to the stage.

When the last item on the program had been concluded, we offered our audience further entertainment by letting McGuire take centre-stage and declaim against the concert, us, and all our works. His rantings were far preferable to the show concluding with 'God Save the Queen'. We had no intention of ending with that vapid anti-Jacobite dirge, but most entertainments, especially in cinemas, then did. Before God was invoked to 'save' the monarch and 'confound' the politics of his or her (Papist) enemies, the more resourceful of the audience would sprint for the exit, but if they failed to reach that door in time they would emulate Lot's wife by freezing on the spot — though not for as long as that unfortunate lady — only until the dirge had died. Unlike Lot's wife, they were *not*, in the eyes of monarchists, the Salt of the Earth. But enough of this digression; Hooton, without doubt, would have echoed McGuire's denunciations, for he was later heard to observe that the concert was 'not the kind of do *I* would have cared to attend'.

From the time of the 'March of the Turks from the Ruins of Athens', or more prosaically, from the time of the departure of Paddy and Parker from the shambles of their Milsons Point flat, our relations with Tatty were understandably soured, so we decided to look elsewhere for a place to live. The advertisement to which we responded offered a Kirribilli flat with harbour views. At first we were sceptical. 'Harbour views' frequently meant that, if one stood on the toilet seat and peered out of the top of the bathroom window, a sliver of harbour was just visible, but only if no neighbours had hung out their washing. That was not the case with this Kirribilli flat.

That flat was a gem. Admittedly its sandstone walls had been painted a sickly mauve, but this I remedied by painting them white. (It was easier than scraping off the mauve paint, and anyway, the unsealed stone always oozed moisture.) Admittedly, when one flushed the toilet one could dash out, if nimble, and watch one's turds floating towards the Heads, or if the tide was coming in, towards Luna Park and the Sydney Harbour Bridge. Admittedly, too, it took three or more large packets of Ratsak to reduce to acceptable numbers the harbour-refuse-fattened rats that held mass meetings on our window-sill. But it was still a gem.

This basement flat was part of a building owned by a man of dubious reputation, a millionaire (on paper) who had a talent for buying semi-slums and out of them creating much more noisome places of residence for the poor. For a time he made money out of this practice, and was kind enough to employ his aged father as a cleaner; day or night, if one walked across the building's mezzanine floor one would have to greet this old fellow, who spoke very little English, and who was slowly wielding a mop. Legend had it that the building was purpose-built as a brothel for the sexually deprived officers of visiting nineteenth-century merchant ships. Our flat had been the boat-bay in which they could moor their boats to make a clandestine entrance. Well, there was no room to doubt that it had been a boat-bay. Much of the floor of our not very large living area would not have existed at all had the bay not been filled in. Our roman-arched window, through which we watched the construction of the Sydney Opera House on the site of the old Fort Macquarie tram depot, had no doubt replaced two barred gates, probably kept discreetly closed during daylight hours. And some of the flats on the floors above ours seemed to be again (or still) in use as brothels, though brothels less class-conscious in selecting their clientele.

For much of the time that Robin and I were living in that Kirribilli flat I was still earning a living as a schoolteacher, and that roman-arched window on one occasion proved a boon for some of my less able pupils — though they never knew it. The single-frame window was hinged at the top, and when it opened its lower edge extended over the waters of the harbour. Those waters were always close to the window-sill, and very, very close during king tides. One day, when there was such a tide and a high wind as well, I was sitting on a couch marking history exam papers for my Intermediate Certificate class when I saw a huge wave approaching. I dived to close the window, but was too late: the wave had already enough momentum to carry it across the room even without the extra upwards scoop that my slamming of the window provided. It drenched many of the history papers. Those pupils whose answers had been obliterated, I had, of course, to pass, despite knowing that many of them would otherwise have failed.

By then, having moved from government schools, I was teaching in the Roman Catholic parochial system. At the time of the big splash I was teaching English and history in a De La Salle secondary school, but I had begun teaching in that system at a primary school conducted by the Patrician Brothers. Until I had taught in the schools of three different Catholic orders I had not realised how different they were, one from another. The worst, in my view, were the Marists, whose 'Prefect of Studies' patrolled the playgrounds always displaying a menacing leather strap. The De La Salle Brothers came a close second in nastiness, but the Patrician Brothers were a delight, though academically hopeless.

On my first day of teaching in a Patrician Brothers primary school, I became rather alarmed when the angelus bell sounded. My whole class leapt to their feet and lunged towards me before dropping to their right knees to genuflect, just as my early childhood toy soldiers were moulded as having done when seeming about to shoot their enemies. Was this, I wondered, a Celtic rebellion against my Anglo-Saxon intrusion? But no, they then recited their Hail Mary. They were not Celts, but a hotch-potch of the young offspring of Middle Eastern parents, mainly Lebanese, with only a smattering of Australian boys who just *may* have been of Irish descent. When all of them rose, later, to sing the Patrician Brothers' anthem, 'Hail Glorious St Patrick, Saint of these Isles', most of them looked completely bemused. But as for the Patrician Brothers themselves, all of them, except one rather sickly Australian youth, *were* Irish. The accents of some of them were so strong that frequently I would parody them in Push circles; on occasion, I accidentally did so in front of the Brothers, but if they noticed they said nothing to me.

The Brothers were frocked in black garments to which they refused to refer by their English name 'cassock', preferring, being Irish, the French term 'soutane'. Around their frequently ample waists they wore a broad green sash of about the width of a cummerbund. They were permitted both to drink alcohol and to smoke tobacco, when most Orders allowed either one or the other, or sometimes neither. In summer, though, they wore white soutanes of a lighter material, and this gave rise, later when I was teaching in a Marist Brothers school, to a rather catty remark from an elderly Marist. I was talking to him as he sweated through a Sydney summer in his heavy black cassock; commiserating with his discomfort, I mentioned the less uncomfortable summer garb of the Patricians. 'Yes,' he replied, 'and they look like advertisements for a well-known brand of Irish whiskey!'

The Patrician Brothers were, one assumes, obedient to the demands of their own Order, but rarely so to those of anybody else. The principal of the school, whom I first met on a Friday, told me, in passing, that he was very hungry: fish he would not stomach, so he was eating nothing until one minute past midnight, when he could savour the joys of a rump steak. The Brothers were barely on speaking terms with their parish priest, and they had advised their diocesan bishop to channel any instructions he might have for them through their Superior-General in Ireland.

That worthy visited the school while I was still teaching there. The principal of the school was fairly fat; the head of the Order in Australia was very fat; but the Superior-General's green sash was long enough to encompass both of them provided that they were standing close together.

I was tempted to the conclusion that, within that Order, promotion was gained mainly by girth.

An exception to this within the hierarchy was the deputy-principal, a lean and Cassius-like figure. He made up for his lack of corpulence by addressing the school assemblies in the manner of a stage Irishman. After one sports day — a rugby-league game for which the Brothers had forgotten to bring a ball — reports had come in of pupils racing on their bikes up to the boom-gate which denied them access to the level railway crossing, and then, deftly to demonstrate their skill, broadsiding their bikes alongside the gate. 'Yesterday,' the deputy announced at assembly on the next school morning, 'you were broadsiding your bikes against the boom-gate. From now on you won't be allowed to ride your bikes to sport.' There was a murmur and some laughter, so he added, 'Well, you may laugh now, but one day, when you are not killed, you will be glad!'

It was at the Kirribilli flat that Brian Fitzpatrick failed to turn up for dinner. Brian had arrived in Sydney from Melbourne, and I had resumed my former Swanston Family Hotel friendly acquaintanceship with him at the Newcastle Hotel in George Street. (The Newcastle at that time was frequently preferable to the Royal George for afternoon drinks, and was also conveniently close to Circular Quay and the ferry to Kirribilli.) One afternoon I invited Brian to come to dinner at Kirribilli. Despite accepting, on the appointed evening he failed to appear. For a time I fulminated against drunken and unreliable historians, but Fitzpatrick's excuse was undeniable: he had died that afternoon.

Sue Robertson shared the Kirribilli flat with Robin and me, but did so only when it suited her. This allowed Robin to pretend to her parents that only she and Sue lived there. It is highly improbable that they were really deceived — they were not stupid: probably they found it less embarrassing just to go along with the pretence. While Sue was living with us she had a fling with John Maze, who often slept there with her. John apparently liked his sex-life and his love of the game of bridge to be catered for under the same roof, so he began to teach me the game. That way I was able to become the necessary fourth player. (Who the third player was I cannot remember, but I don't think it was Robin.) Initially this seemed not much for him to ask; I could already play five hundred, and learning to play this other game also descended from whist seemed to me to present few problems. But at my second or third game, who should be there but Roelof Smilde, either still at that time or a little earlier, bridge champion of Australia. During the game he stood behind me, and almost every time I led a card, he chuckled. I never played bridge again.

During our life together at Kirribilli, and after my divorce from Marion, Robin and I were married. During this time, too, Robin was appointed an editorial assistant at Sydney University Press. That second event changed the paths of both our futures.

14   Trots (with) Ky

Robin and I were married in the Pitt Street Congregational Church on 8 August 1964. The Congregationalists, descended as they are from an ultra-protestant and anti-episcopal sect originally established by Oliver Cromwell and his cronies in the seventeenth century, were not our first choice for the ceremony. I had approached Father Alf Clint, an Anglican priest with whom I was on chatting terms. Alf was mainly working to establish and support Aboriginal co-operatives, especially Tranby College in Glebe. But he also, when needed, made himself available as a third priest when a High Mass was celebrated at Christ Church St Laurence, near Railway Square. I had hoped that he might marry us there, with that church's impressive rituals to grace our nuptials. Alf replied that if a High Church priest were to marry a divorced person (me) within the Anglican Diocese of Sydney, he 'would be defrocked so quickly that it would have the appearance of a rape case'. He suggested the minister of Pitt Street Congregational Church, who held liberal views on divorce, and since Robin had agreed to a church wedding, there it had to be.

Robin's stepfather, Alan, and her mother, Ailsa, attended, as did my sister, Betty, then married to Phillip Arnot, and a select group of our friends. (Our 'un-select' friends made rude noises of protest outside the church door.) Whether Phillip Arnot, who was also invited, turned up, I cannot remember — he was the kind of man easy not to notice even in a crowd of two, or sometimes fewer. After the ceremony we all walked, yes walked, to the nearby Adams Hotel, where Alan had booked at my suggestion. There, along with the usual speechifying and toasts, we drank cider, also at my suggestion, rather than champagne. After that, our relations went on their way, and our friends came back with Robin and me to party-on at Terry McMullen's flat in Elizabeth Bay. That was our 'going away'.

I liked Robin's stepfather, and this feeling, I think, was reciprocal; with her mother, although we were usually polite to each other, if only coolly so, there was always an underlying canker of mutual dislike. We conformed, one might say, to all the clichés about the relationship between mothers-in-law and their sons-in-law. But at least I no longer needed to hide behind a curtain and breathe softly while curbing my smoker's cough whenever Robin's parents unexpectedly visited the flat when she and I were still in bed. I never did much enjoy French farce.

For some time Robin and I had been friends of Ken Cobb. He was one of the many young Englishmen brought to Australia by the Big Brother movement to be exploited by their sponsors as poorly paid agricultural workers. From this miserable apprenticeship he had escaped to a better-paid job in Sydney, but he remained rather adrift in Australian society until he came into contact with the Push. The Push was then prone to bestow nicknames upon all and sundry, and to Ken we gave the name 'Chicken'; I have no idea why. He retained that name until his death.

Chicken, for a time, owned a rather work-worn but clinker-built motorboat. In it he would often chug up to our roman-arch window for a visit. On occasion, too, he would take us for a cruise. But the boat's engine was not entirely reliable, and on one such outing it decided to stop chugging not far off the wave-battered rocks of Middle Head. For what seemed a very long while, as we drifted closer and closer to those rocks, Chicken tried in vain to resuscitate the engine. It relented only just in time to save us from being smashed to floating fragments of fish food.

Chicken also took part in another, quite different, Kirribilli occasion. The Vietnam War was then nearing its height (or depth) and South Vietnam's nominal leader, Marshal Ky, recently installed in office by the United States, was visiting Sydney. He was staying at Admiralty House, which was close to our flat in Kirribilli. The whole peninsula was cordoned off, probably without the power to legally do so, by Commonwealth Police, and entrance was refused if one could not prove that one lived there, or was invited to visit somebody who did. So Robin and I threw a party.

Most of those we invited, and some whom we didn't but who came anyway, were against Australia's involvement in Vietnam. Some of the guests arrived before the cordon was fully in place, but those who did not had to persuade the police they were genuine visitors or bluster and bluff their way through the cordon. Bruce McFarlane, then a senior lecturer in economics, knew his rights and insisted on having them acknowledged. He duly arrived at our door accompanied by two hefty police officers, who gruffly said to me, 'This man claims that he has been invited to visit you.' When I responded that Bruce was definitely invited, they had no option but to go in peace — though I strongly doubted that they would 'sin no more'. Chicken, by contrast, was not one to defy authority, at least not if he could find a way around it. And that he did. With his satchel of grog slung over his back he clambered from Kirribilli Wharf around the foreshore rocks until he reached our flat.

When Ky's launch cruised by, escorted by an armada of police watercraft and protested against by a solitary Trotskyist youth in a canoe, we gathered on the porch outside our front door, shouting imprecations against Ky — which obviously he could not hear — and brandishing placards — which he probably chose not to read. People living several floors above our flat took umbrage at our tiny demonstration, and poured down buckets of water on us. But it was a warm summer day, and Bruce McFarlane placated them by continuing to shout 'More water!' Gradually it became quite an amiable contest. The party lasted throughout that afternoon, and whenever the grog ran out we deputed one of those few visitors who owned a car to drive to the nearest pub and get more, arming them with my rent receipts to serve as passports so that the police would allow them to bring back the necessary supplies. That party was the least uncomfortable, most enjoyable, and possibly the most successful demonstration I ever attended. Those organised by Stalinist, ALP, or Trotskyist groups (and I usually attached myself to the last) were much more puritanical affairs, and probably resulted in more antagonists than supporters.

Because we lived on the harbour (and still I can almost hear the fog-horns, bells and sirens that would ring in a foggy morning) Robin and I enjoyed cruises in vessels other than Chicken's sometimes recalcitrant boat, including one with Peter and Eileen Groenewegen. In these hired craft we took our ease, sipping chilled Houghton's white burgundy and landing to picnic wherever we chose, anywhere between Clifton Gardens and Rose Bay. At Rose Bay, though, we had to be wary of the flying boats that still plied between there and Lord Howe Island.

During part of our life together in Kirribilli, Robin worked for a record club. Because of the recordings we thus obtained cheaply I began, for the first time, to hear and enjoy the early Bob Dylan's mouth-organ and voice renderings of his own songs — so much so that I persuaded several of our friends to buy them. I still have and still enjoy some of those early recordings, but as Dylan's excursions into rock increased, so did my liking for his later songs decrease.

During this period, too, I bought and read Isaac Deutscher's three-volume biography of Leon Trotsky, and as a result would acquire and read Trotsky's own writings. Trotsky argues quite convincingly his Marxist theories, unlike Lenin, who simply decrees his to be true. As for Stalin, rather than the millions he did shoot, he should have shot whomever he paid to write his books for him. For a time, I became again a convinced Trotskyist, but later, with my involvement in the politics of the Australian Labor Party, I came to the conclusion that, if those who would try to create 'Heaven on Earth' gain control, they usually achieve instead that other reputedly fiery and perpetual retirement village. This applies not only to those such as Stalin and Pol Pot, but also to William Lane with his attempt to create socialist utopias in Paraguay, first with New Australia, then with Cosme.

Robin was not all that enthralled with her proofreading work for the record club, and I was becoming increasingly jaded with trying to teach English and history to adolescents who were not even remotely interested in those subjects. Had I been a good teacher I would probably have manifested the ability to engage their interest, but I wasn't. In 1966 Robin responded to an advertisement inviting applications for appointment as an editorial assistant at Sydney University Press; this eventually released both of us from the drudgery of work that did not interest us.

That position's requirements, as I recall them, appeared at first sight daunting, and the wages offered were pitiful — this was while Australian publishers still emulated their British counterparts in assuming that publishing was an occupation reserved for gentlemen and, grudgingly, gentlewomen. 'Gentle' in this context meant having an independent (that is, unearned) income. But Robin applied for, and won, the job.

The editor for whom she worked was arrogant, but knowledgeable about his profession, and Robin learnt the craft rapidly. Within a short time she was employing me (casually) as copyholder for her proofreading, and thus, in turn, began training me. Because of this I soon gained additional editorial work. This ranged from editing Carter Brown 'whodunnits', for which one was paid a fixed fee regardless of the work involved, to editing judicial reports for the Law Book Company. With the first, given the amount I was paid, I could do little other than correct obvious grammatical errors and check that the author had not inadvertently changed, from one chapter to another, the names, hair colours, etc, of his characters. With the second, I had to be scrupulous never to insert even a comma, or any other punctuation, that might in any way interpret the meaning of a judge's ruling, which had been delivered orally, and painstakingly taken down in shorthand word for word by court officers. If later use by a barrister of an unwisely edited version of that ruling was

taken as evidence for or against some poor client, my injudicious insertion of a comma might have deprived opposing counsel of opportunities
to argue for divergent interpretations of such a ruling. It may well have
unfairly deprived that barrister of the income to which he or she felt
entitled.

While at Kirribilli, I had sometimes resumed my previous practice of
sitting up all night, sipping brandy (or whatever other alcohol was available), popping Methedrine, and writing poetry. Unlike my earlier efforts
during intrusions into the Hallwood–Smilde household, I did actually
succeed in rewriting and finishing a poem that I had begun in 1960.
During these overnight binges of words and wine, and obviously influenced by gazing at the harbour and the buildings surrounding it and the
water lapping just below our window-sill, I finished 'Green Grow the
Bushes', the earlier parts of which were published in *Hermes 1961*, and
the completed version in *The Pluralist* of May 1965. It was the only
longish poem that I had ever written, and reads:

1

Green grow the bushes
Aloft in his land
And, limpid, the sea
Laps, soft, the warm sand
  Of his soul;
Beloved, life-entombed, but alone,
  This man was an island:

Spawned in those interim years
Where the grain swelled gold
  In the bread
Yet the fat of the land
Spread thin
  At noon,

Sucked pap from the plastic teat
  Of an ersatz England.

And their villas were pink,
Set polite — by-the-right
  To the sea,
Where the cliffs hung — adamant.

Green grow the bushes
Aloft in his land
And, limpid, the sea
  Laps, soft, the warm sand
Of his soul.

As spice to his legend,
The spoor of his blood
  On the sand
Stains Pinchgut Island;
The taunt of his land
To the rum-dark sea,
He gleaned,
  To buoy his environment.

The ripples were decades deep
  And greened to patina;
Crouched to the sea
  And age-warmed
The stone.

Dark to discernment
And lithe one last time
On home's garden-green lawn,
Cleansed in the tears of his dam,
  He fore-swore preferment —
And blessings glowered grey

In the eyes
Of paternal dénouement:

Betrothed to empyreal bride,
   Thus alone,
He aspired to a tenement;
His lust for the lips of mankind
Breathed plangent tomorrows.

Brine-tanged
And brash as a breeze
   Sang the sea,
Sibilant on scarred stone.

2

Spawned in those interim years
Where the grain swelled gold
   In the bread,
Yet the fat of the land
Spread thin distress
   At noon,
Was weaned from his plastic teat,
   Hence sought for a mistress:

Taut to his sex as the key,
   To emboss on her credence —
Presumptive caresses to bridge
   An imminent silence —
With paean in place of a pulse
   He tendered continuance.

Sought:
   Bones from the Hound of Fate
   (Triple caresses) —
   Memos for Juggernaut —

Pleas for forgiveness —
Roses for secateurs
And the fingers' fervour.

Ahead, this city
Fingers the pall of the sky.

Dark to discernment
And blithe one last time
   In the now
     (Or, at latest, near five),
He spliced his embrace to his theme,
His lust
   To alignment.

This skyline distorts
  Mirages of ends.

Taut to his credence,
Void to bar souls
   But the loins conjoining —
Hanged in love's ante-room
   The meaning —
Embossed on her silence
   But stilled, the theme.

3

Those who came after
Those who belled the crime —
Who dressed the stepping-stones
   And stepped —
Who dredged the tides of aspiration
   In the dark river,
Those died.

Those who came after —
Shoes smooth-shone
  On truth-worn stone
And faith a-flutter
  (nostalgic banner
  of make-believe rebellion),
Learnt, first, with laughter
To toll the lies —
  And, later, with languor.

The ripples were decades deep
  And greened to patina;
Crouched to the sea
  And age-warmed, the stone.

For the lies were daily sold,
  Were disbelieved
But taught in school,
So the joke was old —
  And the road to hell
  At least was paved —
Thus the gesture,
  'Hemlocks at five, by invitation'
Was tainted, to tasteful ears
  With 'And later, the theatre'.

And their villas were pink,
  Set polite, by-the-right, to the sea,
Where the cliffs hung, adamant.

Those who came after
Learnt reservations —
True as the Blessed Isles, the dream,
But also, well-charted;
Sweet as the flood-tide of Styx,

As the final embrace,
  To the Dreamer;
Still sweeter,
And chaste as post-copulative caress,
  To those who came after.

4

Spawned in those interim years
Where the fat of the land
Spread thin doleur, at noon,
Set keel with his Styxian bride
  In quest for a harbour.

I have sucked in
The noon of my day
  In the bright of the sun.
(Beginnings seem trivial now,
  Or turned too soon.)
Green to the current,
White bows transgress their foam
  To dubious buoys, on time.

Ahead, this city fingers
  The pall of the sky;
Wake seethes astern while
  Clouds seek its pulse,
But old loves are lies.
Bright in the rum-dark tide
  (or, at latest, near five)
This skyline distorts
  Mirages of Ends.

This city is concrete and steel
  (And our long-drowned noon)
And glass.

The fleck from our bows
   Stings white
In the flux of the harbour.

Green grow the bushes
Aloft in his land,
And, limpid, the sea
Laps, soft, the warm sand
   Of his soul;
Beloved, but becalmed in his Now,
This man was an island.

5

Flood-tide brings Siva to me:
Silver flesh of the surge of oceans
   From out of all Asia.

In the white of the sky,
Sea-gulls bend slivers of sun
   (Pale from the East)
To the sands of slumber, in Sydney.

And Alexander was king
And ruled by fire and sword
   (and Napalm, later)
   Lest we remember.

So much for mornings:
For mine was the kingdom
   (The power and the glory?)
Where love wrought blessings
   In brick villas, with green lawns
   (Short front and sides)
And Sansar tea.

A burst of sunlight
On white linen
  (Or whiter than white)
And fond good-byes.

Mine was the kingdom
Of love's labour leased,
  At least till later,
To lesser tomorrows,

Lest we remember.

At least some of these verses, I still think, have poetic virtue, despite the criticism quoted in a later chapter.

After sometimes writing all night, when dawn finally allowed me to douse my desk-lamp I felt a strong urge for company and activity. By then, Johnny Earls had joined us as a co-tenant. His job as a quality-controller in an ice-cream factory had helped him to save up his fare by ship to Peru, and he was soon to set sail. Ruthlessly, I would deposit a couple of Methedrine tablets in his open mouth while he was still sleeping (much as one would drop coins into a slot-machine). Once I was sure that he had swallowed them, I would drink a mug of coffee while they took effect, then I would shake him until he wakened. The purpose of my cruelty was to hijack him to come with me to an early-opening (6.00 am) pub; there we would together solve the world's problems in the company of shift-workers, who had just knocked off and were having a quiet beer before going home to sleep.

Usually we would then continue drinking, and postulating increasingly absurd theories, in whatever pubs took our fancy, throughout that day, before fronting at the Royal George in the afternoon. When Johnny sailed for Peru in 1963, he took memories of these occasions with him. In 2002–3 he made a brief return visit to Australia, bringing back these memories — albeit a little frayed around the edges — and we both indulged in (permissible?) nostalgia. By then, he was *Doctor* Earls and a leading authority on prehistoric agriculture in the Andes.

Our stay at Kirribilli came to an end when Robin and I moved to a terrace house we rented in Darlington Road, Darlington.

15 Darlington Days

The Darlington Road Push terraces, and all the others nearby, were owned by the University of Sydney; it had acquired them intending to demolish the lot, and in their place expand its campus. Lack of sufficient funds put paid to this for the then foreseeable future, thus demolishing instead my fantasy about the eruption of conflict between Sydney's, at that time, only two universities. With the University of Sydney expanding through Darlington towards Redfern and beyond, and the recently established University of New South Wales also expanding, I had envisioned those two institutions colliding at some disputed border. Bloody warfare, I predicted, would ensue.

In lieu of large-scale demolition, Sydney University decided to rent out its Darlington houses. Robin and I shared one of them with Marilyn Little and Ken Quinnell. Two doors away was the terrace house which harboured Geoffrey Whiteman, Mike Baldwin and his future wife, Joanna. Farther towards Parramatta Road there was another household. Its occupants I did not know well, but did know well enough, when my car was not functioning, to borrow a Citroën belonging to one of them to drive Rabbie Namaliu, a future prime minister of Papua New Guinea, to the airport.

The car that I then owned should have been dubbed 'Appleton's Folly'. As yet unable to drive, and liking its sleek lines, I purchased, of all things, a 1955 Citroën Light Fifteen. This was an oldish make of vehicle not at all popular in Australia (Geoff Whiteman described it as 'an orphan'), and a stupid buy for one who lacked any mechanical ability at all. Learning to drive it took me some time — my co-ordination being what it is — and for much of that time, since to drive legally I was required to have a licensed driver sitting beside me, that person was Ron Opie. The fact that he was frequently drunk, and usually asleep, did not, in my view then, diminish the legality of my L-Plate excursions. For some time after I gained my licence, I thought a Light Fifteen to be the only make of car that I was capable of driving, which was why I borrowed one from down the road to see Rabbie Namaliu on his way back to Papua New Guinea, and eventually to high office.

Geoff Whiteman was apt, when any unaccompanied young woman arrived at his door, to order her: 'Upstairs, and get your clothes off.' Probably some of them did obey him. The Whiteman–Baldwin ménage was the principal centre for Darlington Road Push activities. Of it, what I remember best is a winter evening when that household was without electricity (presumably because of an unpaid bill); Whiteman, huddled in a duffel-coat, was sitting close to a lighted gas jet, one that he had discovered still connected from the time of gaslight illumination, enjoying what warmth he could, free of cost.

The Whiteman household was the venue where I came as close as ever I have to 'doing a Dylan Thomas'. I had been awake for at least two days and nights, taking Methedrine and drinking, and probably not eating at all, when those in that household held a party. There, somebody offered me pot, which I rolled into a cigarette thick enough to fit into my cigarette-holder and smoked until only a little butt remained, thus violating all the niceties of polite pot-smoking. After that, somebody offered me a sliver of blotting-paper said to contain LSD, and I consumed that as well. I was also, by then, rather drunk, so when a bloke who, I think, was a final-year medical student challenged me to drink a middy (ten fluid ounces) of straight Scotch in the same time as he drank a middy of beer, I tried. Consequently I collapsed, and was carried two doors up the street and upstairs to bed by Joanna and Robin. I doubt if I managed to finish my Scotch, but certainly that student would have finished his beer.

At the Royal George at around that time, I engaged in my chairman-
ship tussle with George Molnar (the philosopher, not the architect and
cartoonist). In the back room of the George during the afternoon peak
Push hours, chairs were always in short supply. One afternoon, arriving
there before Robin, I 'reserved' a chair for her. George Molnar turned up
before Robin did, and he coveted that chair. The resultant tug-of-war
between the two of us must have been won by one or the other, since the
chair did not break. George had just come into an inheritance that, as
well as money, included his uncle's wardrobe; he had taken to wearing an
inherited pair of plus-fours, but with them, and incongruously, sandals.

During our Darlington days I began my first full-time work as a book
editor. Robin was working just across Darlington Road at Sydney University Press, and my office, located in Marrickville, was almost as conveniently placed. My employer was Science Press, a publisher of school
textbooks and the odd university text. Its proprietor, Alex Boden, also
owned (partly on the same premises) a chemical manufacturing company, and so could if necessary subsidise his book-publishing enterprises.
He was an odd man, intelligent and dictatorial. Every couple of years he
bought a new Jaguar, always white — 'pristine' was a favourite expression
of his. Before he would employ me he sent me to someone who appeared
to be a phrenologist. This bloke did not confess to belonging to that
obsolete and discredited profession, but asked me to let him feel my head
— in case, he said, I had suffered an injury that might impair my judgement.

While he was exploring my then hirsute head, he engaged me in conversation. So I had been a student at Sydney University, had I, and what
did I study? Once the word 'philosophy' was mentioned, he asked me for
my views of the then notorious Professor John Anderson. So I told him
those Andersonian theories with which I agreed, presumably including 'truth' and 'empiricism', and those with which I disagreed, certainly

including his aesthetic theories and 'the good'. Subsequently he reported back to Boden that I was a perfectionist who would have no loyalty to anybody. Surprisingly, Boden still employed me.

He could be a demanding employer. Initially he instructed me, 'Don't talk to me about consistency; I want my books to be consistent only when it's a good consistency.' He never told me when that might be. On another occasion he asked me brusquely, 'Why do you always look unshaven?' (At that time I had no beard.) 'Because,' I replied, 'my skin is pale and my facial hair is dark.' Boden just grunted. Then there was a book he intended to publish which explored the evils of partaking of illicit drugs. He had written an introduction which stated authoritatively that amphetamines caused their users to become drowsy. 'Not so,' I told him, 'their effect is the reverse. Commonly they are prescribed to combat narcolepsy.' He wouldn't believe me. So to prevent a gross error I rang one of the authors, a fairly senior academic in pharmacology who also happened to be a friend of mine. 'Slip him a dexo [Dexedrine], Dick,' he advised me, 'then he'll know.'

Surprisingly, too, my editing of textbooks at Science Press proved to be a good apprenticeship. My work included commissioning books, editing them, marking up manuscripts for the typesetter and correcting the resultant galley proofs, then selecting a printer and seeing them through the press. I wrote advertising brochures recommending the finished books to schools and, finally, packaged the books for delivery by post or courier, or, sometimes, delivered them directly to schools in my ageing Citroën.

I am still proud of some of the books I was responsible for publishing. One of them is *Models of English Style: From Old English to the Present* (Science Press, 1971). The two original authors were J.C. Bright and P.M. Bright, both schoolteachers. Their manuscript seemed to me promising, but not at that stage ready for publication, so I persuaded them to accept the co-authorship of P.D. Roberts, a Push associate who was also an academic in linguistics in the English Department of Sydney University.

Working with the original research of the two Brights, he tightened up the manuscript, breaking it into sections under such headings as 'A Few Recipes', 'Narratives', 'Description', 'Speaking', 'Dialogues', 'Song', 'Exposition' and 'Argument'. This resulted in an authoritative text outlining the evolution of English from King Alfred's time to the present day.

As an example of modern song, Roberts recommended the inclusion of a Beatles lyric. So I rang their publisher's representative in Australia and, not unexpectedly, was told that the royalty payment required was a sum I would not even bother asking Boden if he was willing to pay. I asked Roberts for an alternative, and he came up with 'Finally I Called' by Leonard Cohen. The royalties required to republish this poem were reasonable, so we used it. For me, this led to my becoming an admirer both of Cohen's verse and of his ability to put it to music and sing it.

There are two other volumes, comprising one book, that I am also proud to have commissioned and overseen. It is entitled *The West and the World*. It was edited and planned by N.K. Meaney. Volume one was published in 1972, and volume two in 1973, after I had resigned as editor of Science Press.

When I attended high school the standard history text for seniors was *History of Modern Europe*, written by S.H. Roberts and first published in 1933. It was a standard 'Whig' history and very pro-British. Somewhere in its pages Roberts refers to Leon Trotsky as a prominent Russian trade unionist. Well, visualising a Trotsky at Sydney's Trades Hall has its humorous aspects, but it also says something about how well a supposedly serious historian understood the meaning of the term 'soviet'. *The West and the World* would, I thought, provide a more accurate and believable text for senior students, and one that was definitely *not* pro-British.

In retrospect, perhaps it leans a little too far in the other direction. In the chapter 'Nationalism and Independence in South-East Asia' the photographs used show British-controlled Malay police kicking-in the door of a dwelling in their search for subversives, as well as a British so-called 'resettlement camp' in Malaya. In 'China, 1914–1970: Towards the

People's Republic', all the illustrations are laudatory. On balance, though, the two volumes constitute a reliable text.

Among the incidents that took place in Darlington Road was a non-violent war of attrition between the Darlington Push and the Sydney University Regiment, whose premises were just across Darlington Road from the Push houses, though they fronted on to City Road. That busy thoroughfare would have been far too dangerous a site for soldiers to use for drill, so they used Darlington Road as their parade ground. When they did so Chicken, if he was visiting us, drilled on our front balcony facing them, emulating every movement of their rifles with a borrowed broomstick. On the balcony of the house two doors down the road Mike Baldwin did likewise, though Mike preferred an umbrella as his make-believe weapon.

During this time I fell ill with pneumonia. This led me to regress into sulky adolescence: I remained in bed, consciously becoming sicker day by day, determined to do nothing towards seeking treatment. Robin phoned the medico that I was using and he made a house visit, even then a rare occurrence. He was, I think, a Hungarian; I had chosen him not so much because of his medical ability, but rather because he shared with me an admiration for the novels of Evelyn Waugh. Nonetheless, he did appear medically competent: he had no difficulty in diagnosing my pneumonia, but because of my other symptoms he suspected that I might also have the highly dangerous meningitis. He called an ambulance, and two burly ambulance men manoeuvred me, on a stretcher, down the narrow stair-way of the Darlington house. I was less than impressed, though, on arrival at Sydney's Royal Prince Alfred Hospital, when an intern who was a friend of ours predicted to Robin, 'I *think* we can save him.' But at least my suspected meningitis won me the privilege, in a public ward, of a private room.

By then, as I relapsed into semi-consciousness, I thought that perhaps I might really die. The next day, though, antibiotics had, with the aid of an oxygen-mask, worked their wonders, and I felt reasonably alive again. So much so that I was eager to substitute tobacco fumes for oxygen, and did so. To determine whether I did have meningitis (which I didn't) I was subjected to a lumbar puncture. This process, during which some of my spinal fluid was siphoned off, caused me to suffer horrendous headaches. Being in a public ward had its disadvantages despite my private room: that room was soon invaded by an uninvited medical professor and a gaggle of medical students. I was in no mood to be treated as a promising specimen for the professor's punditing-on to postulate his theories about the shape of my skull. I was, he told his students, a brachycephalic, and consequently unlikely to father children. 'Have you any children?' he asked me, so I lied and told him I hadn't, ignoring the existence of my Melbourne-born son. His students diligently took notes, but by then this dialogue-cum-monologue was exacerbating my already excruciating headache, so I told them all to go away. And surprisingly they did.

A more welcome visitor was Bruce Cobbin, then a senior lecturer in pharmacology at nearby Sydney University, though I had first known him as a student in the run-down students' hostel in Melbourne mentioned earlier. He chatted with me, sitting on my bed (which nurses regarded as a 'no-no') and smoking a cigarette (then quite acceptable in hospitals). When a nurse came in, she saw his white coat, as well as a lapel badge designating him as 'Dr Cobbin'. 'I'm sorry, doctor,' she apologised, and went away again.

After about a week in hospital I signed myself out. A party had been organised at our Darlington Road house and I had no intention of being unable to attend. Given my still weak physical condition, I did not especially wish to party-on, but neither was I about to let anyone usurp my place at that party. The medico who witnessed my signing myself out obviously thought that I was shallow and stupid to leave hospital prematurely just to go to a party. 'Some people,' he chided me, 'think that when they have suffered severe pneumonia their lives are virtually at an end. But you are treating it as if you had recovered only from a common cold.'

At the party, a diversion took place when I refused entry to a couple of blokes I either did not know or did not want to know. They retaliated by first turning off the electricity, then invading the house from its back lane and tearing off the seat of our outside dunny, so I confronted them there. A brawl threatened, and for a while it seemed likely that I would suffer the indignity of being beaten about the head with a dunny seat. Taus Vorbach (aka Toss Davidson) intervened; she told these unwelcome visitors that I was 'a very sick man' and, improbably, this persuaded them to desist. All in all, it was not a good party.

The unwelcome visitors, despite their declining to hit me, were an indication of the decline of the then current hotel as a venue for the Push. This had happened earlier with the Royal George, where yobbos (though we called them 'Alfs') had taken to drinking in the hope of involving themselves with this sexually permissive group. One Saturday afternoon Paddy McGuinness, Sue Robertson, Ian Parker and another woman, as well as Robin and I, were sitting in the George's back room when three young Alfs came in, no doubt thinking that intellectual-bashing might be a change from poofter-bashing. After no time at all, or so it seemed, the three of them surrounded our table, accusing us of 'looking at them and laughing'. This we denied. So they then began picking up our drinks and pouring them over us. I was the first to lose patience and attempt to stand up. Immediately, as I started to rise from my chair, one of the three, who had been standing behind me, smashed me in the face. They then left, mission accomplished.

It was by then clear to most Push members that the George was no longer acceptable as a resort for conversation and drinks, or, as Terry McMullen tagged us, for 'critical drinkers'. Terry and I had advocated colonisation of the Gresham Hotel, across the road from Sydney Town Hall, but had only limited success. Darcy Waters and Roelof Smilde were more successful in colonising the United States Hotel, in Sussex Street, and for a while that pub, along with the Newcastle, became one of the two dominant Push meeting places.[19]

In 1968 Jim Baker, having resigned from his chair of philosophy at the University of Waikato in New Zealand, came back to Sydney. With him, from the same university department, came Alan Olding. Alan, who was an Englishman, lobbed at the Darlington house that Robin and I were renting and stayed for a week or so. He described his philosophical position as 'English realist', and while he definitely was not an Andersonian, his admiration of Anderson's empirical and realist position helped him to blend seamlessly into the Push. My friendship with him began then, but grew closer in later years.

But for Robin and me, Darlington was beginning to pall. The following year we were to buy a cottage in Katoomba and move there. David Malouf, whom we knew only slightly if at all, took over the Darlington house. But the 'little magazine' that I christened *The Pluralist* had its beginnings in the Royal George days; its history is outlined in the next chapter.

16   Pluralism and Propositions

Late in 1961 André Frankovits suggested to me that we publish a quarterly magazine. It was some years since the *Libertarian*, published (as one might suspect) by the Libertarian Society, had last appeared. *Broadsheet*, the then current Libertarian publication, seemed to André and me increasingly inward-looking, its contents focusing mainly on sexual theory and political philosophy. As has been mentioned, it was I who christened our magazine *The Pluralist*, with the intention that it would really *be* pluralist, publishing not only material unlikely to find space elsewhere, but also, issue by issue, tackling topics in politics, literature, etc, with their authors holding divergent views on each topic, thus illustrating the pluralist view that societies, or their sub-groups, do not have many interests in common. An example could have been government-subsidised literature. *The Pluralist* number one, edited by André Frankovits and myself, was published in summer 1961–2. We were unable to offer payment to our contributors. As for *The Pluralist* appearing quarterly, this was managed only once over the seven years and seven issues that the magazine survived — with number three, summer 1965, and number four, May 1965.

In her book *Sex and Anarchy*, Anne Coombs wrote:

> André Frankovits and Dick Appleton did not stay on as the editors [of *The Pluralist*]. It was gradually taken over by Jim Baker and Bill Maidment. Baker disapproved of the way Appleton had given space to a communist in one issue. André Frankovits withdrew because he realised he either had to get more involved or get out, and he chose the latter.[20]

Well, Coombs was probably more or less correct about André, but the remainder of the material quoted above appears to be cut from whole cloth. I *did* stay on as an editor for all seven issues, and for number four I was sole editor, as well as being publisher of numbers four to seven. As for Baker disapproving of my having 'given space to a communist', at that stage I had not, and I doubt if Jim would have objected had I done so. In issue number one, David Makinson had contributed 'On Marx's Idea of Classes', which was highly critical of Marxist theory, and Peter Groenewegen, in an article headed 'Planning, Marxian Economics and Normal Cost Theory', reviewed, not very kindly, *BOOM and BUST*, journal of the Commerce Students' Society, Melbourne University, edited by M. Keating and P. Samuel (1962). Much later, in issue number seven, edited by Baker, Maidment and myself, we did give space to a communist, with Lloyd Churchward's 'Marxism and Leninism', but I had advocated the inclusion of a Marxist, rather than a Stalinist, hoping for at least an Isaac Deutscher as a contributor, if not a Marx or a Trotsky. After number two was published, I let the magazine lapse until Jim Baker suggested that he and Maidment join me as editors. There was no gradual 'taking over'.

Since Coombs did not, it appears, examine *The Pluralist* carefully, relying too much, if not entirely, on oral history, I quote from John Penfold in *The Australian Highway*, journal of the Workers' Educational Association, of winter 1965, for a fairly objective review of the 'general content' (meaning content other than fiction or verse) of numbers one to three. Number four yielded no general content, so Penfold made no comment on it. Of the general content of the first three numbers he wrote:

> In its first issue, *The Pluralist* described itself as 'a dissident quarterly', and its editorial asserted 'the existence of a plurality of equally valid and frequently conflicting interests' as against the 'assumption of dominant common interests and goals' ...

In promising priority to speculative articles, the editors were realistic enough to forecast that such articles might not be readily available. They were right. Of the eleven articles published by the journal so far, only one (Davison on 'Modern Drama, Judgment and the Academy') puts forward an analysis of a situation and recommendations for action. Nine of the other ten articles are critical or expository …

The critical and expository articles vary from those tightly reasoned but largely of interest to specialists, [such] as Khamara's examination of certain arguments concerning 'The Existence of God', to very general introductions in the visions of others, as in Baker's 'Remarks on George Orwell', Sonnino's 'D.H. Lawrence: Social Ideas', and Ferraro's 'Anarchism in Greek Philosophy'. The 'in-between' articles, for example Furedy's 'The Scientific Status of Psychoanalysis' and Makinson's 'On Marx's Idea of Classes', state clearly and readably simple points which have for a long time been familiar to those concerned with the writers discussed, but which may usefully be restated as time-savers for beginners …

But *The Pluralist* can be blamed … for failing to develop a consciousness of an identifiable group of people that it is trying to address … even the single editor who provides the only physical continuity running through all issues of the journal so far, has failed to provide a similar intellectual continuity. [Appleton's] article in the second issue was to be the first of a series of essays on 'Time and the Realist Novel'; so far there is no sign of the rest of the series.

The determined opposition to any concessions which might seem to imply 'dominant common interests and goals' has also led to one field being excluded; formal social arrangements — rituals, laws, institutions, governmental policies — have not been subject to criticism. In one sense this fits in with the deliberate absence of emphasis on the topical, and in this *The Pluralist* has been true to its original statement of values. As is so glaringly not true of topical magazines, every article in *The Pluralist* is as readable now as it was when it appeared …[21]

As a result of the lack of topicality remarked on by Penfold, *The Pluralist* failed to notice editorially that the Vietnam War was taking place. This political abdication or evasion is elaborated on, but in a later chapter.

In the same edition of *The Australian Highway*, Stephen Knight reviewed the literary content of *The Pluralist*, but only of number four. Consequently the writings in verse in numbers one to three were not reviewed. In chronological order they were written by Lex Banning, Barbara Woods, Geoffrey Lehmann, Ron Blair and Clem Gorman. (I have omitted the names of those writers published in these issues whose work appeared in number four and thus *was* reviewed.) Neither were the two stories by Peter Newton in those numbers reviewed, and David Perry's woodcuts for the covers and in the pages of the magazine do not rate a mention by either Penfold or Knight. Other writers published in issue four whose work is not mentioned by Knight are Dick Southon and Ian Lightfoot. Of those who *were* mentioned Knight wrote:

> *The Pluralist* 4 is entirely literary. In his editorial, Richard Appleton ... places the stress entirely on the poetry ...; rather than publishing stray poems by a number of authors he has chosen to print a number of poems by each of a small group of writers, and this seems an eminently sensible decision. He ends ... by saying: ... 'I consider the collections published here ... manifest some resistance to the contemporary Australian virus of crypto-Georgian reaction'.
>
> This seems optimistic. It is true that most of the poets he publishes do not belong to the rather bloodless round of Australian poetry publishing, and this is good. There are poets here, notably Peter Newton, whose work is stronger and more worthwhile than the elegant and over-educated poetasting that fills most of the little magazines. But the quality of the poetry as a whole is certainly not enough to show a resistance — more a pocket of guerillas — not many of whom have the writing talent that the so-called crypto-Georgians exhibit ...
>
> Newton is offering a real alternative here to the gutless modern verse his editor complains of. But little else in the magazine does. Appleton himself, in his long 'Green Grow the Bushes' shows a considerable skill in controlling a lyric type of poetry: in terms of prosody he is the best writer in the magazine. But he seems too derivative ...
>
> Bruce Beaver, too, is disappointing ...

But there is prose, too. Ian Bedford's story 'In Darkest Hungary' seems a
failure ... Frank Moorhouse's story 'Nish' is a different matter. This very
short, tautly written piece seems the best he has written yet ...

Pluralist 4 is mixed: but even though some of the material is weak,
Newton, Moorhouse, Beaver and Appleton are worth printing anywhere
and we should all be grateful for this magazine ...[22]

To what Knight wrote about Moorhouse's 'Nish' I must add my own
comment. Frank offered me at least two other stories for publication as
well as 'Nish', but all of them except 'Nish' used the word 'fuck', and I was
too frightened of being imprisoned for obscenity to publish them during
the allegedly 'swinging sixties'.

For *The Pluralist* numbers five to seven there is, to the best of my knowl-
edge, no objective criticism available, so I have tried to fill the gap, in
some cases damning others, as I was damned by Knight, with faint praise.
Their general content consists of articles by Max Nomad ('Comrade
Anatole: The Political Evolution of Anatole France' [number 5] and
'Radicalism — A Summing Up' [number 7]), David Armstrong ('The
Freedom of the Will' [number 5], Peter Kenny ('Determinism and Free-
Will' [number 5]), Lester Hiatt ('Violence in Animals and Early Man'
[number 5]), Arthur Sewell ('Linguistic Analysis Reconsidered' [number
6] and 'Language, Truth and Poetry [number 7]), J.R. Maze ('Freud and
Dostoevsky' [number 6]), Judith Barbour ('Another Look' [number 6]),
John Brink ('Apartheid and Plomer's *Yurbot Wolfe*' [number 6]), Leon
Cantrell ('The Myth of Prometheus: Camus' *The Plague*' [number 6]), J.L.
Mackie ('Aesthetic Judgements — A Logical Study' [number 7]), and
Lloyd Churchward (Marxism and Leninism' [number 7]). There are
verses from John Tranter, Clive James, Lee Sonnino, Ronald Tamplin and
Norman Talbot; and one story, by Geoffrey Mill, 'The Afternoon Your
Old Man Dies' [number 6]. In reviewing *The Pluralist* some thirty-odd

years after it ceased publication I obviously have the advantage of hindsight, but I think that I have not made too much of a welter out of this.

Max Nomad's political position is similar to that of the Libertarians, and is expressed in both of the articles of his published in *The Pluralist*. In 'Comrade Anatole' he urges:

> But there was in [Anatole France] ... something that should make ... radical intellectuals turn to him for consolation ... after they have become disenchanted with the gospel of Revolution, whether it be that of Marx, Kropotkin, Sorel or Lenin.

Nomad's 'Radicalism — A Summing Up' concludes with his exhortation that, despite the futility of any revolution's attempt to change the world,

> [radicals] can fight back. They can achieve a reduction in the temperature of the hell in which the majority of the human race is fated to live only by fighting for more and more, now, of the good things of life ...

I find little to quarrel with in his views other than his insistence that intellectuals, when preaching revolution, always are *consciously* determined to themselves become the new autocrats.

Like Max Nomad's Anatole France, John Maze's Dostoevsky, in 'Freud and Dostoevsky', has no intention of becoming a revolutionary martyr. Nomad's France is described as:

> ... not a hero. Hated by the reactionaries, he was afraid lest a similar fate [to that of Jean Jaurès, who was assassinated] might befall him as well ... for two or three years [during World War I] he was forced ... to spout patriotic propaganda ... 'During the war,' he said later ..., 'I wrote and spoke like my janitor. But it was necessary.' Necessary, that is, for the preservation of his life.

Maze's Dostoevsky, after his return from the exile to which he had been condemned for subversive conspiracy,

> was thoroughly circumspect and submissive in his dealings with the authorities, and that seems to me simply a direct consequence of this exceedingly painful lesson, of having felt their crushing power to punish, rather than from a conviction of worthlessness and guilt. In sum, the considerations listed above give little reason for thinking [as Freud argued] that guiltiness over father-hatred was a major force in his mental life.

Cowardice, or self-preservation, is of course not the point of Maze's article. As the last sentence quoted above suggests, Maze disputes Freud's conclusion that:

> powerful, repressed, murderous impulses against his father were the major force in Dostoevsky's life. In Freud's view, of course, that could pretty well be said of everybody, but their effect, he believed, was exacerbated in Dostoevsky's case by their having been vicariously realized in his father's violent death at the hands of his serfs, in 1839, when Dostoevsky was seventeen ... Freud asserts[:] 'Now it is a dangerous thing if reality fulfills such repressed wishes. The phantasy has become reality and all defensive measures are thereupon reinforced.'
> ... Freud uses this to explain Dostoevsky's epilepsy (regarded by Freud as psychosomatic), his compulsive losses at gambling, his reaction to imprisonment in Siberia, and in large measure the motivation for his writing.

Maze writes wittily and with great clarity, and his argument against the conclusions of Freud's inquiry into the origins of Dostoevsky's artistic production is well founded according to psychoanalytical theory. But this counts for little if one agrees (as I do) with J.J. Furedy's conclusion in 'The

Scientific Status of Psychoanalysis' (*Pluralist* 2) that '[psychoanalysis's] claim to be a science at this time is highly questionable'.

Regardless of the conclusions reached, though, the problem of 'What is Art?' and 'What gives rise to it?' is discussed in two other articles in *The Pluralist*, one by Arthur Sewell and the other by J.L. Mackie. In 'Language, Truth and Poetry', Sewell makes the observation that:

> Like many of the questions that puzzle us the question 'What is the nature of truth in poetry' was first asked by Plato and Aristotle.

He goes on to pose, and then rebut, various propositions. One is the view, which Freud shares, that psychological examination of author and text is helpful:

> Modern psychological accounts of Shakespeare's characters … are all committed to the notion that, leaving aside what might be carried and brought home in the poetry, there is a 'truth to life' in [them] which is, you might say, 'imitation'. But, of course, you *cannot leave aside* what is carried and brought home in the poetry.

Sewell argues, with qualified approval, that a French writer, Jacques Rivières, 'puts the whole matter [of the function of poetry] in perspective'. He quotes Rivières's postulation:

> 'If in the Seventeenth Century Molière or Racine had been asked why he wrote, no doubt he would … [have answered] that he wrote for the enter-tainment of decent people … It is only with the advent of Romanticism that the literary act came to be conceived as a sort of "raid on the abso-lute" and the result as a *revelation*.'
> … Poetry, then, is neither more nor less than the revelation of the Platonic idea …

Later in the article, he writes:

When a poet revises a line, he is not, then, as we might think, finding a truer way of expressing what was in his mind; he is discovering something different, something more exciting, something more novel, which never was thought of before he thought of it by finding words for it.

Many of Sewell's arguments are cogent and illuminating, as in the examples quoted above, but his conclusion that

In great poetry, the poetry is in the morality — the morality of complex attitudes — and the morality is in the poetry.

is not, to my mind, either meaningful or helpful. I do not assume that Sewell attributes to the word 'morality' the same meaning as would F.R. Leavis, but what he does mean he fails to make clear.

Early in his article 'Aesthetic Judgements — A Logical Study', Mackie poses questions that he obviously intends to answer:

Can judgements of value about art be themselves justified or defended, or are such judgements essentially arbitrary and subjective? Is there, or should there be, a *science* of criticism, or is the evaluation of literature and art and music a field in which everyone is free to follow his fancy, and one man's fancy is as good as another's?

Mackie then goes on to postulate various methods of evaluating art, dismissing them one by one. For example, he writes:

Also, there is the psychology of art: we can investigate psychological questions of why artists produce works of art, and of what mental processes contribute to artistic creation. We can inquire whether art is a form of fantasy, or whether, as Freud says, it is a path back from fantasy to reality. And, of course, as well as the psychology of the artist, there is the psychology of artistic appreciation to be considered too.

After this discussion of psychological evaluation of art, Mackie treats similarly sociological and historical evaluation, and evaluation by examination of the biography of the artist, and concludes:

> A discovery or an insight, however sound or however penetrating, about the history or the psychology or the sociology of art, or even about the intentions of artists, will not in itself tell us anything about the merit of particular works of art ... Value judgements, about how good or beautiful or great a work is, are distinct from all sorts of factual judgements, and do not follow from these alone. But, as we shall see, this does not mean that all factual judgements are irrelevant to judgements of value: there can be indirect connections between them.

The role of fashion and the relevance of a 'cultivation of taste' also come under review, as well as the no longer fashionable 'Social Realism':

> ... we may note that there are fashions in art and music and literature, much as there are fashions in dress or in hair-styles, though the fashions in the arts change more slowly. That being so, a critical judgement may express not an innocent private response, but rather a sophisticated, learned response: the reputable critic is the one who manages to react in whatever way the top people are reacting at the moment. On this modified view there can be such a thing as the cultivation of taste: but it consists essentially in keeping abreast of the changes in style, in being in touch with the centres of artistic fashion. But again we must ask, is this *all* that is possible? Can an aesthetic judgement not be anything more than an emotional response, whether sophisticated or naïve?

Social Realism, Mackie dismisses with undeniable logic, as he does evaluation by the artist's intention (which one might argue is one characteristic of Social Realism). And a later passage of his, which has little to do with Maze's refutation of Freud's evaluation of Dostoevsky, reads:

If we think we can discern creativity in some works, and can use this to discriminate the good works from the bad ones, then I believe we are using this word as a name for something else, something not to be explained in psychological terms ... And this goes for psychological criticism in general. Suppose we say that one work is inhibited, that another is uninhibited or spontaneous. If these terms are used literally, they apply not to the work but to the producer: we are guessing, rightly or wrongly, at his psychic condition, and whether this condition is healthy or unhealthy, it tells us nothing about the artistic merits of his work.

Mackie's conclusion is, in my view, less convincing than the argument by which he arrives there. It reads:

Several of [the criteria] that I have mentioned are relational, but the formal feature which was mentioned under the name of organic wholeness is a qualitative feature, an intrinsic property which does not depend on anything outside the work of art itself. Similarly, while the choice of criteria can be called subjective, a judgement that applies criteria can be a fully objective one. This account, therefore, enables us to avoid both extreme relativism and extreme absolutism ...

Well, yes, it does; but again, like Sewell's, it is not very helpful and only dubiously meaningful. What if one of my subjective criteria for the value of a poem is rhyme?

I am reminded of a book launch I attended in the Philosophy Room at Sydney University. The book was edited by Jenny Anderson, Graham Cullum and Kimon Lycos and its title was *Art & Reality: John Anderson on Literature and Aesthetics*.[23] Two people launched it, David Armstrong and A.D. Hope. Armstrong said much what one would expect him to say on such an occasion. Hope prefaced his speech by admitting that he had examined only two theories of aesthetics: one was Anderson's, and it led to only James Joyce meeting the theory's requirements; the other was that of F.R. Leavis, and he, said Hope with manifest glee, 'God help him, ended with only D.H. Lawrence.'

Not surprisingly, since both have an Andersonian background, the methodology adopted by David Armstrong in 'The Freedom of the Will' is similar to that applied by Mackie in seeking an objective theory of aesthetics, but Armstrong's conclusion is more fruitful. He begins:

> We are now in a position to develop a very orthodox account of the Free-dom of the will, an account that does not clash with Determinism. Locke raised the problem in the form 'When is a man free?', and I believe this to be the best approach. We shall work towards a final answer by a series of approximations.
>
> (a) *A man is free if he can do what he wants to do.*
>
> ... The limit of man's freedom is the limit to which he can do what he wants to do. Now, on our view of purposive activity, ... it is activity initi-ated and sustained by a mental cause. Free action must therefore be *caused* action. To deny the action was caused would be to deny that the action was free.

Step by step Armstrong pares down the extent to which (a) is true by dismissing some causes of a man's doing 'what he wants to do' as indicat-ing that his action is not free. These include a concentration camp inmate who co-operates with his captors' slaughter of fellow-inmates in order to live a little longer; a drug addict whose habit intrudes on his other goals in life; actions that are caused by 'chance'; and cases where an act is *not* the result of the *past mental state of the agent* [Armstrong's emphases]. The article concludes that 'Man is free to the extent that he determines his own fate'. Unlike Sewell or Mackie, Armstrong does reach a proven, meaningful and helpful conclusion, though he does so rather dryly for my taste.

It was fortunate for readers that Armstrong's article appeared in the same issue of *The Pluralist* as did Peter Kenny's 'Determinism and Free-Will'. Kenny writes:

... neither the notion of 'determinism' nor that of 'free-will' has been established beyond doubt ... Within the monastery it is assumed *a priori* that a post-judaic divinity ... is the reference point by which any thesis may (and must) be evaluated. Within the universities similarly religious viewpoints masquerade under philosophical terms: e.g. 'Andersonian Realism' ...

To my mind (and obviously also to Armstrong's) Kenny's premise is invalid. His conclusion, that 'Factually it is not manifest that we make decisions, or have ideas, or feel satisfactions, simply because there is no sensory modality through which we can observe the workings of our own *minds* within those of others', is, by Kenny's own criterion of observation, untrue.

In the end, then, the arguments put forward above do suggest that in some ways *The Pluralist* did achieve its aim of really *being* pluralistic. All seven issues, and especially numbers three to seven, seem to me on a rereading to be still relevant and of value.

17 Katoomba: Problems, Protests and Progeny

Although *The Pluralist* published nothing directly related to the Vietnam War, my poem 'Green Grow the Bushes', published in issue number four and quoted in a previous chapter, did refer, albeit obliquely, to that war. Part 5 of the poem begins: '*Flood-tide brings Siva to me: / Silver flesh of the surge of oceans / From out of all Asia. // ...* And Alexander was king / And ruled by fire and sword / (and Napalm, later) / Lest we remember.' But this *was* oblique, and certainly not verse designed as political propaganda. These lines applied as much to the Dutch in the then Dutch East Indies (Indonesia), and the British in India, Burma, Malaya, Australia and elsewhere, as well as to the French, and the Americans later, in French Indo-China (Vietnam, Laos and Cambodia), and, of course, to the Spaniards and Portuguese, and the invasion to which the poem explicitly refers, that of India by the Greeks under Alexander the Great.

For most Australians, the Vietnam War began in 1962, when this country first sent troops there, but it was in fact a much longer war, with its immediate origins in the defeat of Japan in World War II. The French had begun their Indo-China colonisation by attacking Da Nang in 1858, and nationalist forces episodically continued to oppose the French until Japanese invasion put French domination to a temporary end, or so the French thought. These same Indo-Chinese nationalists also opposed Japanese occupation. In Vietnam by the 1930s they were led largely by communists and known as the Viet Minh. They switched their armed opposition to the French to fight instead against the Japanese. When those invaders were defeated by the Allied countries, the Viet Minh resumed fighting against French occupation of their country. Despite financial aid from the United States, the French were defeated in 1954, and support for the anti-communist government that they had imposed in southern Vietnam was taken over by United States forces. A token force of thirty-two Australian 'advisers' joined them eight years later; but that force did not remain token for long, and as the number of Australian servicemen in Vietnam grew and grew, conscription was introduced to provide sufficient numbers to meet Australia's new 'obligations'. With conscription came controversy, and increasing Australian opposition to the war.

While I failed to write directly about the Vietnam War, I did demonstrate against it, and this well before opposition to that war had become widespread. I cannot, of course, answer for Jim Baker or Bill Maidment, but certainly there were many who could see no reason to choose between supporting a neo-colonialist American-installed south Vietnamese government and a neo-Stalinist Viet Cong (the name for the Viet Minh in southern Vietnam). The then French leader, Charles de Gaulle, saw a communist victory as inevitable, and so did I. Because both the Australian Labor Party and the Communist Party of Australia campaigned only for 'peace', I campaigned with the Trotskyist groups who advocated a north Vietnamese reunification of Vietnam. Nothing less than that, I thought, would end the war, certainly not the victory of any government imposed in southern Vietnam by the United States or any other foreign power.

I cannot remember all the demonstrations in which I took part, but one does stand out in my memory. That was on the occasion in 1966 when Lyndon B. Johnson, then President of the United States, visited Sydney. Crowds of protesters against and supporters of the war lined Oxford Street in huge numbers. It was planned that LBJ would be welcomed by the Mormon Boys' Choir singing 'The Yellow Rose of Texas', their voices being conveyed to Oxford Street by cable; but anti-war activists cut the cable. I approved of their action, for both political and aesthetic reasons, but would have lacked either the courage to cut that cable or the expertise necessary to do so without electrocuting myself. Then came Bob Askin's advice, now infamous: with crowds of protesters blocking the street, the Premier of New South Wales, seated in the official car with Johnson, urged his driver to 'Run over the bastards'.

After that incident, the president and the premier, with their minders, moved on to the Art Gallery of New South Wales. Why, I do not know, as it seems unlikely that either of them was an art lover. Standing on the very top of that edifice was an Australian naval rating clad in formal long whites and carrying a rifle at the slope; no doubt he was extremely hot and uncomfortable, and whom or what he was supposed to protect isolated on that improbable perch was impossible to imagine. At the beginning of the demonstration I had searched through the multitude of placards provided by the communists and others, seeking one that I could brandish without embarrassment, and eventually finding one that simply said 'No'. On the lawns outside the art gallery I encountered John Maze, who was holding up another copy of a similar simple placard, presumably having selected it for reasons similar to mine. Any self-importance we may have been feeling was promptly punctured by a police officer, very senior judging by the liberal lengths of silver braid decorating his cap and tunic, who instructed his police cohorts: 'This lot is harmless. Move over to the other side of the gallery.'

The year 1968 was a momentous one in world politics. In France, radicals, largely students, seized virtual control of Paris. The French communists refused to support them or allow the trade unions they (the communists) controlled to do so. This was seen by many on the left, including myself, as a betrayal. Had the communists joined that revolution in the making, it would probably have ended much as did that of the Communards in 1870, especially had the United States intervened to protect the imperial control of western Europe granted it at Yalta. But the failed revolt of the Paris Commune in 1870 *has* resounded through history.

In the same year, Soviet forces invaded Czechoslovakia to remove the Czech leader, Dubček, who was threatening the Soviet empire (granted to them, too, at Yalta) with his call for 'Socialism with a Human Face'. I well remember the demonstration in Sydney against that invasion. This time I was not about to be limited again to choosing between placards displaying slogans with which I could not fully agree. While at work at Science Press in Marrickville I designed my own placard. I was not going to risk being identified as one of the anti-communist right, so my placard read: 'Keep Stalinism out of Socialist Czechoslovakia'. My placard, and the demo, were reported on favourably in the Press, and as we marched through Kings Cross, pedestrians on the footpaths applauded us. Such support was rare, but we had a problem: there was no Soviet Union establishment within marching distance of Martin Place, where we had assembled. So we chose instead to demonstrate at Rushcutters Bay against the poor bloody Poles and their consulate in that suburb.

My involvement in left politics continued in subsequent years, but when, late in 1969, Robin and I moved to Katoomba I found it more difficult to ensure that it did so.

Katoomba is a town about one hundred kilometres west-north-west of Sydney's central business district; it is the administrative centre of the (notional) City of Blue Mountains. When Robin and I moved there its population, with nearby Leura and Wentworth Falls, was fewer than twelve thousand people, most of them elderly. Developed before World War II as a tourist attraction, Katoomba by the 1960s was a mountain resort which had gone a long way downhill. Honeymoon couples and other tourists, in a car-driven era, were no longer attracted by sleazy boarding houses with some of their beds on enclosed verandas, and dimly lit dining rooms where the evening meal, with no liquor available, was served no later than six o'clock. And no sex, of course, except for proven honeymoon couples and others duly documented as being married and thus entitled to love in a cold climate.

As well as the ageing population, many of whom were British immi-grants who preferred Katoomba's cooler climate to that of Sydney, there was a growing population of young or youngish couples, who like Robin and myself were attracted to the Blue Mountains because the decline of the tourist industry had driven down the price of houses, making them much more affordable than even those in the arid monotony of western Sydney. The cottage that Robin and I bought cost a little more than seven thousand dollars, though the old man from whom we bought it would talk only in terms of pounds, shillings and pence. As with his rejection of the terms of decimal currency, which had been introduced only three years earlier, that old man also refused to have anything to do with lawyers or finance companies. We asked the solicitor who drew up the sales documents to explain to him what he had agreed to, and after handing him our deposit in cash we paid agreed instalments of the balance into his savings account at the local branch of the former Rural Bank.

Our arrangement when we bought the cottage was 'walk in; walk out', by which the old man meant that he would walk out taking nothing but his clothing, cooking and eating utensils and food, and we could walk in carrying whatever we pleased after disposing of whatever furniture we did not want. One thing that he left was of some value, his piano; this we gave to Robin's mother. But with our new home we had also purchased two problems.

One of these was our next-door neighbour, a one-legged war veteran with a mind still to fight somebody, anybody or everybody. While we were moving our furniture in, we locked our dog in the laundry to pre-vent his worrying the neighbours. But the dog disapproved and barked to tell us so. Within a day we were in receipt of a stern letter from the Blue Mountains Council, informing us that our neighbour had complained of incessant barking. ('Incessant', in this case, apparently meant thirty minutes.) Some days later our one-legged welcomer, after complaining about where I had parked my car, threatened to hose our, by then two, dogs. He kept beehives in his backyard, and bees, he told us, go amuck at the stench of wet dogs, and sting everything in their vicinity. Whether bees really behave in this way I never discovered, but as Robin was allergic to bee-stings I took the threat seriously, and instructed our solicitor to send him, in turn, a stern letter.

Later several other neighbours, all of them pensioners, congratulated us; that veteran, they told us, had sought and found, or rather made, new enemies long before he found us. He had been in the habit of reporting those pensioners to the authorities if they earned money or did anything else to infringe the conditions under which they were allowed pensions. He would stand, suitably hatted, at his front gate each and every day, watching everybody's comings and goings. We heard nothing more from him, or nothing more directly, after our solicitor's letter had been delivered, but the next day the words 'Commo bastard' had been scrawled in the frost covering the rear window of my car. Unfortunately I was able to leave those words there only until the weather warmed.

Our other problem was the cottage's location. In Katoomba, that part of Vale Street in which it stood was for much of each winter's day in the shadow of a railway embankment. Early in our first winter there I filled the dogs' water bowl every evening, only to find in the morning that the water had solidified; and dogs find it difficult to lap up ice. Quite often, in the late afternoon when we returned from work in Sydney, the ice-block, although diminished in size, was still floating in the bowl.

The cottage was fairly close to Katoomba railway station but well below it. In winter, to reach the station on foot we had first to climb a steep stairway the steps of which were usually coated by ice, or snow, or both. As well as avoiding falls on those steps, there was also the problem of protecting ourselves from the cold and the frequent gale-force winds. Rugged up in beanies, overcoats and gloves, we would traverse our treacherous climb, and then board a heated train. Our winter clothing then became an unnecessary nuisance both while travelling to and after debarking in Sydney. Travelling home, though, we donned those previously nuisance garments to brave the freezing evening before climbing down (or falling down) those often still-icy steps. More and more frequently we decided to be cowards, and I drove the two of us to the railway station, or sometimes to Sydney.

Robin did not commute for long. Since our Kirribilli days, we had been trying in vain to get her pregnant, using all the recommended methods, including the obvious one. So we put our names down with the appropriate authority to adopt, not just a baby, but twin babies. Twins, we thought, rightly as it happened, would be less in demand than single infants, and so more quickly available. But the reputation in the 1960s of those social workers who were to decide whether we were a fit couple to become adoptive parents was a grim one. They would, we were told, scour our house, including its cupboards, for any sign of untidiness, dirt or immorality. It therefore seemed unlikely that either our Darlington house or our Kirribilli flat would have impressed them at all favourably. Our Katoomba cottage, we were determined, would become a shining example of smug suburban respectability. Once we were informed that twins were available and thus that the arrival of a social worker was imminent, we tidied, washed and polished everything, including even our dogs and ourselves.

Our information proved to be out of date. When the social worker turned up, she was wearing neither grey stockings, nor a long dark skirt, nor even a bonnet or pince-nez. She seemed quite capable of smiling and examined no cupboards, nor did she interrogate us to establish our moral turpitude or lack of it. One question she did ask, and her face told us that this was *the* important one: Did we believe that nurture, not nature, determined the direction of a child's development? Since it was obvious what answer she wanted, we were not about to engage in any complex debate about the competing causal strengths of genes and general parental attitudes and other environmental factors. We became instant converts to the infallibility of loving nurture. Only days later we were informed when and where in Sydney we should pick up our twin baby girls.

While I was teaching with the Patrician Brothers I had made friends with another teacher, a bisexual who preferred to be known, though not by the Brothers, as 'Edie'. Edie introduced us to a quite likeable lesbian couple, Pat and Alda, who also lived in the Blue Mountains, though at Lawson. Unfortunately they were friendly for a time with another lesbian known, at least then, as Lee. Pat and Lee (Alda was at work) helped us bring the twins home.

And help we did need, though I would have preferred it delivered by somebody to whom I felt closer. The day appointed for us to pick up Helen Ingrid (Ingie) and Kirsten Tudor (Katie) Appleton was dangerously hot. If capsules in which to transport infants more safely in cars were then available, we hadn't heard of them. Robin could not drive, and there was no way that just the two of us could cuddle the babies and bottle-feed them with water, which was essential in those temperatures in a car with no air-conditioning.

For a time, and while I was still commuting to Sydney for work, learning to be parents was our main concern. With adopted infants, bottle-feeding was obviously the only option, and this duty, at night, we shared. I quickly mastered the contortions necessary to offer bottles to two babies at the same time, but always found it difficult to roll a cigarette while doing so. (I had heard that heavy doses of amphetamine could induce male lactation, but I did not think that any fluid so produced would be particularly nourishing for babies.)

And Pat and Lee, and to a lesser extent Alda, insisted on keeping on 'helping' us. Quite unnecessarily, though with Robin's consent and help, they used diluted hydrochloric acid and scrapers to remove the plaster from the chimney around the fireplace in our tiny living room. Stripping plaster was trendy at the time, and when all of it had been removed the stripping was supposed to result in the revelation of the texture and colour of beautiful bricks. Unfortunately in our case, not all the plaster was removed, and — predictably in a former miner's cottage — those bricks that were revealed were uneven and extremely ugly. I should have protested but was too lazy, or cowardly, or both, to bother.

The other protests, those against the Vietnam War, I did persevere with. A small anti-war group, consisting largely of Quakers, met regularly in a run-down church hall in Katoomba's main street, so I joined them. There I met a schoolteacher by the name of Tony, who persuaded me that the most effective way, in the Blue Mountains, of opposing that war was by joining the local branch of the Labor Party.

18   Soft Labor in the Blue Mountains

When I joined Katoomba Branch of the Australian Labor Party, I had in mind Trotsky's theory of *entrism* — the tactic of joining a social-democratic party with the intention of subverting it into a revolutionary socialist organisation. Like many before me, I found this task to be impossible and soon, in my case, no longer even remotely desirable.

Katoomba Branch, then, was little more than a token branch. In the days of the Chifley government, the Australian Minister for External Affairs (not 'Foreign Affairs' in those days of fading empire), Dr H.V. Evatt, is said to have recommended that a vice-president of that branch, Dr Eric Dark (who during World War I had been awarded the Military Cross for giving aid, under enemy fire, to wounded soldiers), be appointed as Australian Ambassador to the Soviet Union. But 'Chifley certainly did not favour his appointment [and] … It did not come about.'[24] Chifley's unwillingness to appoint Dark at that time was understandable. Dark was a friend of his and of Brian Fitzpatrick as well as of Evatt, but in 1947 'Bull' Abbott, a Country Party MP representing the New England electorate, had denounced Chifley in parliament for allegedly tolerating communists in his own ALP branches. In his speech he claimed:

> I shall choose a particular branch of the Australian Labour [*sic*] party, and show what happened in it during a period of three years. The branch that I choose is the Katoomba branch in the Macquarie federal electorate, which is represented by the Prime Minister (Mr Chifley). I have chosen it because, up to a little over a month ago, one of the dominant branches in the electorate of the Prime Minister was Communist-controlled. It was

deregistered on the 7th March last, not because it had in its ranks a large number of Communists, who held most of the executive positions in it, but because it had criticized actions which the Prime Minister had taken ... The Prime Minister must have known for more than two years that this branch was under Communist control ...[25]

Among the many members of Katoomba Branch denounced as communists under parliamentary privilege by Abbott was Eric Dark, of whom Abbott said, 'Although he may not be an acknowledged Communist, he is closely linked with the party underground, and is of the same type as Dr Alan Nunn May [who had then only recently been discovered to be a spy]... His wife, Mrs Eleanor Dark, the novelist, [is] also an underground worker for the Communists.'[26] Also denounced were Peter Carroll (who actually did join the Communist Party) and Hal Pratt, a teacher at Katoomba High School.

Obviously Chifley *would* have known the composition of the largest branch in his electorate, and so, most probably, would the New South Wales ALP executive. But apart from anti-communist zealots such as J.P. Ormonde (and Jack Lang, who would use any available stick with which to beat the Federal Labor Party), I doubt if anybody much cared. Anyone who has been in the ALP for some time knows how little one electorate council, let alone one branch, can influence the direction of the party as a whole. The State executive presumably decided to withdraw Katoomba Branch's charter (on the pretext of friction and inefficiency) not because they were afraid of Reds, but because they were afraid of being called Reds themselves.

Having got rid of the offending ALP branch, the New South Wales executive proceeded to get rid of Dark himself. Under pressure, he resigned from the Labor Party on 18 February 1950. But the accusations that he was a communist were enough to enrage Katoomba's would-be vigilantes. He explicitly denied those accusations, both then and until the end of his life. In 1987 he declared: 'Democratic Socialism not Communism! I never became a communist because I always thought out my own politics ... If you joined the Communist Party you had to go entirely along their line, and I would not do it!' But in the 1950s he continued to be the subject of death threats. His wife, Eleanor Dark, said to him, 'Get me fifteen inches of inch-wide lead piping and bring it to me.' She put that lead pipe in her muff and assured him, 'I'm still in pretty good training and the things I can do to those bastards with my foot of lead piping, you'd be surprised!'[27]

For some years there was no Labor Party branch in Katoomba, but eventually Tony Luchetti, who had succeeded Ben Chifley as Federal member for the seat of Macquarie, saw some advantage, at least when an election was imminent, in having a branch there. In 1953 Katoomba Branch, Lazarus-like, was resurrected.

This Lazarus, though, was still only partly alive. Shortly after joining the branch in 1969 I was elected its president. At that time the branch's total membership was only a little above the fifteen members required for a branch to retain its charter. My opponent for the presidency at the Annual General Meeting was the endorsed, but unsuccessful, candidate at the most recent State elections, and we received seven votes each. ALP rules stipulate that in the event of a drawn vote both names be placed in a hat and the election decided by the luck of the draw. On that occasion the slip of paper with my name on it was the rabbit.

Like Peter Baldwin, later, in the Federal seat of Sydney, I took advantage of the accelerated demographic change in the Blue Mountains. The young seekers for affordable accommodation, many of them with tertiary education, played the same role as their equivalents in Sydney who later 'gentrified' the inner west of that city. The recruiting of such as these, as well as of old lefties orphaned by splits in the communist parties, was an essential element in reviving Katoomba Branch as a large and left-leaning party unit. According to Abbott in his speech recorded in *Hansard*, that branch had 291 members when it was disbanded in 1947; the highest number enrolled during my presidency was around 200, and that was only in 1975, after the dismissal of the Whitlam government.

My Katoomba days had their moments. On one occasion I organised an anti-Vietnam War march down the main street of the town. Starting out from the grounds of the grand old Carrington Hotel, we planned to march only to the church hall mentioned earlier. We had warned the police of our intentions and asked them to halt the traffic for us. This they did, all going well with this mass demonstration of all of thirty people until Teacher Tony (the one who persuaded me to join the ALP) hit a cop over the head with a hefty banner which complained about police brutality. He was arrested. When I found my way into the police station to bail him out, the police sergeant would not accept my cheque, and I lacked sufficient cash to free the fool. Back I trudged to the church hall and rudely interrupted somebody's lengthy oration so that I could pass around the hat among this *de facto* congregation of very respectable and largely elderly people.

Then there was the branch member who was a Catholic Ulsterman. Inevitably, I suppose, his name was Paddy. After some dispute or other at a branch meeting, he visited Robin and me at our home. Sombre in a suit and tie, he addressed me with cold politeness as *Mister* Appleton, and this brought chillingly to my mind the politeness with which Ulstermen of both religious persuasions are said to greet one another in a ritual preliminary to a knee-capping or a killing. Paddy eventually became a friend, especially after (though still a member of the ALP) he joined an Irish communist party. That party, he told me, advocated self-determination by the citizens of Ulster as to whether they joined the Republic of Ireland or remained a segment of the (not very) United Kingdom of Great Britain and Ireland. (That monarchy by then had, I think, abandoned its claim to rule France as well.)

Among the old lefties that Will Silk and I cajoled into joining or rejoining the branch was Peter Carroll, mentioned earlier. During the bitter coalminers' strike of 1949, Peter had taken his khaki truck and joined convoys of military vehicles conveying troops, under Chifley's orders, to work the mines and break the strike. Peter's truck was not carrying troops or supplies for them, but instead food and other necessities for the support of striking miners and their families. In Katoomba today there is a Peter Carroll Park, named for him after his death. Perhaps the World War I saying, 'The only good German is a dead German', should be recycled in Australia to read 'The only good Red is a dead Red'.

Among the younger and tertiary-educated people who joined Katoomba Branch while I was its president, and who became friends of mine, were Louise and Ian McIntyre, both TAFE teachers, and Bob Debus, then a book editor with Angus & Robertson and later a cabinet minister in several Labor governments of New South Wales. As well as being president of Katoomba Branch, I became secretary of the ALP's Macquarie Federal Electorate Council, and in that body I became a friend of its president, Ross Free, later a cabinet minister in Federal ALP governments.

The meeting place for Katoomba Branch was the Carrington Hotel, coincidentally then owned by the same millionaire (on paper) who had owned our recycled brothel at Kirribilli. As was his wont, he was running the place down, with the able assistance of his gangster-like manager. One evening I bought a flagon of rough red from the Carrington's bottle department. When I reached home, and enough light to inspect my purchase, I found it to be filled with piss-coloured liquid in which were suspended decayed purplish globules to punctuate the piss. I took it back to the pub, where its manager tried to argue that this was the way red wine *should* look; when he failed to convince me he relented and replaced the flagon.

That incident was not the only occasion on which the Carrington Hotel was a precursor of 'Fawlty Towers' long before that comedy of implausible errors took over Australia's television screens. For reasons that I no longer remember, but probably political, I took two acquaintances there for dinner. Soup was the first course, and to keep up the pretence that, despite its deplorable dinners, the Carrington remained a high-class establishment, the soup was brought to the table in a decorative and heavy silver tureen. The theory was that the waiter would then ladle it into our waiting soup bowls. The practice was different. The waiter was young, nervous and inexperienced; his first ladleful missed the bowl and landed, steaming hot, in the lap of one of my guests. Thereafter, all three of us stood up whenever that waiter brought *anything* to our table.

Another time, I organised a Labor Party fund-raising dinner at the Carrington. To cater for our more trendy recent young recruits, I advised the head-waiter that about one-third of the third-rate dinners offered should be vegetarian. Things would be, I thought, all right on the night (as actors hopefully say before a First Night). But they weren't. With great pride the head-waiter assured me on the eve of the dinner that he had provided a choice of fish or chicken dinners for vegetarians. I argued vehemently that neither fish nor fowl were vegetables, but he countered by informing me that from his long experience as a caterer he *knew* what vegetarians ate. Further argument was pointless, as by then it was too late to alter the menu. Soon after that dinner the gangster-like manager absconded with the contents of the Carrington's safe and, after a suspicious fire, the pub closed down.

Before it did, though, and while it was still catering exclusively for flesh-eating vegetarians, the ALP's Macquarie Federal Electorate Council, presided over by Ross Free and myself, held another dinner, as part of our electioneering, at the Carrington. The guest of honour, and the drawcard, was Bob Hawke, then still president of the Australian Council of Trade Unions (ACTU). He was not then known as 'the Silver Bodgie', as the adjective 'silver' was not yet applicable. When, after dinner, Hawke rose to address the assembled faithful, I attempted, with my usual lack of mechanical ability, to adjust the microphone down to his level, without much success. He snatched the microphone from me and adjusted it himself. Years later, when Prime Minister Hawke was launching the fourth edition of *The Australian Encyclopaedia*, of which I was editor-in-chief, he looked at me strangely, obviously thinking 'I've seen this bastard somewhere before'. I chose not to enlighten him.

On another occasion, Hawke flew into Katoomba by helicopter, landing at a sports ground where I had spread out a white sheet as a primitive navigation aid. He was then whisked away by car to impress the locals by 'pressing the flesh' at a garden party. Afterwards he arrived at the home of Ross and Margaret Free to recuperate before undertaking his next round of electioneering.

This recuperation was accomplished by sunbathing in the Frees' backyard. Time passed, with Ross and I more and more frequently consulting our watches as the next round of politicking grew nearer. As the secretary for the Federal Electorate Council, I had devised the schedule for Hawke's visit to the area, and that schedule was tight. Finally, when it was already ten minutes past the hour when Hawkie was to be gone, I went to waken him. Immediately his two companions, who until then had given the impression of just being affable fellow-Laborites, arose to block my path. I desisted at once, and eventually Hawke wakened, dressed and departed.

With Gough Whitlam it was quite a different story. When Bob Debus became the Labor candidate in 1981 for the State seat of Blue Mountains he invited Gough to launch his campaign at a barbecue at his and Jenny Debus's home at Leura. Someone told Gough that I was editor of *The Australian Encyclopaedia*, and he demanded that I make my way over through the crowd and talk to him. This conversation, on topics varying from the Coptic Church to the origins of the name Mount Olga, recurred episodically — once at the art exhibition at the closure of Rod Shaw's studio in Sussex Street; again when my third wife Barbara and I were preparing for publication our book, *The Cambridge Dictionary of Australian Places*; and once again when Gough became chairman of the editorial advisory board of *The Australian Encyclopaedia*.

My time of involvement with the Labor Party in the Blue Mountains was not just beer, barbecues and backchatting with prime ministers, future or past. The Macquarie electorate then extended from Penrith through the Blue Mountains to Bathurst, and with Lithgow and its environs being the only strong trade-union pocket within its boundaries it was far from a safe Labor seat. Tony Luchetti enjoyed personal as well as union support in Lithgow. When he retired from parliament, Ross Free made two unsuccessful bids to win the seat. I was lengthily involved in both campaigns, taking at least a week of my annual holidays in each to act as campaign secretary and/or campaign director.[28] When Ross indicated that he would stand for preselection a third time, I considered standing against him. My marital affairs at that time were in some disarray, I was wary of risking our friendship and, in the event, I changed my mind. I then let Ross know that I would not be standing. At the next election, in November 1980, he finally won the seat.

In the State seat of Blue Mountains political relationships were not so harmonious. That seat did not include Penrith, but did include Lithgow, and it, too, was marginal. The president of Lawson Branch, just to the east of Katoomba Branch's boundaries, was Mick Clough. Mick was a right-winger who later, when he narrowly won the seat of Blue Mountains for Labor, gave Neville Wran a majority of one and thus the premiership. Clough then aligned himself in parliament with that subfaction of the right known to their less hidebound colleagues as the troglodytes. Frequently, if not always, Mick and I found ourselves on opposite sides of the factional fence, especially after changes in branch boundaries and alterations in the New South Wales Branch membership rules placed the McIntyres and Will Silk in Lawson Branch.

Will was without doubt a thorn in Mick's side. At his home in Bullaburra he established a Marxist Discussion Group, which was attended by younger members of the Lawson and Katoomba branches, among others. I attended only one meeting of that group, and then only briefly. While I was there I offered a few remarks about the contribution of Edouard Bernstein and Karl Kautsky to Marxist theory in the Second International. Not long after my visit there Mick Clough laid a charge with the

New South Wales ALP Head Office that Silk had set up a communist cell within the Labor Party. I was called as a witness for the defence, and was able to assert, with dubious honesty, that I had attended only one meeting of the Marxist group, and on that occasion only Bernstein and Kautsky had been discussed in my presence.

Then as now, neither the left nor the right of the Labor Party was a unified faction; there were sub-factions abounding, and the dominant right-wing group in the State executive were not overly supportive of Clough's troglodyte sub-faction. Neither did they wish, I suppose, to engage in wholesale expulsions of the young members that they needed as election fodder. So after my specious evidence one of them, Graham Richardson, I think, pronounced that, although Marxists, both Kautsky and Bernstein were respectable social democrats, and discussing them did not infringe party rules. Mick's charge was dismissed.

Unfortunately, though, Mick's spectre of communism continued to haunt him, as indeed it then haunted much of Europe. Soon after that ALP hearing, Ian McIntyre contacted me with the information that Will Silk, while still a member of the ALP, had joined the Communist Party of Australia (CPA). This was quite different from Paddy's improbable adherence to an Irish communist party, so I taxed Will with it. It was untrue, he said. A little later I was able to confront Will with some evidence, and this time he did admit membership of the CPA. I felt obliged to warn both Ross Free, as Labor candidate for Macquarie, and Mick Clough, as member for Blue Mountains, of Silk's defection and its possible political repercussions. Both were nervous of that prospect, but I assured them that I could deal quietly with the problem, and I did. I persuaded Will that, for the good of the left of the Labor Party, with whom he shared some goals, he must resign from our party. He agreed, and wrote a letter to the local paper, the *Blue Mountains Gazette*, explaining why he was leaving the ALP and joining the CPA. The *Gazette*'s normal practice was to publish each week pages and pages of letters, and

Will's missive was largely lost among those from a multitude of irate correspondents.

Some time earlier I had been nominated by the left and was subsequently elected to the New South Wales Branch's Rules Revision Committee. The numbers of the left in Labor Party branches had increased rapidly, not only to the east of Katoomba within the Blue Mountains, but also in Penrith. Both Will Silk (before his resignation) and I, with a large number of supporters, attended a meeting with John Faulkner and Peter Crawford, two representatives of the left faction in Sydney then known as the Steering Committee, sent to recruit our group into their fold. Crawford was abrasive, telling us that we would not be allowed to survive as a 'little local left-wing mafia', and almost succeeded in alienating most members of our group. Faulkner was conciliatory and persuasive, pointing out the advantages of affiliation. Without his efforts I doubt if I would have been able to sway our local leftists into joining the Steering Committee.

Mick Clough was astute enough to read the political omens. Instead of nominating again for preselection in the Blue Mountains seat, he gained preselection for Bathurst, which seat he held until his retirement. Before that election was called, we had formed a left caucus comprised of delegates from Penrith branches as well as those in the Blue Mountains electorate. This was a sound enough move while that caucus confined its deliberations to local policies, but when it became evident that a left candidate could win preselection for the seat of Blue Mountains, that whole caucus (not just its Blue Mountains delegates) insisted on participating in the vote to decide who should stand as the left candidate for preselection.

I could and should have objected strongly to those outside the electorate claiming voting rights, but didn't. There were two candidates, myself and Kate Blakeney, whose stance was rather to the left of mine. When the ballot took place, Kate defeated me by one vote. I was then asked by the leading Penrith delegate whether I would abide by the decision. I replied that I would, provided that Kate, who had not been in the party long, proved eligible to stand.

Around this time Barbara and I moved to Sydney. For a while I played no part in Blue Mountains politics, until, in the Criterion Hotel in Sussex Street, that same Penrith delegate approached me, telling me that Kate had not proved eligible to stand and that therefore I was the left candidate. A little later Bob Debus phoned me at work, requesting that we meet. I chose the Criterion as the venue, and there Bob put it to me that, since I no longer lived in the electorate, I should stand aside and agree to his taking my place as left candidate for preselection. For a few moments I cogitated. I then asked Bob to assure me of his intention to join the left parliamentary caucus should he be elected, which he did, so I agreed. Bob won the preselection *and* the seat, which he has held, except for one term of parliament, ever since.[29] I did not then, and do not now, regret my decision.

While I was involved in politics I still had, of course, a professional and a private life. Both are dealt with, in that order, in the following chapters.

19 The Encyclopaedist Charmed

(With apologies to Isaac Deutscher)

When Robin and I established ourselves in Katoomba I was still employed by Science Press as an editor for Alex Boden. Boden, when I told him of our move, responded less than graciously: 'So I suppose you will arrive every morning too tired to work properly', was the form his congratulations took. Staying in Boden's employment, too tired to work or not, was not my intention. An advertisement in the *Sydney Morning Herald* provided me with a possible alternative. An editorial assistant, it stated, was needed by *The Australian Encyclopaedia*.

Initially I was hesitant. Until then I had tended to assume all encyclopaedias to be, at least to some extent, fraudulent publications. But the good ones, as I was to discover, definitely are not, though the hype with which they are sold frequently is. *The Australian Encyclopaedia* was, and I hope will continue to be, the best reference work with Australia, in all of its known aspects, as its sole subject.

When I applied and was interviewed for the editorial assistant position I came gradually to recognise that I had already encountered Bruce Pratt, the encyclopaedia's editor-in-chief, on two earlier occasions. Some years earlier, while hitch-hiking from Melbourne back to Sydney, I had accepted a lift from a bloke who informed me that he worked as a book editor for Angus & Robertson. He had picked me up, he told me, only because he had mistaken me for one of his authors, but he drove me to Sydney despite this. Not very much later, after gate-crashing either an Artists' or an Art Students' Ball at Sydney's Trocadero, I had met an attractive young woman, Halcyon Pratt, with whom I remained in contact for some weeks. After a day we had spent rowing on Sydney Harbour, she invited me to her parents' home and introduced me to her mother,

Pixie O'Harris, and to her father, Bruce. Halcyon was the Pratts' eldest daughter. To add to those coincidences, the Pratts' second daughter, Robin, whom I had come to know at the Tudor Hotel, was the girlfriend of Peter Tranter, an associate of the Push; later they married. The youngest daughter, Megan, it transpired, had been known to my wife Robin at Sydney Girls High School.

Whether Bruce Pratt recognised me at that first interview, I don't, of course, know, but I suspect not. Certainly he did not accept, without evidence, my claim in my letter of application that I was familiar with 'all aspects of book publishing', though that claim contained very little hyperbole. Before appointing me he subjected me to a test of my editorial capacity: I was to reduce by forty per cent the number of words in the lengthy entry EXPLORATION BY LAND, in the encyclopaedia's second edition, without omitting any information of importance. This I managed to do to Bruce's satisfaction, so I joined the encyclopaedia's editorial staff.

It was a warm and welcoming staff that I joined in 1972 in their offices on two floors of a block of flats at Rose Bay. Our task was, essentially, to do what I had done with EXPLORATION BY LAND with the text of all the articles from the second edition of *The Australian Encyclopaedia*. We were to reduce the 4,500,000 words of that edition to 2,400,000, and this without omitting any important information. In addition, we were to metricate (by the use of printed tables, not calculators or computers) all Imperial measures other than those to be left unchanged for historical reasons. Obviously, too, almost all the articles needed updating, and many new articles were to be written and added. There was a policy change as well, and one that I am not sure was wise: for a person's biography to be included that person no longer had to be dead.

All this, in his sage and mild manner, Bruce Pratt, with his staff, including myself, managed to achieve, though not without intrusive interventions by the encyclopaedia's American publishers, the Grolier Society, then still operating from New York. To understand how, and why, this was almost inevitable, one needs to know something of the history of *The Australian Encyclopaedia*.

As early as 1912 the possibility of publishing an Australian encyclopaedia was projected, with Charles H. Bertie, a municipal librarian in Sydney, as editor. The 'projection' was the brainchild of George Robertson, co-founder and driving force of Angus & Robertson, booksellers and publishers, and the main architect of that establishment's success. World War I put paid to the project for a time, but only for a time.

> When Robertson set in train the production of the first *Australian Encyclopaedia* in 1919, he expected to have it out by the end of 1920 ... Arthur Jose, who was put in charge of the project, was regarded as a fast worker; he decided that some of the articles that had been prepared before the war ... needed bringing up to date and that additional material had to be included. In the event, the first of the two volumes was not published until 1925 and the second not until the following year ... Robertson was displeased with Jose, who went back to England in 1926 before finishing the job. [In that year] Robertson wrote [to his manager in London], 'Mr Jose is on his way home and may look you up. Be civil to him, but don't go out of your way to serve him or commit us in any way. He has loafed on his job here, and left me to clear up the mess.' ... Robertson [later added] that Jose 'had left vol. 2 of AE in a state of chaos for one to clean up. It made me ill and I was in the doctor's hands.'[30]

This was not the last time there was to be a falling out between a publisher of *The Australian Encyclopaedia* and its editor, but presumably any resentment felt by Jose faded over the following seven years. On hearing, in 1933, of Robertson's death, Jose wrote:

> Even in the 1920s [Robertson] read every one of the three thousand columns of the *Encyclopaedia*, worked through them with me, insisted, even

at the last minute, on alterations he preferred or excellent reasons for not making them.[31]

On the title-page of the first volume of that edition of the encyclopaedia the editorship is credited to Arthur Wilberforce Jose and Herbert James Carter, with the collaboration of T.G. Tucker. There is no acknowledgement of Robertson's own editorial input.

In 1946 Angus & Robertson (A&R) commissioned Alec Chisholm to prepare a second edition of *The Australian Encyclopaedia*. Chisholm was an ornithologist, a historian and a journalist. He had been well known to George Robertson, to whom he had suggested engaging Eagle Press as the printer for A&R's publications. Robertson had been contemplating ceasing publishing because of the high cost of printing, and reverting to being a bookseller only. He accepted that suggestion of Chisholm's, and later A&R acquired a controlling interest in Eagle Press, later still renaming it Halstead Press, after Robertson's birthplace in England. It was Halstead Press which printed the ten-volume edition of the encyclopaedia edited by Alec Chisholm. A&R published it in 1958.

It had taken twelve years for Alec Chisholm, as editor-in-chief, and Bruce Pratt, as general editor, to put together that edition. To me, it seems highly likely that A&R's publishing director (by then Robertson's grandson, George Ferguson) would have intervened more than once to hurry Chisholm up, but if so, Bruce never mentioned it to me. What he did mention was an editorial office strung with clothes-lines on which were pegged, in alphabetical order, the printer's galley proofs of the encyclopaedia, each about one-and-a-quarter metres in length and printed on cheap paper. These were used, in those pre-computer days when linotype and monotype printing were the norm, for publishers to check the typesetter's accuracy. Through that inflammable forest of paper fronds the editorial staff went about their day-to-day and year-to-year compilation of the encyclopaedia.

In 1962 A&R sold the encyclopaedia to the Grolier Society, publishers in the United States of *Encyclopedia Americana*, the main international rival of *Encyclopaedia Britannica*, also by then American-owned. Five reprintings of *The Australian Encyclopaedia*'s second edition were issued under the Grolier imprint between that year and 1972, with such minor amendments as were thought necessary by the then editor, Bruce Pratt. And 1972, as was said earlier, was the year in which I joined the staff of the third edition.

With Bruce Pratt I remained a friend until his death. One piece of advice he offered, after I had succeeded him as editor-in-chief, was: 'Never tell the Editorial Advisory Board anything more than you must.' Alex Skovron, whom I met on joining the encyclopaedia, has remained my friend ever since. For much of that edition's time of gestation, he and I were the sole occupants of the offices on the first storey of the block of flats, and later, with others, occupants of a flat on the second storey. A poem of his that he dedicated to me later appeared in his collection *The Rearrangement* (Melbourne University Press, 1988), and refers to conversations we enjoyed in our offices there. The title and first two stanzas read:

> **Sentences**
> (*for Richard Appleton*)
>
> I seem to recall
> a quaint time I thought hitherto
> said like concerto
>   *hithérto*
> and albeit to echo Arbeit
>   *álbeit*
>
> My friend who drank
> red wine and wrote encyclopaedias
> confessed he'd crossed

> segments of youth
> mouthing misled like wise-old
>   *misled*

Alex was entitled to add the letters MA after his surname, but with the exception of Mimi Bailey, Bruce's very capable associate editor, and Elizabeth Bowman, most of the staff editors working on the premises were recent arts graduates. Alex and I were staff editors too, until he became illustrations editor and I became production editor. Degrees go unmentioned on the editorial pages of all editions of the encyclopaedia (except for Dr Tucker, collaborator in the first edition) for the good and sufficient reason that no editor-in-chief to date (2004) has had one, and crediting our staff members with their degrees would have drawn unwelcome attention to the lack of letters after our own names.

The change from Science Press to an initially more junior post on the staff of the encyclopaedia was, for me, a charming one. For the first time, while in paid employment, I could converse with my workmates much as I did with Push members in whichever pub or other meeting place we were then frequenting. Since living in Katoomba had deprived me of daily Push conversation, this change was doubly welcome. And while private meetings for dinner or drinks with friends who were Labor Party members in the Blue Mountains did lead to conversation, political topics usually took precedence. Talk with fellow-encyclopaedists could and did move from topic to topic from moment to moment. We were obviously in training to join the now despised 'chattering classes'.

Metrication, too, had its moments. Perusing metric conversion tables provided no information on what metric unit measuring the intensity of light should replace 'million candlepower' in the article dealing with lighthouses. Neither did direct queries with the Metric Conversion Board. After hours of fruitless telephoning I finally located a reclusive government official who was burdened with the title 'clerk of lighthouses'. He offered me the alternatives of 'lumens per square metre' (I think), or 'megacandelas'. Not only was the latter more Italianate and mellifluous, but the conversion ratio was one to one, as opposed to the former, with which the ratio for conversion had copious numerals following its decimal point. As I had no calculator, and the conversion needed to be repeated several times, 'megacandelas' won the day.

As production editor I had other problems to overcome. The third edition was not only to be typeset, but also sorted alphabetically, by a mainframe computer with a program woefully inadequate for book publishing. Until then I had dealt only with literate and highly proficient linotypists or monotypists, human beings capable of judging where it was permissible to hyphenate a word and carry part of it to the next line, and where it was not. This computer program was definitely not so capable.

The typesetting company's first suggestion was to avoid, by l e t t e r s p a c i n g, the need to hyphenate words over a line at all. That method was much used in those days by newspaper publishers, and now, fortunately, is not. This solution I flatly rejected. Various other suggestions were put forward, the obvious one being to allow the computer to break words so that suffixes such as '-ing' or '-ion' could be carried over to the next line. Clearly, such a method would not apply to words without these suffixes, and what about, I asked, words like 'string' or 'lion'? There were also prefixes suggested as possible hyphenation points, but similar objections would have applied. They had no answer, so I provided my own. I read through, at manuscript stage, all the 2,400,000 words of the coming edition, marking with a pencil every syllable where hyphenation was permissible. This was time-consuming, but enabled me to gain an intimate knowledge of the encyclopaedia's contents. As a side benefit, I picked up some errors, and flaws, not detected until then.

I also complained to the computer company about their typesetter's failure to revert to a roman typeface when a comma or semicolon occurred after a word or phrase in italics. That war I won, but when a different problem arose later and a solution was offered, one representative of the computer company said to another, in my presence, 'Dick

Appleton would never tolerate a roman full stop in an italic setting!' I suppose this was, in a way, a wry plaudit.

Problems with our American publishers began as only minor pin-pricks. The world economy was undergoing one of its increasingly frequent downturns, and Grolier was feeling the pinch. Its New York head office instructed our Australian editorial team that no purchase costing $100 or more was to be made without prior permission from their financial managers. As *The Australian Encyclopaedia*'s contributors continued to send us more and more manuscripts we increasingly needed additional storage space. Since new filing cabinets, even then, cost more than $100, Alex Skovron and I wasted many hours scouring second-hand furniture shops to acquire cabinets, one by one, so that each purchase could be sufficiently cheap to evade the requirement for overseas permission. The resultant miscellaneous multi-coloured collection of cabinets, with the archives therein, was later for some years in my possession; now, I suppose, it gathers dust in the storage rooms of the Australian Geographic Society — a historic and colourful monument to economic hypochondria.

Grolier's financial woes steadily worsened; the company vacated its New York premises and retreated to cheaper accommodation in Danbury, Connecticut. Acting on similarly nervous anticipations, Grolier's Sydney head office was evacuated from North Sydney to the industrial sector of Artarmon, farther north. At Rose Bay, all of the encyclopaedia's editorial staff, other than Bruce, Mimi Bailey, Alex Skovron and myself, were dismissed. Naturally enough, such a major reduction of staff considerably slowed progress toward publication of the third edition. Its American publishers eventually came to understand that they had tied up their already considerable investment, and pushed further into the future any possibility of recouping that investment. What were they to do?

Their response was to spur us, they hoped, to greater haste by dispatching to Sydney the editor-in-chief of *Encyclopedia Americana*, Wallace Murray. Bruce did not complain about this intrusion on his territory, or at least not to me. Obviously, though, it undermined his editorial authority and was an insult to his encyclopaedic capabilities. Wallace himself was a pleasant enough bloke, and he said nothing against Bruce in any conversations in which I took part. At least once, and possibly twice, he lunched at a local restaurant with Alex and me, but did not attempt to suborn our loyalty to Bruce. What he did suggest was that we editors could, by the use of other reference books, write more of the edition's contents in-house, rather than wait for manuscripts solicited from outside contributors. Sometimes this did prove possible; for instance, I was able to use newly available defence documents to write the article BRISBANE LINE. But while it was no doubt practicable to use this approach widely in America, where one could condense the contents of publications describing the individual States, this approach could not be applied widely in Australia. Whereas in the USA some States published, or had caused to be published, encyclopaedias of their own — later I was to be offered the task of being founding editor of an encyclopaedia of California — in this country it was smaller encyclopaedias that all too often condensed *our* articles to provide the contents of their own publications.

Another visitor at that time from Grolier's home country was Betty Chase. I was never told what was her role in Australia, but if, as seemed plausible, she was related to the Chase Manhattan Bank, it was probably of a financial nature. I had little to do with Betty editorially, but had pleasant interludes with her socially. She visited Robin and me in Katoomba, and while there she proudly told me that she was an old-style liberal who had never crossed a union picket line. I drove her around the more accessible Blue Mountains scenic locations, and after our visit to Minnehaha Falls she asked me how those falls had acquired their name. In response I spun her a yarn about an Aboriginal princess called Pocahontas and how she saved the life of an English settler. An American of Betty's generation would doubtless have been brought up familiar with Henry Wadsworth Longfellow and *The Song of Hiawatha*, but Betty, to her credit, managed to keep a straight face until my bogus legend had dawdled to its improbable end.

Subsequently to and probably as a consequence of these visitations from on high, our cash flow from Grolier resumed — although given Grolier's global operations, it was very likely just a cash trickle for that company. Staff were hired again, and my responsibilities as production editor began in earnest.

As well as typesetting and alphabetical sorting (of which more later), the computer company with which we were working boasted that its program could lay out the pages of the encyclopaedia, with very little human input needed for this task. After some discussion the company's representatives agreed to modify their program to meet my specifications for the format of those pages. These included stipulations that no fewer than three lines were to be turned over to begin a new column; that line-spacing be resorted to only when no other alternative was available, and then must be sufficiently small to be barely detectable; and that, when necessary to balance columns, additional space could be inserted in areas left blank for the insertion of illustrations. With my assistance, Alex had carefully calculated the depth and breadth of each photograph, drawing and map, and we had together checked the captions against the body of the text to ensure that one did not contradict the other. What I failed to stipulate, because it seemed so glaringly obvious, was that the space left for any one illustration must be confined to the appropriate column and page.

Then the page-proofs of volume one came flooding in, and it swiftly became evident that the stipulation I had failed to make was not obvious at all to the programmers. Page after page was delivered in which the space left for an illustration fell partly in one column or page and partly in another. As well, line-spacing on several pages was gross, and far exceeded my specifications.

Until then, at Bruce's suggestion, I had been working at home in Katoomba for two or three days each week, and commuting to Rose Bay only on the remaining days. One result of this was that, when the Granville train disaster of 1977 occurred, and many in my usual carriage were killed, I was not on board. In that horrendous accident the train's leading carriage left the rails and crashed into a stanchion, which sliced through that carriage at neck level. The fall of the stanchion caused the collapse of an overhead concrete road bridge, crushing several carriages of the train. Eighty-three people died and more than eighty were hospitalised. One of those killed was Alda, the amiable lesbian woman mentioned earlier.

To remedy the inadequacies of the computer program I resumed commuting to Rose Bay each weekday. With Bruce's consent, I engaged three production assistants and purchased scissors and some lethal-smelling glue. On photocopies of those pages I found unacceptable I marked the necessary rearrangements, and on other photocopies my assistants literally cut and pasted to move the text, and the spaces for illustrations, according to my instructions. The resultant rough paste-ups were then returned to the computer company so that a draughtsman there could replicate our changes on the bromide pages in camera-ready form. On most afternoons I then boarded a train home to Katoomba, and there worked out (again without the aid of a calculator, a device by then available but with which I was not familiar) where the current volume should conclude so that all six volumes would be, at least approximately, of the same thickness. On some afternoons, though, the prospect of three hours of travel followed by an evening of lengthy additions of page numbers and the long-division of the resultant multi-digit sums by almost as complex divisors was too much at the end of a working day. When it was, I would take myself for drinks at the then current Push pub, and sleep, that night, at the home of one Push member or another in Sydney.

Luckily it was not until we were well into volume six that the stress of my taxing schedule struck me down. One afternoon, while I was supervising the removal of dysfunctional picture spaces, an excruciating pain pierced my forehead and I crashed, in mid-sentence, to the floor. It was the first, and the worst, migraine with which I have ever been afflicted. Bruce ordered a taxi, which took me to Central Station and a fortunately waiting Mountains train. Even more fortunately, on board the train was Bob Debus. Bob, when we reached my parked car at Katoomba station, drove me home. He then drove me to a medical practice, where I was injected with some substance that dulled the pain, but also, unfortunately, dulled my wits.

When all the bromide pages, including those which had needed repair, were ready, they were dispatched to Griffin Press, in Adelaide, for printing. As production editor, it was my task to supervise our mutual efforts to their final stage: printed, sewn and casebound books. As soon as each volume was ready for printing, I flew to Adelaide. For volume one I had the very welcome assistance of Aubrey Cousins, who had been the managing director of A&R's Halstead Press. Aubrey instructed me on what to look for in a printery, how to ensure that ink was distributed evenly over the pages, and when necessary, how to call for improvements in the colour mix of the inks. After that I was on my own.

Most casebound books were printed on both sides of a sheet of thirty-two pages, which was then mechanically folded and trimmed to create what was called a 'forme'. Once the first forme of a volume had gained my approval, I would take a taxi into Adelaide's central business district and stroll around its streets. But in that city one could not stroll very far without reaching its parkland edge, so more and more often I would sit in a pub near the printery until the next forme was ready for inspection. This process was repeated over days, and by the time I had finished with a volume and was ready to fly back to Sydney I was rarely sober. This did not matter; I could sleep my way from Adelaide to Sydney and sleep again from Sydney to Katoomba, though on one occasion I was carried on to Blackheath before I awoke. After I had completed this exercise six times, tiredness was beginning to take its toll.

At the end of this lengthy process, in 1977, our role at Rose Bay was over. Bruce Pratt retired, and I was confirmed as his successor. Robin and I, accompanied by Louise and Ian McIntyre, then rented for a week or two a farmhouse near the Snowy Mountains, and there, at last, I could hope to learn again to relax, or more likely, to find some other project or cause about which to become obsessive.

20   Matrimonial Blues

At that farmhouse, the only obsession I was able to conjure up was splitting firewood to fuel the kitchen stove. That triumph of engineering competence not only made hot meals readily available; it also provided hot water for our morning showers. With Louise and Ian on that holiday came their two sons, Ben and Laurence, and with Robin and me came not only our daughters, Ingie and Kate, but our son, also named Laurence, after my father.

It is not uncommon, or so I have been told, that when a couple adopts a baby (or babies) the woman falls pregnant afterwards. Certainly this was so in Robin's and my case; Laurence Douglas Appleton was conceived nearly two years after we brought our twin girls home to Katoomba. Laurence was born prematurely and delivered of necessity by Caesarean. For a week or more he resembled a small pink monkey in a cage, confined as he was behind the glass of an incubator-like humidicrib, but after that he grew apace.

The first time after the birth that I visited Robin in her austerely sterile ward at the King George V Hospital in Camperdown, I was in the company of a small man with a long blond pony-tail. It was Johnny Earls, back briefly, and unexpectedly, from his teaching post at the Ann Arbor campus of the University of Michigan. It is, or was, customary for a father to celebrate the birth of his child by drinking copiously with his friends, and Johnny was, for me, the ideal person with whom to engage in this ritual. So as soon as we were expelled from the hospital by a bell signalling the end of visiting time, we did just that. Political correctness was not then yet in place, but had it been we should still have done so.

We drank first, I think, at the White Horse Hotel, since subsumed by a theological college, but by the time that the official Push drinking hour had arrived we were in the Criterion Hotel in Sussex Street. Neither of us had drunk in that current Push pub for some time, and Nico (Doug Nicholson) greeted this dual surprise with: 'Do my rheumy eyes deceive me? Or is that Appo and Earls in the pub and in the flesh?' For a while Laurence, and Robin, were forgotten.

Johnny had moved to Ann Arbor after teaching for some years at the University of Ayacucho, in Peru. When he arrived in the United States his first thought (expressed in a letter to Sydney) was 'Jesus! The Push has taken over the world.' He was referring of course to the sexual liberation, as well as the informality of dress, that had taken place in the United States, Europe and Australia, but not yet in Peru. What he, and I, found at the Criterion was a Push that in these respects differed little from the society of which it was part, but unlike other elements of that society, held strong theoretical beliefs that upheld the desirability of at least the former of those changes.

Not that all Push members had dressed in bohemian uniform; I well remember, at the Tudor, one young woman giving voice to the *Women's Weekly* mantra: 'If you buy a good handbag, belt and shoes, to wear with a cheap cotton dress …', at which point Lillian Roxon interjected rudely, 'It will still look like a cheap cotton dress.' As for many Push men, informal dress was frequently not their preference, nor usually an option for those in office jobs. Peter Hellier wore suits, as did Peter Tranter, and when necessary, so did I. The change in appearance of those with no bohemian credentials is best illustrated by the complaints of certain Push associates. They had travelled to Brisbane to protest against a football tour by the Springboks, when South Africa still selected its players by the rules of apartheid: those football fans that assaulted them, they lamented, 'wore clothes just like us and had long hair and beards just like us!'

Like many others, no doubt, as a child and more so as an adolescent, I had anticipated that once I attained adulthood all my problems would be triumphantly solved. For both Robin and me, similar expectations continued: marriage would usher in a miraculous improvement in our lives; escaping to Katoomba would do much the same; adoption of the twins, and later the birth of Laurence, would elevate our marriage to a state of bliss. In practice, the changes brought about by these events, though extensive, did not include a metamorphosis in our marriage.

With the arrival home of Laurence we found that our larger, recently acquired home in northern Katoomba was an advantage. It had been made possible through the financial help (unwisely accepted) of Robin's mother, and of course a mortgage. Our new weatherboard palace, together with the termites it harboured, stood in Rupert Street on land that sloped downhill from our back veranda towards the north. This delivered to us what warmth was available from Katoomba's winter sun.

What change there was, unnoticed at the time by either Robin or me, tended towards a deterioration in our relationship. I assumed that Robin, with the children and a house, was at least moderately content. She, I think, assumed that I, having become editor-in-chief, was happy with both commuting and with my work. Neither assumption was correct.

Nobody, other than a masochist perhaps, could be happy to spend about five hours each working day commuting to work by car, train and bus, but I accepted this as a necessary evil brought about by our inability to afford an acceptable house other than one in the Blue Mountains or somewhere else equally distant from Sydney. And as for my enjoying my work, there was little to enjoy once my office was moved from Rose Bay to Grolier's head office in Artarmon.

Some of the reasons for Robin's growing discontent are now so obvious that they could have been used in a case study in a feminist marriage-guidance textbook on 'How *not* to do it'. They were not so obvious, to me at least, in the early to mid-1970s. For many of her waking hours from Monday to Friday she was a lonely housewife mothering three young children. At weekends, too, I was frequently occupied by Labor Party tasks, many of them self-imposed, leaving Robin for long hours alone.

For a time she had the solace of Lee's company. Lee had fallen out with the Pat mentioned earlier, so she visited us instead. And stayed and stayed. Eventually I persuaded Robin to tell Lee that she was not welcome as a permanent non-paying house-guest, and she departed.

Another frequent visitor, more welcome to me, was Ian Parker. At the time that Robin and I had moved to Rupert Street, Ian still owned a small and decrepit cottage in nearby Leura. (Johnny Earls had lived there briefly during some penurious period prior to his departure for Peru. Once, when Robin and I visited him we all three fronted the bar at the Ritz Hotel in Leura. Those premises were later taken over by a nursing home, but at that time the Ritz had some claim to being a high-class hostelry. From a white-jacketed barman Johnny ordered beers; then paid for them entirely in pennies and halfpennies.) After Parker had sold his Leura retreat, to which he had been accustomed to return frequently when drunk by a late-night train from Sydney, he took to catching the same late train when drunk but visiting us instead. By then, Parker was almost inarticulate when sober, and quite incomprehensible when drunk, but reasonably good company when halfway between those two states. Obligingly, he always hid his bottle of vodka under a cushion, while pretending to drink, at my request, only red wine.

For a time Robin worked at home, proofreading the third edition of the encyclopaedia. As an editor at Sydney University Press, she had enjoyed intellectually stimulating work in a socially sympathetic environment. At Katoomba, especially after she had finished her work on that 1977 edition, she was stripped of both these intellectual and emotional amenities. She directed some efforts into local community organisations, including a crisis group. But eventually the day arrived when Lee, like the proverbial bad penny, came back.

I drove home one evening, either from a railway station or directly from Artarmon, to find her sitting with Robin at our kitchen table. 'Look who has unexpectedly turned up,' chirped Robin brightly. Giving her a wintry smile I welcomed Lee with warm insincerity.

The intimacy between these two women grew more obvious day by day and week by week, but at least it kept Robin in reasonable humour. One afternoon, with Lee and our children, we took our dogs to a park in Leura. Robin's mother accompanied us, and while I exercised the dogs, she chatted with her grandchildren and looked on benignly.

From then on, Robin regaled me regularly with stories of what a hard life Lee had suffered and what her needs were. These stories grew day by day, as did the quantities of Lee's belongings cluttering our house. The crunch finally came when I returned from work on the evening of 17 January 1978, which happened to be my birthday. After we had eaten, but before we had put our children to bed, Robin told me that our marriage was over, and that she had never had a happy moment in the time that we had been together. At first I took this calmly (after all, I had foreseen it), so I told Robin that she could have the house and that I would leave my job and resume a bohemian life in Sydney. Shortly afterwards I drove to Will Silk's place in Bullaburra, seeking condolences and taking with me liquor to lubricate them.

By the next morning I had changed my mind. I would keep the house, I decided, and the children too, if this proved feasible. When I reached home the house was unoccupied. To my drunken and troubled mind it seemed evident that they all had gone, and gone for good. In the kitchen I kept an axe for truncating firewood to fit the open fireplace. So I grabbed it, and vented my fury on Lee's belongings; then, without success, I tried to tear apart a volume of *The Shorter Oxford Dictionary*. With rather more success, I tore up instead a poem of mine lauding the life of Robin, myself and the children; the poem was far too derivative of one on a similar subject by Robert Graves, so destroying the only copy did not, once I became calmer, much distress me. At that point I heard Lee's car pull up outside.

What was I to do? Hurriedly I grabbed a bottle of wine and a glass, slopped a little wine into the glass and a lot on the floor, and lay down on a lounge to pretend to be asleep. I then realised that one more prop was needed, so I ran and fetched the axe, and leant it against the lounge before resuming my sleeping posture. Lee came into the house, and was silent as she took in her murdered belongings. She then hurried back to Robin and the children, and they drove away. This time, it *was* for good.

In his poem 'The Hippopotamus', T.S. Eliot opinionates about heaven, and I suppose about missionaries, when he writes:

> I saw the 'potamus take wing
> Ascending from the damp savannas,
> And quiring angels round him sing
> The praise of God, in loud hosannas.
>
> Blood of the Lamb shall wash him clean
> And him shall heavenly arms enfold,
> Among the saints he shall be seen
> Performing on a harp of gold.
>
> He shall be washed as white as snow,
> By all the martyr'd virgins kist,
> While the True Church remains below
> Wrapt in the old miasmal mist.[32]

Certainly I make no claim to be a 'True Church', or for that matter a false one, but the 'miasmal mist' does have some relevance. The mist in which *I* remained was so dense that even now my memory pierces it to reveal only ill-defined fragments.

I remember my sense of loss. Almost every time I drove past a school I would park, walk tentatively to its fence and scrutinise the school playground, wondering whether my children might be among those playing there. I could well have been taken to be a predatory pedophile, but fortunately pedophiles were not then in the news.

I remember that I was stupid enough to ring Robin's mother, asking her where the children might be. She replied that they were 'somewhere where you will never find them'. So I did. I suborned a friend who worked in that government department responsible for dispensing the dole, and found that Lee's cheque was being sent to Toms Creek, a locality not far from Wauchope. Stupidly, too, I let Robin know that I knew, thus jeopardising my friend's job.

I remember an elderly police sergeant coming to my door to inform me that Miss (whatever surname Lee was using) had lodged a complaint that I had wantonly destroyed her property. He looked rather peeved when I responded that surely this was not a police matter, but a civil one. He did not agree or disagree, and went away still looking peeved.

I remember receiving a telegram, signed 'Robin Appleton', which read: 'CHILDREN WELL STOP ALL FUTURE COMMUNICATIONS THROUGH SOLICITORS STOP'. This I pinned to the household notice board, giving it almost the prominence of the winning portrait in an Archibald Prize.

On several evenings, on impulse, I jumped into the station-wagon, drove to Sydney, had one drink at the Criterion Hotel, and then panicked and sped back to Katoomba, just in case there had been some development during my absence.

My sanity was very gradually restored thanks to the help given to me by friends. Louise and Ian McIntyre, assisted by other friends, not only repaired the havoc created by my axe-rampage, but also cleaned the long-standing grot of months. Later, Lyn Collingwood and Barbara Warren, who later became my third wife, similarly, and also gradually, repaired the damage to my ego, and at least partly stabilised what passed for my mind.

Some weeks afterwards Robin appeared. She proceeded to tax me with: 'All these weeks, and you haven't even written to the children.' I rose to my feet and stalked to the notice board, retrieved the winning Archibald exhibit, and presented it to her. 'Well,' she responded hesitantly, 'we were both rather mad then.' I gained the strong impression that she was surprised, and that it was not she, but Lee, who had been responsible for the telegram. Not long afterwards, Robin and Lee moved from Toms Creek to an old timber farmhouse some distance out of Wingham. By then, they had abandoned the pretence that their address must be kept secret from a potential axe-murderer.

After a long absence from my editorial office while recovering from this episode, I reluctantly returned to work. But obviously I was not fully recovered. Every time Robin telephoned me there, which she did several times, she felt compelled to comment that my voice when speaking to her was apprehensive and strained, in her view unnecessarily so. After one such telephone call, a rather attractive female middle-manager at Grolier came into my office, looked at my (apparently grey) face and asked, with some concern, 'What's wrong?' She would not accept my assurance that nothing was wrong, but I thought it inadvisable to enter into lengthy and complex explanations.

Ultimately it was Barbara, together with Beth, our baby, who made more solid my sanity, such as it is. Because commuting, especially in winter, was undermining my health, some months after we married (on 6 May 1979) we sold the Katoomba weatherboard and moved to a rented house at Lindfield, in the north of Sydney.

Even before our move from Katoomba my relations with the three older children were becoming more distant. On most school holidays I drove to Wingham, picked up the children and drove them home with me. At the end of holidays the process was repeated, but in reverse.

Sometimes I paid for them to fly down, and met them at Sydney Airport. By the time that Robin herself, with the children, had moved to Petersham, where Barbara and I were by then living, I had become to the children a 'holidays-only father', having little to do with their everyday lives. In the circumstances this was, I suppose, inevitable.

Some nineteen years later my axe-accompanied 'drunken stupor' came back to haunt me. When, at my sixty-fifth birthday party, Robin walked in, Barbara, unwisely in my opinion, informed her that she was not welcome. This incensed my son Laurence. Later he told me that the only thing Barbara had accomplished of which he approved was her converting me from my drunken excesses. He remembered, he said, seeing me in my apparent stupor with an axe beside me. Later, though, he apologised. He acknowledged that he had been only four years old at the time, and remembered little, if anything, of the occasion. His words, when he had given his reluctant and partial approval of Barbara, had echoed almost identically those of Robin's mother when she spoke of me. And she, of course, had not been present at the 'axe murder' scene.

21 The Encyclopaedist *Un*-charmed

Returning to my other baby — my professional one, *The Australian Encyclopaedia* — the tone of this narrative becomes, at least for a little while, rather lighter. On the day that the encyclopaedia's third edition was to be launched I left Ian McIntyre minding the children of both families at the farmhouse mentioned earlier while Louise and Robin further explored the farther reaches of the snow country, and I drove, expectantly, to Canberra and the launch.

This event was orchestrated by Sir Harold White, the chairman of the encyclopaedia's Editorial Advisory Board. Sir Harold had been largely responsible for the foundation of the Australian National Library as a separate entity from the Commonwealth Parliamentary Library, over which he had also presided, and it was his expertise in manoeuvring his way among the other senior public servants in Canberra that had enabled him to do so. On this occasion, though, his skill in manipulating the dignitaries of Canberra's cocktail circuit got the better of his judgement.

Almost all members of that circuit were invited to the launch, and most of them turned up. How many knew what the encyclopaedia *was* and why it was being launched with such fanfare I can only surmise, but little of the pre-launch conversation had to do with anything so esoteric. Bruce Pratt, as befitted the edition's editor-in-chief, was on the dais with Sir Harold and the other board members, so it was left largely to those contributors who chose to attend and myself to entertain as best we could the naval and military dignitaries, diplomats and senior public servants at the tables to which we had been assigned. At my table I learnt from a vice-admiral that all university students were communists and that cocktail-circuit worthies were not. When I attempted to lead conversation toward the contents of the encyclopaedia, embarrassing silences were the not very warming outcome.

But we were entertained by some unrehearsed comedy from the dais. There, the guest of honour was the prime minister, Malcolm Fraser. After orating at some length Sir Harold beamed, and announced, 'I shall now ask Mr Pratt to present the prime minister with his copy of this great work of Australian scholarship.' Bruce, smiling bravely, obliged. Unfortunately, though, Sir Harold had not yet exhausted his verbal repertoire. He enlightened his less than riveted audience about his mission to establish a national library, about the history of the encyclopaedia, and about anything else that his long-term memory chose to dredge up. Then, once again he proclaimed, 'I shall now ask … ,' and Malcolm Fraser hastily pushed the pile of books back to Bruce Pratt, who at the words, 'to present the prime minister with …' shoved them back at Malcolm again. After that, we all were permitted to finish our meals in peace.

The launch concluded, my drive from Canberra back to the farmhouse in the Snowy Mountains was, naturally enough, uphill. More surprisingly, once I resumed work on the encyclopaedia, not at Rose Bay but at Grolier's head office in Artarmon, life was uphill too, for much of the way. Grolier did sell books, including as well as *The Australian Encyclopaedia*, their principal reference work, *Encyclopedia Americana*, and another reference work of some quality, but it sold them solely by mail order. It also sold by mail order whatever else its jealously guarded list of potential buyers might be cajoled into desiring – trinkets, knick-knacks, make-up, ornaments in atrocious taste and, for all I know, the Sydney Harbour Bridge. Its list was comprised largely of low-income earners, and Grolier's efforts to push encyclopaedias were directed at persuading such buyers that it was vital for their children's survival that they be surrounded by a Stonehenge of expensive tomes, purchased of course on time-payment. My new editorial base was tucked away in a small corner of the outer office, the climate of which did nothing to foster fruitful and wide-ranging debate. The epithet with which I was burdened by the sales staff was 'The Boffin', and it was not intended as an honourable title.

Necessity may well be, as is claimed, the mother of invention, but if so, debate must be its wet-nurse. At least until 1980, when I was vouch-safed a budget with which to engage editorial staff (and I refrained from adopting the title editor-in-chief until I was provided with some Indians), I lacked sufficient stimulus fully to develop new topics, new approaches, or necessary major revisions for a fourth edition of the encyclopaedia. With any such extensive reference work, budget restraints usually limit the number of major revisions that can be undertaken within any one edition, and Bruce Pratt's third edition was no exception to this rule. Among other things, it lacked an index, though Bruce had argued strongly with the parent company that it needed one.

Over those three years of my solitary confinement within this retreat from anti-Boffin bigotry I did gain new, if not very useful, knowledge. I learnt for the first time the meaning of that now ubiquitous phrase, 'the bottom line'; I learnt that not all hedges sprout leaves, but that when the word 'hedge' is used as a noun in financial jargon it is kindred to 'hedging one's bets', and bears no relationship to cultivated borders; and I learnt that bureaucratic absurdity is definitely *not* confined to government offices. This last lesson was delivered to me in the form of a letter from somebody in the Danbury head office's protocol department (though Grolier probably didn't call it that) and informed me at some length about the link between status and the appropriate letterhead for corre-spondence to be used within the company's hierarchy of executives. Only very, very senior management was entitled to an embossed letterhead. I did not qualify, but then, neither did I aspire to embossification.

Those years of isolation were not entirely wasted. My reading of recent works on Aboriginal studies led me to realise that much of the long article on that subject in the third edition was out of date. With the advice of Donald Horne (an editorial board member for the third, fourth and fifth editions), I arranged for Professor John Mulvaney to reorganise it completely and select new contributors to rewrite most of its sections. The section entitled 'Aborigines since 1788' was written by Professor Charles Rowley. When I came to prepare the fifth edition, Rowley had by then died. Mulvaney and his colleagues recommended Professor Henry Reynolds to replace him, though one of them qualified his recommendation with the comment, 'Reynolds is now the best, but he doesn't have the fire in his belly that Charles had.' I rather doubt whether he would repeat that comment today.

During the preparation of the third edition we had all been sufficiently busy metricating rail distances in the numerous articles about Australian towns and other urban centres to fail to ask ourselves whether railway distances remained relevant to a presumably car-owning readership. My period of hibernation from active publishing led me to the conclusion that they did not. After discussing the matter with my first two assistant editors, Edna Wilson and Pamela Clements, I decided that public transport was already so undermined that our giving these distances by road would do little to hasten its demise. So we commenced that rather tedious task, using the NRMA's accommodation directories as our principal, though not always totally reliable, guide. At that time it did not occur to me that the construction of motorways, then beginning to increase Australia-wide, would render most of these distances obsolete for each subsequent edition.

Then there were the biographies. The majority of these had been taken almost as they stood from the second edition to the third. Since in the second edition biographies were included only of those already dead, I suspect that its editor, Alec Chisholm, had simply assembled the relevant obituaries and had his assistant editors abridge them. Almost all of them were laudatory, and some of them inaccurate. Of these latter, many we were able to repair by consulting *The Australian Dictionary of Biography*, but because of budget restrictions I postponed replacing many of the more eulogistic biographies with more critical entries for the fourth edition, and again for the fifth — so that laudatory they have, to the best of my knowledge, remained.

Other major revisions of existent articles undertaken in the fourth edition include those discussing medicine and health, by Charles Kerr; social welfare, by Adam Graycar; defence, by Robert O'Neill; music, by Roger Covell; constitutional law, by Geoffrey Sawer; mammals, by John Calaby; and immigration, by Charles Price. We added more than one hundred new articles, discussing subjects that had not been seen as relevant at the time of the second or third editions but that by then were. These included BUILDING SOCIETIES, CONSUMER CREDIT, FUTURES EXCHANGES, HOMOSEXUALITY, POSTAL AND COURIER SERVICES, ROAD TRANSPORT, SUPERANNUATION, and TELECOMMUNICATIONS.

Grolier's Artarmon office initiated me, sadly, into the mindless miasma of office politics. The managing director, David Ashley-Wilson, despite being a salesman was a pleasant and intelligent man, and this probably contributed to his downfall. Constantly he was peering over his metaphorical shoulder, puzzling how to placate his US superiors. On the telephone to them, several times I heard him, his eyes slightly glazed, claiming that Australia was 'cloud-cuckoo-land' to justify why this country's salary structure and working conditions precluded his meeting the company profit goals demanded by his colleagues in Connecticut. On more than one occasion he persuaded me to drive from Katoomba to Artarmon on a Saturday or Sunday morning solely so that we could demonstrate, in front of a visiting American fireman bent on pepping us up, that we in Sydney were just as workaholic as any other set of United States sycophants.

The lack of an index in the encyclopaedia's third edition still rankled with me, and I was resolved to do my damnedest to avoid such a lack in the fourth. To this end, I set out the arguments in favour of an index in three single-spaced quarto pages (or were they by then A4?) and had David dispatch them to Danbury. Back came the laconic reply, 'Of course! All good reference books have indexes.' After my lengthy argument for the inclusion of an index this was something of an anticlimax, but that battle seemed, for a time, to be won.

By 1981 Pam Clements had resigned to take up a more permanent position, and with her went Edna Wilson, since the two of them had shared the one job. Jo Beaumont replaced Pam as my associate editor. Jo was a loudly self-proclaimed lesbian. She liked wearing very butch gear, including ultra-heavy boots, with which she stomped up the stairs to give everyone ample warning that she was approaching the office. Together we made an attempt to salvage Grolier Australia's fading fortunes by producing a partwork version of *The Australian Encyclopaedia*. (A partwork, as I learnt only then, is a book or other written material simplified into 'user-friendly' language, lavishly illustrated, and divided into magazine-size sections to be sold on a weekly, or monthly, basis through newsagents.) Jo was a wizard on design and layout, and she put together several attractive mock-ups of such magazines to use as a drawcard. We approached the middle management of Consolidated Press with a view to co-publishing such a partwork with that organisation. The meeting went well, and as a next step David Ashley-Wilson and I attended a meeting with Consolidated's senior management, with whom a preliminary agreement was tentatively, but only orally, arrived at. For the next week or more David blew hot on the idea, and then he blew cold. Finally he said, 'Dick, there are big sharks out there and we are only little fish.' And the project was abandoned.

Some months later when I arrived at work and was climbing the stairs to my office, I met the company's financial director (aka accountant) moodily descending them. With obvious gloom, he informed me that David had been summarily dismissed that morning and that a bloke called Tony Fox was the new managing director. This was not welcome news. On the same morning Fox assembled the staff and boasted to them that in his previous management position he had sacked more than half of that company's employees and turned around its finances, and he promised to do the same for Grolier.

Early in his turbulent reign Tony Fox sat in at an editorial board meeting. During the board's discussions Bruce Pratt, as was his wont except in a one-to-one situation, said little or nothing. Afterwards Tony, in his endearing way, demanded of me, 'What's with this Pratt bloke? Is he a moron or something?'

Tony, I think, needed meetings at which he could spruik to convince himself that he did indeed exist. Certainly he was addicted to meetings, and called so many that it was almost impossible to meet editorial schedules. At one such meeting he boasted to the editorial staff about his ingenuity as a sales magician: he had, he told us, successfully marketed a brand of tampon which was no different from any other brand, simply by his skill in 'positioning'. Tampons were at that time in the news because of claims that some of them had caused toxic shock, so on the spot one of the editors dubbed him 'Toxic Tony'.

Sackings were delivered by Tony as promised. One of the first to go was the financial director. Tony in his kindness supplied that director with a second-in-command to assist him in his duties, and within a week or so she had supplanted him. Similar tactics were used in the sales department and with the clerical staff, but in the pruning of the editorial department Tony's approach was of necessity more subtle. He knew little or nothing about anything as arcane as editing, and most certainly did not personally know, as he had in the case of his tame accountant, any editor to appoint as *my* second-in-command, so he decided instead to suborn the one that I already had.

Jo Beaumont turned out to be too hard a nut for Tony to readily crack, though obviously I could not know what conversations took place nor what inducements he offered. Then came the Ginger Meggs episode. When Tony first floated the idea of a *Ginger Meggs Australian Encyclopaedia* I took it to be a devious but clever method of forcing my resignation, but he really meant it! Later he complained that the Bancks family wanted Grolier to pay far too much for the use of their cartoon character's name, and this had compelled him to abandon his brilliant concept. It was at this point that I made my first attempt to become an encyclopaedia salesman: I suggested to a reputable publisher, Kevin Weldon, that he make a bid to buy *The Australian Encyclopaedia* as a going concern almost ready for publication. He did so, but Tony rejected the offer — despite the fact that it had already been amply demonstrated that those on Grolier's list did not buy enough books to make the publication financially viable.

At this point, too, the edition's index again came under threat. In the normal course of events indexing does not begin until all the volumes to be indexed have reached page form, pages and columns being the places to which the index refers the reader. Tony asserted that the company, having expended the necessary capital to have the edition written and typeset, could not afford to wait for an index to be prepared before beginning to harvest returns on its investment. One of the editorial staff suggested that perhaps articles could be numbered to expedite indexing. This jogged my memory sufficiently to recollect that Valentines, the typesetting and sorting company for the third edition, could not, without numerical aid, program its computer to sort the encyclopaedia's articles alphabetically. To get around this difficulty, each article had been given an alphabetical and numerical code — for instance, the article PUBLISHING had been allotted the code PUB040, and these codes enabled the computer to sort the articles, but in the third edition it did not go on to print them. Why not, I thought, actually print the code at the head of each article and then index to the code? And Jeremy Fisher, the indexer I selected, very competently did just that.[33] Subsequently a former editor of Melbourne University Press was to complain that he found that index incomprehensible (though I would have expected an editor to read the preface, where the indexing method was explained), but librarians, the people who most frequently consulted that index, told me that they found it faster and easier to use than an index based on pages and columns. Either way, it won me an index for the fourth edition.

Jo Beaumont knew that I had approached Weldon, though she did not let Tony know, but eventually his pressure on her to undermine me became too much for her. She did not succumb to it, but did absent herself from the office for days, and then weeks, claiming to be in her sickbed. Then she resigned.

Her successor as associate editor was Keren Lavelle, an editor for whom I had, and still have, a high regard. Unfortunately though, she did succumb to Tony's blandishments. Already a more junior assistant editor was compiling for him a report on my alleged editorial inadequacies (it later came into my possession), but Keren chose confrontation rather than espionage as her weapon. When I asked her to conduct preliminary interviews with prospective editorial staff members, leaving to me the final choice, she objected to taking this subordinate role. When I repeated my request she stormed out of my office and, I assume, into Tony's. Minutes later *he* strode into my office. I could not, he told me, talk to educated women like that. Then he demanded of me, 'Don't you like women?'

Then I did resign.

Obviously this suited Tony's budget strategy, as it meant that that he was not compelled to pay me the same serious sums as he had to all the other sacked executives, but it saved my self-respect. As I was leaving the Grolier offices for what I thought was the last time, Keren kissed me, and said, 'I know that the encyclopaedia is your baby, and I'm sorry.' Later she was to explain to me that she would not have acted in the way she did had she not been 'so silly as to believe Tony Fox's promises'. But what those promises were I shall probably never know.

I half-expected to be compelled to take legal action to be acknowledged as editor-in-chief of that edition of the encyclopaedia, but, possibly at the insistence of Donald Horne, it was not necessary. Having acknowledged me as editor, Tony had perforce to invite me to the launching. This event took place at the National Press Club, with the guest of honour, Prime Minister Hawke, looking at me in a puzzled way as I have previously related. There, I and the other editorial board members sweated under the heat projected by lights directed at our table while Sir Harold White, in his usual lengthy and polysyllabic way, managed to convey the impression that it was he, almost alone, who was responsible for the existence of this new edition of *The Australian Encyclopaedia*. This time though, he presented its many volumes to the prime minister only once.

22 Hard Labor in Sydney's Inner West

By the time many of the events described in the previous chapter had come to pass Barbara and I had been living in Sydney for some months. Soon we joined the local branch of the Labor Party, Marrickville East Branch, of which Peter Baldwin was the secretary. Peter's face, when he visited us at our house in Stanmore (which we had bought with our friend Ben Lau), still looked a little like the much-publicised photographs taken of him immediately after his infamous bashing. One of those alleged to have been among his attackers was reported as having claimed, 'We didn't want to beat him up. We just wanted to kill the bastard.' For Peter, Sydney's inner west was indeed 'hard Labor'.

While we were renting the house in Lindfield mentioned earlier, we had joined the local ALP branch there, but that branch was most definitely 'soft Labor'. Like most branches in electorates unwinnable by Labor, it was a left-wing branch, but very politely so, and held very, very boring meetings. Only one branch meeting stands out in my memory as decidedly not boring, the meeting to which I had invited a Push member, Paddy Dawson, as guest speaker. Paddy had formed, or claimed to have formed, the Unemployed People's Union (UPU), though I am sure that he first thought up the slogan 'Up You' and only later worked out the words to fit the acronym. If there were other members of that 'union', I was not aware of them. Paddy opened his address to the branch meeting with the word 'Comrades'. While in any ALP branch in Victoria such an introduction would have raised no eyebrows, in Sydney's North Shore it certainly did. Then Paddy noisily consumed the cans of beer that he had thoughtfully brought with him, and smoked heavily as he informed the meeting of the trials and tribulations of being unemployed. Instead of making the usual appeal for more jobs, he emphasised, rather, the need for more money, and after that, more money still, and 'bugger the jobs'. Looking absolutely appalled at such heresy, the branch president was far too polite not to ask the secretary to move a vote of thanks when Paddy had done his worst. The branch members, though muttering, were too polite not to support the motion.

North Shore ALP branches could afford to be polite. In those suburbs there was no competition among those hoping to stand for preselection for either State or Federal parliamentary seats, but rather the reverse. Few were willing to expend the time, trouble and multi-zero-suffixed number of dollars in an attempt to win the unwinnable. This was not the case in the inner west. There, almost all the seats were winnable by Labor, but none of them winnable in party preselections by candidates from Labor's left. Peter Baldwin changed all that.

At a State Conference of the New South Wales Branch to which I was a delegate, Paul Keating, well before he became prime minister, denounced Baldwin as a 'branch-stacker *extraordinaire*', and predicted that Peter would never win the seat of Sydney. Certainly Peter did have Sydney in his sights, and certainly he did 'stack' branches, if by 'stack' we mean energetically and selectively recruit new members. His first task, though, was not to 'stack' but to 'de-stack' those inner-west branches. All controlled by Labor's right wing, many of them elected their branch officials and also preselected parliamentary candidates only by dint of the votes of those party members who either had never existed at all or had long since ceased to do so. It was Peter's campaign to demolish such rorts which had led to his bashing. After deleting from registers the names of non-existent branch members, he proceeded to persuade new residents of those suburbs, consisting largely of tertiary-educated 'gentrifiers', to join their local Labor Party branches. Their names were then added to the list of those eligible to vote in ALP branch elections and also in parliamentary preselections. In those days before ALP membership was computerised, this list was compiled solely from the branch registers and attendance books.

Marrickville East Branch, when Barbara and I joined it, already had a majority of left-wing members, but several of its former right-wing executive still remained in office. That was no longer so after the next branch elections, at which Peter Baldwin remained branch secretary and I became president. Preselections for Federal parliamentary candidates were by then in the offing, so the ALP's Sydney Federal Electorate Council (FEC) was a multi-conspiracy of manoeuvring factions. As well as Baldwin, there were two other left delegates aspiring to challenge the sitting right-wing member for Sydney, Les McMahon. The left decided to stage its own factional pre-preselection in order to field only one candidate against McMahon in the *official* preselection. At a meeting at Leichhardt Town Hall I moved that no pre-preselection be held, as all three would probably stand anyway, but my motion was defeated. Baldwin won the left-wing pre-preselection vote by a large majority, but as I predicted, all three candidates stood against McMahon.

As a scrutineer for Sydney FEC, I attended the final vote count at the official preselection. Rather to my surprise, the left preferences remained firm and Baldwin became the ALP candidate for the seat of Sydney. I was surprised only because of being aware of the venomous warfare between the two main left sub-factions. In the New South Wales Branch one sub-faction was led by a cabinet minister in Neville Wran's State government, Rodney Cavalier, and the other by another minister in the same cabinet, Frank Walker. Quite frequently one left sub-faction would align itself with the right for no better reason than to prevent the other sub-faction gaining more influence, but this had not occurred at that preselection. Today neither Cavalier nor Walker is in any parliament at all, but the sub-factions remain. The former is now known as the 'soft left' and the latter as the 'hard left'. Just occasionally they vote together to defeat the right, and sometimes, too, they even make common cause with the right against the Liberal Party.

Before the left's internecine warfare had intensified to its later level, Marrickville East Branch's meeting place had been in a municipal library building which was isolated from populated areas and surrounded by the shrubs of Enmore Park. There, after one branch meeting, other members of the branch executive and I were credentialling, or declining to do so because of their failure to meet ALP requirements, a number of right-wing Greek applicants for branch membership. (It was the right's turn to 'stack'.) Some of those Greeks who were expected by the right wing to attend that meeting had not done so. After the Credentials Committee meeting had concluded, a young and attractive Greek woman who had been interpreting for the applicants approached me. 'Would you give me, please,' she asked, 'the names and addresses of those applicants who failed to turn up?'

I replied that she was not a member of our branch of the party, and thus not entitled to any such information. She then left the building. Moments later the reputed 'enforcer', Tom Domican, burst into the room. Brandishing clenched fists, and with his whole body shaking with real or simulated rage, he demanded: 'Who insulted my wife?'

I was coward enough to fail to confess that it was I who had insulted his wife, if his wife she was, and if an insult it was. (I was also too cowardly to ask him for the name of the scriptwriter who had penned the immortal line that Tom had spluttered.) As it happened, nobody was bashed, though I can't remember why. Nevertheless, before our next meeting, we of the branch executive thought it prudent to move our meeting place to somewhere less isolated. We selected an Anglican church hall, where the services were High Church and the congregation reputedly high camp. We selected the hall not for those reasons, but because its surroundings were well-lit and heavily populated.

Not long after Peter Baldwin was elected to Federal Parliament, the right-wing sitting member for the State seat of Marrickville died unexpectedly. This gave rise to furious factional activity over which I eventually had to preside, since I had become the returning officer of Marrickville State Electorate Council (SEC).

In retrospect it seems as though a death caused us to be subjected to non-stop meetings of the left caucus, but actually they took place only on almost every Sunday. That was more than enough. At one such meeting the majority, of whom I was one, staged a mass walkout in protest against the way the other sub-faction was manipulating those meetings. It was only then that I came to realise that, by taking part in the walkout, I had become a member of the Cavalier or 'soft left' sub-faction. Rival left candidates for official preselection to the Marrickville seat did not, as it happened, eventuate, but only because the premier, Neville Wran, wittingly or unwittingly, prevented it. He stated unequivocally that he would not accept the 'hard left' candidate because of his criminal record. Thus Andrew Refshauge became the only left candidate for preselection.

The right-wing faction was not so fortunate. Five or six of them stood for preselection, including the not very popular mayor of Marrickville. They all agreed to swap preferences, placing Andrew Refshauge last on their 'how-to-votes'. One of them assured me that, because of this, Andrew had no chance of winning. That candidate, in making such a claim, was relying on the number of right-wing voters as shown in the branch registers and attendance books. But when, as returning officer, I examined the books of all branches in the Marrickville electorate, Andrew's scrutineer, Peter Baldwin, showed irrefutably that many of those listed as eligible to vote were listed fraudulently. In Erskineville Branch alone almost half of the members that they claimed to be eligible were eliminated from the ballot. This purging of fictitious voters gave Andrew a chance, albeit a slim one, of becoming the endorsed ALP candidate in the by-election for the now vacant seat.

For the preselection count itself, I rented a small hall in Tempe. Each branch's members were to cast their votes at the polling places designated by their branch returning officers. There, under ALP rules, voters were compelled to sign the official form listing all those eligible to vote. Only then could they be issued with their ballot papers. After the last eligible member had cast a vote, or when the time allowed by the branch for voting had elapsed, the branch returning officer was to place that form in the ballot box, padlock the box, and seal its aperture. He or she then, by the hour I had nominated, was to bring the ballot box to the Tempe hall. By late afternoon that hall was crowded, so to preserve the integrity of the count I refused to allow anybody other than authorised scrutineers in the immediate vicinity of the ballot boxes as I opened them.

The counting of the contents of the first two or three boxes went smoothly. My assistants and I removed the ballot papers from their boxes, counted them, and folded them into bundles of ten. The progressive count for each candidate I noted on a whiteboard. The next box, though, lacked the essential form signed by each voter. I put it aside, uncounted. At the end of the count of all the properly documented ballot papers there were two additional boxes lacking that essential form. All three of them had come from right-wing-controlled branches. Later, I was to learn that the returning officers of those branches had intentionally omitted to include the form because they were of the opinion that the votes would favour the Marrickville mayor, and they themselves did not favour him one little bit. No doubt they anticipated that I would send the disputed boxes, as well as those undisputed, to the returning officer for New South Wales at the ALP's head office. He, they assumed, would allow or disallow sufficient votes to ensure that the preferred right-wing candidate won.

From past experience I thought that any count conducted at head office would be likely to be adjusted to allow a right-wing candidate to win. Only a massive majority of votes for a left-wing candidate would make such a rort too embarrassing to consider. So I decided not to unfold the ballot papers from the deficient boxes, nor to allocate them among the candidates, but to count them and so determine their total number.

This caused a flurry of objections from Refshauge's scrutineer, Chris Barrett, who threatened (ironically) to complain to head office. But once

I knew how many disputed ballot papers there were, I was able to declare
the result of the preselection. Because the number of undisputed primary
votes cast for Refshauge outnumbered by six *all* the disputed ballot
papers, I was able to declare him the winner and, subject to head office's
assent, the endorsed ALP candidate for the seat of Marrickville. He was,
of course, duly endorsed. No other option remained open for the commissars of Sussex Street.

By the time all this had come about, a dispute within the Sydney Push —
a very silly dispute when viewed in retrospect — had led Barbara, our
daughter Beth and myself to move from the Stanmore house to rented
rooms behind and above a shop in Addison Road, Marrickville. When
the shop became vacant we rented that too, and used it as an office for my
work as a reference-book editor.

Later I also used the shop as a campaign office for the ALP in the
Marrickville electorate. This was for the first general election, as opposed
to by-election, in which Andrew Refshauge was the Labor candidate. No
longer Marrickville SEC's returning officer, I had been elected to become,
instead, its president. I also arranged to be elected as Andrew's campaign
director, though well aware that winning Marrickville for Labor did not
demand any extraordinary skill in campaign strategies.

While living in Addison Road, Barbara and I remained in the Marrickville East Branch of the ALP. When we bought, with the aid of a heavy
mortgage, a house in Petersham, this was no longer possible. ALP rules
compelled us to move to Petersham Branch, then still under right-wing
control. This also placed us in the Balmain electorate, represented at State
level by Peter Crawford, whom I remembered, without fondness, from a
left caucus meeting in the Blue Mountains.

The right wing did not long retain control of Petersham Branch, and
the ALP did not long retain control of New South Wales. Neville Wran's
unexpected resignation as leader, announced at a session of the 1986 ALP
State Conference, did not of itself cause the government to fall. But the

way the Sussex Street commissars went about selecting his successor certainly did.

Before becoming leader Wran had been a member of the Legislative Council, the State's upper house. Candidates for election to that chamber were selected by means of deals between competing ALP factions, but with the right always gaining a majority of the available seats. While premier, Wran had asserted strongly that Legislative Councillors would be allowed to vote in the ALP's parliamentary caucus 'only over my dead body'. Obviously he knew that chamber and its members well. But once he had resigned as leader Wran *was* dead politically. His right-wing faction colleagues selected another member of that chamber, Barry Unsworth, as Wran's successor.

Nobody in the parliamentary left had the guts to stand against Unsworth in the caucus vote, and among the right only Peter Anderson did. He lost. Anderson's bucking of the Sussex Street machine probably led to his political doom, though this did not come about until some years later, after Bob Carr had become State premier.

For me, the appointment of Unsworth as leader, together with my dissatisfaction with Crawford's performance as member for Balmain, was more than I could stomach. At the next State election (1988) I worked openly for Jack Mundey as a left independent candidate for the Legislative Council, and for Larry Hand as a left independent candidate for the seat of Balmain in the Legislative Assembly. My actions had little to do with the outcome, but in that election the Unsworth government was swept from office, and Labor, for the first time ever, lost the seat of Balmain. Hand's preferences helped Dawn Fraser win that seat.

Later, I asked Andrew Refshauge, by then deputy leader, whether I had been expelled from the ALP as the rules dictated that I should be. 'No,' was his reply, 'but you will be if you draw attention to yourself.'

After its massive defeat New South Wales Labor was not overly keen to expel anybody if they could avoid it. And not only was I careful not to draw attention to myself; I also withdrew altogether from Sydney's inner west and from any other part of Sydney. Once I had completed my work on the fifth edition of *The Australian Encyclopaedia* (which is discussed in the following chapter), Barbara and I realised that without the income provided by the encyclopaedia we would lack sufficient funds to live comfortably while meeting the mortgage payments on our Petersham house. After some agonising, we sold it, bought an old house in Cessnock and, towards the end of 1988, moved there.

23   The Encyclopaedist Outcast

When I resigned from the Grolier Society and hence as editor of *The Australian Encyclopaedia*, Barbara and I, with her son Wesley and our daughter Beth, were no longer living in the Stanmore house. Our move to the rear and first storey of the Marrickville shop, and then my relief at sloughing off the mire of office politics, for a while dominated my days. Almost immediately after leaving Grolier's employment I had circularised several Australian publishers seeking work. In my letter to them I had claimed that, after working from 1972 to 1983 on *The Australian Encyclopaedia*, I had had 'more than enough of a good thing'; working on another type, almost any other type, of publishing project was my hope. It was not to be: I was forever typecast as an encyclopaedist. The editorial work which I was offered, and undertook, included preparing for publication by William Collins the manuscripts of an Australian encyclopaedia and an Australian chronology, and updating the Australian content of the twelve-volume 'Micropaedia' section of *Encyclopaedia Britannica*. At first, though, I found it difficult to make myself begin working at all.

Once we were able to occupy the shop itself and, with the help of my nephew, Charles Arnot, had converted it into an office, I was able to resume believing in myself as a professional editor. Of the three projects I had undertaken, the work for *Britannica* was the most time-consuming. Almost every article on Australia needed updating; in many of the articles on flora and fauna the taxonomy described was no longer applicable; but I corrected only two really egregious errors. The article on dingoes claimed that those canines had reached Australia with the Aborigines, whereas they had reached mainland Australia only about four thousand years ago, and never reached Tasmania, which had separated from the mainland some ten thousand years earlier. (Aborigines, of course, had occupied Australia, including many of its offshore islands, for at least forty thousand, and probably seventy thousand, years.) The other major error was *Britannica*'s assertion that one of our early prime ministers, Deakin I think, had been a member of what later became the Australian Labor Party.

It was while I was engaged in this task that I was able to manifest my obsessive-compulsive tendencies in a fairly spectacular way. Torrential rain had been pouring down for days; the shop was low-lying, and many of the buildings nearby had in years gone by illegally channelled their stormwater downpipes into the sewerage system. That system could no longer cope. Because our shop had previously been a hairdressing salon it boasted at its rear a series of wash-basins. As the downpour continued these basins spewed up an undigested brew of sewage, mud and water. While this shit-peppered soup swirled around my ankles I doggedly remained at my desk and kept working at the task in hand until it was done. Though more than fifty, I had not yet been medically diagnosed as suffering from obsessive-compulsive disorder — still, for a reference-book editor, this form of insanity has its benefits.

Flooding was not the only hazard that beset us in our Marrickville dwelling. At its back and at ground level were a tiny kitchen, a meagre living and dining area, and the only available bathroom and toilet. The stairs to the first-storey bedrooms were narrow and precipitously steep. On more than one occasion, after an evening's drinking, I had tumbled down them on my way to enjoy a nocturnal piss. Breaking my neck, or even a limb, was not something to which I aspired. A new cycle of Push deaths had by then begun, and I had no wish to conform to that all too mortifying fashion. Our move to the single-storey house in Petersham was thus a welcome one.

I do, though, have some warm memories of that Marrickville shop. One is of Harry Reade coming early one morning to the door of the shop while I was still in the upstairs front bedroom. Harry's repeated singing, and flatly at that, of 'Open the door, Richard' was enough to hurry me downstairs, if only to shut him up. Another is of the old Greek fisherman who lived next door. Almost every morning his boat and its trailer blocked the exit from our garage to the lane outside, while he sat there mending his net. Before asking him to move the boat so that I could drive out, I usually asked him how his fishing had gone on the previous night. On a Saturday morning he inevitably replied, 'No bloody good. Too dronk!'

After moving to Petersham in 1984 I had again sent circulars to publishers. One reply was from Mike White, a partner in the New Zealand publishing company David Bateman Ltd, and another from the new managing director of Grolier, an amiable Afrikaaner. This conjunction, as the astrologers say, led to good fortune. At my interview at the Grolier office I outlined to the Afrikaaner the many ways, by publishing spin-off books from its various categories — towns, fauna, flora, etc — that more money could be made out of *The Australian Encyclopaedia*. At the end of my spiel he responded by telling me that, if I could find somebody to buy the encyclopaedia outright, he would pay me a commission of $10,000. When I met Mike White, he informed me that his company was interested in bringing out an Australian encyclopaedia in partwork form. He offered me the contract to take on this task, but only if I could lead him to an encyclopaedia to form the basis of that partwork. So I became that almost universally despised creature, an encyclopaedia salesman.

Mike, or rather David Bateman Ltd, did buy *The Australian Encyclopaedia*, and I engaged Averil Moffatt as an assistant to prepare partwork samples to be used in market research. In the meantime, the editorial board was reconvened, though without Alan Day who had resigned because of the pressure of his academic work. Its first meeting was organised by Mike White at an apartment he had rented in York Street, Sydney. After the meeting he took us all to lunch in a city restaurant, and it became obvious that both Sir Harold White and Bruce Pratt had become very frail in their old age. Shortly after that luncheon Bruce resigned from the board on the grounds that he was no longer able to meet his obligations as a member. Once I told Mike of Bruce's resignation he suggested that we designate Harold White with some seemingly superior title that precluded us needing to have him present at board meetings. This I attempted to do, but although old and garrulous, Sir Harold was too wily a bird not to see through such stratagems, and he too resigned. Donald Horne succeeded him as chairman of the editorial board.

Donald had already congratulated me on regaining the editorship, and after those two resignations he and I met over lunch to discuss their replacements on the board. One of us — I can no longer remember whether it was Donald or I — suggested Robyn Williams, of the ABC science program, to remedy our serious lack of a colleague who not only knew about science but could write about it in comprehensible English. Robyn accepted the appointment, and with him we scored the bonus of David Throsby, a professor of economics, who also joined the board.

At some point during that lunch I suggested asking a well-known legal figure, whom I shall call X, also to join the board. Donald vetoed this. X, he claimed, would so dominate discussions that nobody else would be able to get a word in. Donald himself is prone to dominate any discussion in which he takes part — so this was a little like Ezra Pound chiding, as he did, James Joyce for obscurity when he, Pound, first read the manuscript of *Finnegans Wake* (and this from the author of *The Cantos*, for God's sake!) — but I concurred. (This comment must be qualified by my acknowledgement that Donald's domination of discussions, unlike Sir Harold's, was always germane to the subject under review.) Later, Susan Dorsch, an eminent medical rather than a legal figure, was invited to join the board and did so.

The new cycle of Push deaths mentioned earlier was begun in the late 1970s by Ian Parker. The proportion of Push deaths when compared with the total number of Push people seemed to me then, and still seems now, considerably higher than deaths among the same age group in the population at large. This might be expected given our chosen life-style. It remained so even after most of us were well past the age when we had given any serious thought to killing ourselves. Our general attitude to suicide by then resembled that of a quietist Marxist towards the socialist revolution: if the bloody thing was, as Marx insisted, inevitable, why bust our guts (or cut our throats) trying to hasten what would happen in due course anyway?

While we still were living in Katoomba, Parker had continued to be a fairly regular visitor. After one such visit, when he and I had spent the evening drinking and talking — and Parker's devolution from brilliant young economist to hopeless alcoholic was by then almost complete, so talking did not figure hugely — I drove him back to Sydney the following morning. When we arrived at my workplace at Artarmon I asked Ian whether he felt capable of making his own way to the city proper. It was a silly question; one look at him persuaded me that he was barely capable of making his own way across the road. At his request, I then drove him to Balmain. After we had imbibed what Parker always described as a 'heart-starter' at a pub there, I declined to join him in an all-day drinking session. Instead, I drove him to an address that he had given me where there lived, he told me, a friend. Unfortunately, that 'friend' had never heard of him. Parker's second choice of address for another friend was more successful, so I deposited him there and drove back to work. Parker somehow managed to make his way to the by-then Push hotel, the Criterion, in Sussex Street. After drinking there, presumably until closing time, he left and wandered out. He was hit by a motor vehicle, probably a truck, and killed. His body was later found in Dixon Street. Of this I learnt only some days later.

During Barbara's and my time in Petersham, that cycle of Push deaths continued. Another death with which we were closely concerned was that of Chicken (Ken Cobb). From a boyhood as an easily exploited farm-hand shipped out to Australia by the Big Brother Movement, Chicken had educated himself sufficiently to gain an honours degree in social anthropology (I had helped him put the finishing touches to his final thesis). This had enabled him to win employment with the Commonwealth Taxation Department, though why qualifications in social anthropology should be relevant to taxation neither he nor I even attempted to fathom. During our stay in Petersham, Chicken gradually grew ill. He suffered from headaches, for which he took unwisely large doses of paracetamol. Soon, sitting at a desk, as his work compelled him to do, caused his legs to swell. Advised by his general practitioner, he gave up drinking alcohol. After that, when he visited us I usually made available a bottle of non-alcoholic wine, though unfortunately the only red wine of this kind that I was able to drum up was both sweet and bubbly. Then he was admitted to Balmain Hospital. While visiting him there we inquired with the sister-in-charge about his chances of recovery. With uncharacteristic candour for a hospital spokesperson she informed us that his liver was buggered. Chicken knew. He said to us, 'I think I've got a touch of the terminals.' Some days later, early (and I mean *early*) one morning I received a phone call from the police constable manning the city morgue. Chicken, he told me, had died at the Royal Prince Alfred Hospital, and as he had named me as next-of-kin, would I please come to the morgue to identify his body for the post-mortem?

But he had been in Balmain Hospital, I replied, and his death was presumably under medical supervision, so why was a post-mortem necessary? Patiently the policeman explained to me the bureaucratic safeguards that made a post-mortem legally essential: when his condition had deteriorated, Chicken had been sent by ambulance to the Royal Prince Alfred, and had died before the necessary twenty-four hours had elapsed that would have permitted the resident doctor to write a death certificate. So I drove to the morgue. There, on a black-and-white television screen, I was shown a snarling face that at first I did not recognise — I had never seen Ken snarling. But it was he; and if one can't snarl to greet one's own death then when can one snarl? Dry in the mouth, I left the morgue and, as he then lived nearby, visited Alan Olding. Partly it was to tell him of the death of our mutual friend, but largely it was because I needed urgently a drink of water.

Several Push friends, including Alan Olding, put up money for Chicken's cremation, which Barbara and I arranged. It was attended by some of Ken's Taxation Department workmates as well as by several members of the Push. (Later the cremation costs were refunded from Ken's superannuation.) At the crematorium, I spoke briefly, played a Noël Coward recording (Coward being Ken's favourite singer and composer) and then pushed the button to convey Ken's body into the flames. Most of the Push members who attended the cremation, but none of Ken's workmates, then took part in the real memorial ceremony — a wake at our house in Petersham.

As his supposed next-of-kin, I became, after a few weeks, the custodian of Chicken's ashes (at least, I assumed that they were his — I had not then read Graham Greene's *Travels with My Aunt*, though Greene was one of Chicken's favourite novelists). Unwisely perhaps, I had confided to Midnight (Jack Millard) that I proposed to tip those ashes into the waves beating on Middle Head, where once, many years earlier, Chicken in his small boat had nearly drowned himself, me, and others. But I then did nothing about it. Some time later, Midnight, on learning that the ashes were still at Petersham, exclaimed: 'You can't leave the poor bastard in limbo!' (Midnight was brought up a Catholic.) In an extremely hot and uncomfortable flat-bottomed metal boat he chauffeured Barbara and me out to the waves of Middle Head. There, I dutifully committed Chicken's mortal remains to the waters of the harbour that in the past had almost claimed them even more prematurely.

Parker's and Chicken's deaths were about a decade apart, but there were many other Push deaths over that period and after. I attended the funerals of only four, those of Peter Lake (heart attack), Rocky Meyers (heart attack), Declan Affley (aneurysm), and Peter Hellier (cirrhosis of the liver). At Peter Hellier's cremation a woman also attending upbraided me for still being a smoker. Pointing to the wisps of black smoke emanating from the crematorium's chimney, I observed that this, surely, was *not* a non-smoking area. For many years my memory misinformed me that the woman in question had been Peta Hussey, but when I encountered Peta once again many years later, coincidentally at the death-bed of Alan Olding (bowel cancer), she assured me that it was not she who had chided me about smoking. Since she was puffing on a cigarette as I spoke to her, I felt impelled to believe her.

The encyclopaedic partwork, too, was destined for a premature death. My friend Lyn Collingwood had joined Averil and me in the role of our *de facto* illustrations editor, and with the co-operation of the New Zealand design staff of David Bateman Ltd we three had put together some quite passable samples of the partwork we intended to produce. Once we had done so, Mike White escorted Averil and myself to the premises of a market-research organisation.

There we were treated like portents of prosperity, then seated behind the spying side of a one-way mirror. On the spied-upon side sat a group of people described by the market-research spruikers as 'a cross-section of the Australian community', self-consciously thumbing through our partwork samples. The compere (I can think of no other noun that adequately denigrates his role) asked them whether they would buy, at the price we had nominated, such a series of educational magazines. Naturally they replied as was expected of them. Why should they risk appearing as a set of stupid nerds too mean to buy the wherewithal to educate their offspring? Mike then paid the perpetrators of this charade, and we left.

Outside, he asked what I thought of this 'market research', so I told him that I thought it to be all bullshit. 'You may well be right,' said Mike, looking worried. And I was. Copies of the first two or three magazines were printed in reasonable quantities and put on sale through Brisbane newsagents. Very few bought them. After hasty discussions, Mike, looking even more worried, tried again, this time in Adelaide. This time, too, sales were too low to warrant going ahead with the project. David Bateman, I was told later, had mortgaged his Auckland mansion to raise the credit to buy the copyright of *The Australian Encyclopaedia*. If so, he was by then at risk of losing his home.

In retrospect, I think that the partwork concept might have worked if I had summoned the wit to remember my advice to the Grolier management. Had we divided the encyclopaedia into its several categories — Australian towns, Australian geographical features, Australian mammals, Australian plants, Australian birds, Australian noteworthies, etc — and published them not within the straitjacket imposed by their alphabetical order, but so that there were several major articles of interest in each issue, and also in each issue advertised items of interest to come in the next issue, the partwork may have 'taken off'. Even then, I think, it would have needed another of my recommendations to Grolier — collaboration with a large media group, Packer, Fairfax or Murdoch — to achieve significant sales. But these ideas did not recur to me until the year 2003, rather too late to help Mike White and David Bateman.

In the end, though, they did find a solution, albeit a not very satisfactory one for their financial aspirations. They approached the Australian Geographic Society, then still presided over by Dick Smith, and did a deal by which they were to co-publish, effectively as a junior partner with Australian Geographic, a fifth edition of *The Australian Encyclopaedia*. Australian Geographic, with its list of subscribers far more sophisticated and better heeled than Grolier's, would own and market the resultant volumes. They would also own the copyright.

This, if what I had been told was true, presumably saved David's house, and it also gave me the opportunity of singing my swan-song as editor-in-chief of the encyclopaedia. Coinciding with my swan-song was that of the last-ever Push pub, the Criterion, though its swan-song was sung by a motley crew in older, frailer and usually quavering voices, and frequently interrupted by louder, and distinctively non-Push, lesser tunes. The following chapter combines as a duet the swan-songs of both the 'paedist and the pub. It is titled accordingly.

24 A Discordant Duet of Swan-songs

Before my appointment as editor was finally confirmed, I had been flown to New Zealand so that the Bateman family could take my measure. My aeroplane was hours late in its departure from Sydney and as an apology of sorts the airline crew liberally poured alcohol into all of us in the first-class seats all of the way across the Tasman. This flight landed at Auckland not many months after French intelligence agents had blown up the Greenpeace vessel *Rainbow Warrior.* Against the cold of a windy Auckland night, I had donned my Basque beret before debarking from the aircraft; consequently I was taken to be French when I fronted at the arrivals desk. I was drunk enough by then to reply, 'No. I am not French and, even if I were, I would not admit to it in New Zealand.'

At first, I think, I had been Mike White's protégé, and during the partwork interlude both Janet and David Bateman had suspected my ability to edit Averil's rewritings within the schedule they wanted. This was presumably because they did not understand my methods of work. In Auckland I managed to dispel their apprehensions, despite my lack of tact over drinks with them at their mansion-like home. I told them my anecdote about a nonagenarian English factory worker who, when asked to give his recipe for longevity, replied: 'Drink like hell, smoke like billy-o, and hate the Tories good and proper.' With a wry smile, one of the Batemans remarked: 'That would seem to be your motto, too.' If, as I suppose, they *were* Tories, they did not take offence, but rather seemed to like me better for it.

The Batemans were not new to encyclopaedia publishing. With Mike White as production manager they had issued in 1984 the *New Zealand Encyclopedia,* and they introduced me to its editor-in-chief, Gordon

McLauchlan, so that he could initiate me into their publishing methods. All that I can remember now of my conversation with him was his warning that 'Sometimes they [the Batemans and Mike] fly by the seat of their pants'.

In Auckland the Batemans had booked me in to what they assured me was the best motel available, and at their expense. At the end of a working day it was a boring place to be, and the locals refused to believe that I really was Australian — had I modified my accent and, perhaps, managed a technicolour yawn into their drinks, I probably could have persuaded them. But I didn't. The motel's dinner menu listed only four main dishes, and on my second and prolonged visit to Auckland, after the second time around and the eighth dinner I found that the crumbed coating of the Chicken Kiev I had ordered (my second go at this dish) had become so armoured by age that a jemmy was needed to burgle its contents. When I did manage this, the mummified fowl that I found within had not been worth the effort. I then tried a nearby restaurant, even though there I had to pay for my own meal. What meal I was served I cannot remember, but on the wine list, to the name Tyrrell's Long Flat Red, of which I ordered a bottle with my meal, was appended the remark that 'Only the Aussies would call a wine a long flat red'. But the New Zealanders do constantly tell 'Irish' jokes about Australians just as we do (or did?) about the Kiwis.

Back in Petersham, Barbara and I had to modify our home to accommodate the wherewithal for compiling the encyclopaedia once again. There was no way that all the filing cabinets necessary for this task could fit into the house itself, or not if we were to continue to live there, so we purchased a lined and floored metal shed. (Mike White preferred to call it 'a container'.) Our house was oddly situated, its land surrounded on three sides by at least seven separate house-blocks, and on the fourth by the extremely narrow Crystal Lane. From this lane a crane-driver manoeuvred the shed through a tangle of live electric overhead wires across a high wooden fence and into our yard. In it we housed those cabinets.

With the addition of two desks and further bookshelves to our sitting room we thus contrived sufficient office space, provided, that is, we were happy to forgo relaxing there during working hours.

I had reclaimed my encyclopaedic baby. Much later, Dick Smith was to recognise that it *was* my baby, but only after he had fostered it out for its sixth edition to a less punctilious parent. For a time, though, this fifth edition was available for me to revise, research and renovate to the best of my editorial ability. In this, with the help of a revitalised editorial advisory board, I succeeded.

The Criterion Hotel, or rather those Push members who drank there, also had a not inconsiderable input. As I knew, many of them were acknowledged authorities in their several separate disciplines. Peter Groenewegen wrote the article TAXATION AND PUBLIC FINANCE, Liz Fell wrote NEWSPAPERS and TELECOMMUNICATIONS, Dave Clark wrote ECONOMIC HISTORY, ECONOMICS and HENRY GEORGE MOVEMENT, Terry McMullen wrote about William James Chidley, and Jim Baker contributed LIBERTARIANISM, SYDNEY. Paddy McGuinness offered often helpful advice on choosing contributors, though never trying to thrust a right-wing agenda on to my choices, and I found that my own experience working at the 'sharp end' of heavy manual labour contributed to a balanced view when editing articles dealing with rural and industrial matters.

I have described the Criterion as a Push pub, but as its demise grew closer it became less so. Right-wing trade unionists and their ALP colleagues had been in the habit of drinking at the Trades Hall Hotel and their left-wing opponents at the Star, both pubs being located close to the Criterion. When they ceased operating, permanently in the case of the former, these groups converged on the Push pub. More welcome than most of them was Jack Mundey's group from the Builders' Labourers' Federation, notably Jack himself, Joe Owens and Bob Pringle. This was because Push members such as Roelof Smilde, Wendy Bacon, Arthur

King, Liz Fell and others had allied themselves with these green-ban unionists to prevent the destruction of old working-class residential buildings in and around Victoria Street, Kings Cross. With the connivance of the New South Wales Labour Council, this celebrated union had been deregistered, and its place taken by a Norm Gallagher-controlled building union, the reputation of which was less than pristine.

As my friend Jim Rule remarked, all the Mundey BLs had very 'short fuses', and Bob Pringle's fuse could be measured only in millimetres. One afternoon, as I later learnt, several Gallagher supporters came into the Criterion, and characteristically Bob insulted them. One of them broke a beer glass and with it slashed at Bob's throat, fortunately severing only veins. An ambulance was called, as were the police. With the ambulance officer, Bob refused treatment until he had finished his beer. With the police, he insisted that he had not been attacked, but had accidentally cut his own throat while drinking. It was not until later, when Jack Mundey visited him in hospital, that he was persuaded that union solidarity — against agencies of the state — did not extend quite *that* far, and he agreed to give evidence to the police against his attackers.

On another occasion I was involved, though only peripherally, in a fight between Joe Owens and the well-known Trotskyist bookseller, Bob Gould. Like many members of the former Communist Party of Australia, Joe did not approve of Trotskyists, and on this occasion words led to blows. Somebody, I think, restrained Gould, and I embraced Joe in a bear-hug, pinning his arms to his sides. But when he growled 'Let me go, Dick!', his voice thick with menace, I obliged. The fight did not resume, and shortly afterwards Gould left the pub.

Once, too, in the dying days of the Criterion, I stupidly joined forces with Judy Andrews to rescue a damsel who may or may not have been in distress. The damsel was Pam Wilkinson, a woman I had known in the Lincoln days and again in Melbourne. That evening, at her request, I had already bought for her several double nips of whatever spirit she then favoured when suddenly she became fall-over drunk. This attracted the attention of the predatory eyes of several unaccompanied males, and Judy suggested that we rescue her. We hailed a cab. With Pam between us on the rear seat, we directed the driver to where Judy had taken up residence in Sydney. (She by then lived in northern Queensland.) On the way there Pam slurred, 'I'm going to be sick.' The taxi stopped, and I opened its door so that Pam could lean out. She did, but not far enough. Instead, she vomited warmly into my lap. At Judy's place, once we had put Pam to bed, we sat sipping wine until Judy complained that she could not stand the stink of my pants. She took them from me, and kindly covered my lap with a towel to save me, I presume, from the embarrassment of slopping wine on to my underpants. When it was time for me to go home it became necessary for me to telephone Barbara, asking her to bring me a pair of trousers. As Peter Groenewegen observed later, I had 'done a Mal Fraser'.[34]

Many of the Criterion's patrons did not see it as a Push pub. This could not be better illustrated than by a conversation I was involved in, either in my editorial or my political persona, or both, with a young woman. 'I know you!' she exclaimed. 'You're one of those mad old men who drink near the men's toilet at the Criterion Hotel.' From notorious bohemians whom the world came to watch (or at least some of the more prurient of the Sydney world) our status had shrunk to being seen only as mad old men who drank near a public toilet!

Bruce Pratt, as related earlier, had recommended that I tell the editorial board of the encyclopaedia 'as little as possible'. My successor as editor-in-chief did not use meetings of the board (of which I was by then a member) for any purposeful consultation at all; he simply showed off the page formats that he had designed and told us just enough to justify his placing of our names on the introductory pages of the sixth edition and thus giving the impression of responsible editing. This was in marked contrast to the board meetings relating to the fifth edition. All these were occasions for consultation and discussion on matters on which I needed advice, though naturally I also made some unilateral decisions. Without the board's able help it is unlikely that the fifth edition would have received the laudatory reviews that it did. In the newsletter of the Library Association of Australia, *inCite*, David J. Jones wrote, *inter alia*:

In intellectual terms, there are strong links with earlier editions ... The present editor-in-chief, Richard Appleton, held the same position in the fourth edition, and was production editor for the third. Bruce Pratt was editor-in-chief of the third, and had been general editor, under the legendary Alec Chisholm, of the second. We are the beneficiaries of this tradition of and experience in what Appleton accurately calls the 'arcane arts of encyclopaedia editorship'.

Pratt's own motto ... was 'we are paid to be accurate'. In the article on Mount Olga there is a nice case study illustrating Appleton's continuing application of this worthy maxim. The second edition ... stated that Mueller persuaded Giles to name Mount Olga after the Queen of Spain. This was not in fact the case, although Reed's *Placenames of Australia*, *Australians: a historical library* and some editions of [*Encyclopaedia Britannica*] perpetuated the error. There never was a Queen Olga of Spain. Appleton relates how, through contact and correspondence with, among others, Gough Whitlam and the German Ambassador to Australia, Mueller's Olga was identified as the Queen of Wurttemberg by the State Archives in Stuttgart. Reference workers have, or should have, a healthy distrust even of the most 'authoritative' works, but this example of Appleton's and his team's editorial exertions is reassuring and not, I think, isolated.

... There is also the quality of the contributors: Ray Whitrod on the police, Richard Walsh on periodicals, Jill Sykes on dance, Ronald Strahan on mammals, Peter Spearritt on Sydney, popular culture, tramways and ... the Sydney Harbour Bridge, Gavin Souter on New Australia, Maurice Saxby on children's books, — the list goes on and on ...

A new feature, which I did like, was the series of introductory essays, headed 'Australia and the World', in which distinguished and polished writers like Russel Ward, Donald Horne, Elaine Thompson and Mary White provide broad perspectives of the country in which we live. These essays range widely over topics such as the geological formation of the continent, the migration of peoples (Aboriginal, European and others), politics, wars, sport, economics, science and technology, all setting Australia within the context of movements in the world as a whole.[35]

As well as these well-known contributors whom the board and I contrived to find and persuade to write for us, there was also the less-known botanist and photographer who reorganised and rewrote all the plant entries in the edition, Tony Rodd. Not only could Tony write 'like an angel' (if angels can write well — surely those cumbersome wings must inhibit their hand movements), but he also enabled us to make use of his beautifully precise library of plant photographs. When first I contacted Tony he had warned me that he was neurotic and prone to depression, and thus unreliable. This proved to be true: almost every one of his numerous contributions arrived late, and some of them so late that I could meet page-layout schedules only by faxing them to the Bateman offices in Auckland, New Zealand, as soon as I had hastily edited them. Almost all of his contributions exceeded the word count that I had allotted to them. On many occasions, when Tony delivered a manuscript long after its deadline had expired, he would ring the bell on our gate, then throw his manuscript over the fence and run away, reluctant to face what he assumed would be my wrath. His writing was good enough for me to forgive all his foibles. This is illustrated by comparing the article FRUITS, NATIVE in the fourth edition — which read, in part: 'Among native fruits there are a few toxic species which must be avoided, one example being the Queensland finger cherry (*Rhodomyrtus macrocarpa*), which causes blindness if eaten.' — with Tony's emended version in the fifth edition:

Few native fruits are both highly poisonous and palatable; one exception is the north Queensland finger cherry (*Rhodomyrtus macrocarpa*), which when eaten ripe has on several occasions caused sudden and permanent blindness due to destruction of the optic nerve; at other times, though, it has been eaten with no ill effects.

Mike White and David Bateman had met in the British army, where David was serving as an officer during his so-called 'national service', while Mike was a regular officer. With Mike, particularly, his time in the army showed: on more than one occasion his manner to me too closely resembled that of a senior officer towards his subaltern. This ceased when I objected to his speaking to me 'like a British colonel'. He defused the situation by replying: 'Only a major actually, Dick.'

Inevitably, some difficulties arose because, although the edition was being edited in Sydney and printed in Adelaide, its production work, including the placing of photographs, was undertaken in Auckland, with Paul Bateman (Janet and David Bateman's son) as production manager. Today this would have been no problem at all; we would have edited entries on a computer and emailed the finished document to Auckland. But in 1987 the closest thing to modern technology we used in Petersham was the fax machine with which Mike had provided us. I was still using the manual typewriter I had bought for five dollars when Grolier closed down its Rose Bay offices, and Alex Galloway, who with Averil Moffatt was my associate editor, brought with him his own manual portable typewriter. The problems were further exacerbated because Paul Bateman could not spell.

Not being able to spell, though, had nothing to do with a fax that he sent me one Sunday afternoon as I was enjoying a wine with friends. 'Is the pope,' the fax asked, 'left-handed or right-handed?' Paul was uncertain whether or not he had 'flipped' the photograph of the pontiff taken on his visit to Sydney. Now flipped photos — that is, those printed from the wrong side — can be a problem. I have seen pictorial representations of the Sydney Opera House that placed it on the *north* side of the Sydney Harbour Bridge. About the pope I didn't know and, not surprisingly, at home I had no pictures of him. Across I walked to the Leichhardt shopping centre, where an Italian Catholic bookshop did have photos of the Polish pontiff. But obstinately, in all of them, he had kept his hands well within his copious sleeves. I faxed back to Paul: 'Don't know. Will check Monday. But surely anybody brought up in a Polish Catholic school in the 1930s *had* to be right-handed.'

Later, there was the problem of the index. Like George Robertson at Angus & Robertson earlier, when Arthur Jose was editor, Australian Geographic was pressing David Bateman and Mike White to finish the edition according to its schedule, not mine. And David and Mike were, perforce, pressing me. When Geographic's demands for the finally completed volumes became too strident to ignore, I had no choice but to make a most unprofessional compromise. By then, the only pages not completed were those of the index, though I, in turn, had been pressing the indexers to hurry. These pages I agreed to finalise myself in Auckland. This was the reason for my second, and prolonged, visit to that city. For two weeks Janet Bateman and I toiled over those pages, straining our eyes to decipher the eight-point typeface. An index, like the proverbial horse, is not easily amenable to changing riders in midstream.

With his usual flair for publicity, Dick Smith staged the launch of the fifth edition in the accessible section of Sydney's Tank Stream. All of us were provided with white hard-hats, with the words 'The Australian Encyclopaedia' stencilled incongruously in gold on their fronts. But John Ferguson managed to steal the show. In an impromptu but forceful speech he described in some detail how his family, the Robertson family (of Angus & Robertson), had been responsible for the very existence of the encyclopaedia. All that he claimed was factual, but Dick Smith did not appear pleased. This, no doubt, was understandable — not many of us would enjoy being upstaged at an event we had organised and paid for.

The delaunching (or drydocking) of the Criterion Hotel took place 'not with a bang but a whimper'. Expecting to make a night of it, many Push people turned up at the pub's doors for what was to have been its wake, only to find that those doors were locked and barred. Fortunately I was not there.

I am told that on a wall of the multi-storey building that supplanted the Criterion there is now, or was once, a plaque claiming that Germaine Greer, amongst others, used to drink there. I doubt that she did. But no doubt her rival warrior queen, 'Good Queen Bess', did not sleep in every bed that English tour promoters would have us believe she slept in. And the Germ did drink in a lot of Australian pubs.

25 Penultimatums

As well as Chicken's wake, one for Declan Affley took place at our Peter-sham house. Because, after the cremation, there appeared nowhere else for his friends to go, I invited them home. This turned out not to have been such a brilliant idea. Some of Declan's friends were definitely not *my* friends, and when this group began behaving belligerently I suggested that they leave and wake-on elsewhere. This prompted their red-bearded leader to punch my friend Jim Rule in the jaw, fracturing it. Why he elected to hit Jim, and not me, I'll never know, but having vented his disapproval he and his mates left, and the rest of us, once we had taken Jim to hospital, waked-on where we were.

When not hosting wakes, Barbara and I did manage some productive work at Petersham. During our time there, as well as the fifth edition of *The Australian Encyclopaedia*, we co-edited the *Macmillan Australia Children's Encyclopedia* (Macmillan Company of Australia, 1986) and I, for a time, continued editing *The Post* (official publication of the National Council of the Union of Postal Clerks and Telegraphists), work I had first taken on while at Marrickville. The children's encyclopaedia did not turn out *too* badly, but during its preparation I over-reacted to interference by the Macmillan publishing manager by sending her a letter which was sufficiently sarcastic to preclude Macmillan offering me work ever again. With Alex Galloway, I also co-edited *There Was a Crooked Man: The Poems of Lex Banning* (Angus & Robertson, 1987).

This book was a long time in the making. From the time of Lex's death in 1965, I had promised myself that I would collect and publish his work, but promises to oneself are rarely binding. After Lex and his wife, Anne, returned from England and then, shortly afterwards, separated,

Lex for a while continued to live in the Kings Cross flat that they had shared. When I visited him there, he showed me verse on which he was working, but he also complained of the green mould that was invading the flat. He tried to show me the mould, but unfortunately there was none, of any colour, to be seen, and Lex's physical and mental well-being were obviously in question. Not long after that he formed a relationship with Joy Anderson, and with her moved back to his mother's house at Punchbowl, in Sydney's south-west. It was there that he died.

When I was living in Katoomba my acquaintanceship with Joy Anderson resumed. Both of us were then commuting to work in Sydney, and on such railway journeys one either talks, reads or sleeps, and usually all three. Conversations with Joy inevitably touched on her life with Lex Banning, and she, from time to time, urged me to collect his work and publish it. At Katoomba, too, I had become a friend of Alex Galloway, then a leading figure in a local writers' group. By the time that Barbara and I were living in Petersham it was Alex who finally stirred me into belated action.

As a first step Alex and I approached Anne Banning for permission to publish, and for help in finding, Lex's poems: both were readily forthcoming, and in addition Anne gave us access to Lex's letters to her, all written before he departed to join her in England. Without what I learnt from these letters, my introductory 'Brief Biography' would have been sparse indeed.

Our next step was to find a publisher, and after the University of Queensland Press rejected our manuscript, I approached Richard Walsh, then serving as publisher for Angus & Robertson. Walsh knew and admired Lex's work, and after Alex and I had undertaken the revisions that Walsh requested in our prefatory sections, he accepted the manuscript for publication.

The launch of *There Was a Crooked Man*, which we organised at Sydney University, was attended by an unprecedented convocation of Push members and associates dating back to the years of the Lincoln Coffee Lounge. The main speakers at that launch were Rod Shaw, the publisher and craftsman printer who, with his partner Ron Edwards, had brought out Lex's *Apocalypse in Springtime*, and the poet Les Murray. Among those present were Graham Stone (then a librarian at the National Library of Australia), Brian Sproule and Don Della (both Macquarie Street medicos), Joy Anderson, Anne Banning, Black Judy (Judy Smith), Sylvia Lawson, Lyn Collingwood, Brian Slater, Royce Williams and Doug Nicholson. Alex Skovron, by then living in Melbourne, also attended. Almost all the copies of the book that were ever sold (at least at the full price) were sold at this gathering, because shortly after it had been published Richard Walsh resigned from Angus & Robertson and his successor promptly remaindered the unsold copies.

This was despite a generally favourable reception of the book by critics. In the Melbourne *Age*, Vincent Buckley wrote:

Appleton's brief 'biography', which introduces Banning's poems, is altogether admirable ... He does not skimp any of his friend's weaknesses or the social difficulties he sometimes created for his friends by his gratuitously sharp tongue; he stresses that 'Lex spoke with difficulty; and grimaced, spluttered and spat as he spoke' ... I knew Lex Banning for a mere three years, I suppose, but from the first regarded him as a friend ... It was he who introduced me to John Anderson, the philosopher, as well as a whole range of Sydney bohemians, anarchists and poets.[36]

In the *Weekend Australian*, R.F. Brissenden said of Banning's poetry:

And there is not much of it. If, as his editors claim, it 'constitutes an important part of Australia's literary heritage', it must be admitted that his reputation rests on a mere handful of poems. If he had a major talent (and I believe he did) he had a pitifully minor output ... His physical condition did not help, nor did the life he led, which involved an increasing amount of alcohol and, as Richard Appleton makes clear in his memoir, amphetamines. And the hard-drinking, puritanically libertine Sydney Push, while intellectually and socially supportive, did not (as I remember it) provide an atmosphere sympathetic or stimulating to the production of poetry.[37]

Finally, in the *Sydney Morning Herald*, Myfanwy Gollan argued:

> First, the editors ... must be congratulated, not only because they have made memorable poems more accessible, but because their introductory essays help record one of the lively intellectual groups which have always existed in Australia and, in spite of the view dominant until the 1960s, did not yearn for greener, northern-hemisphere fields.[38]

One reviewer, though, definitely disapproved of the book. I cannot remember the name of the journal for which she wrote and I have lost my copy of the review itself, but under the heading 'A New Book of Old Poems by a Dead Poet', she made her feelings clear. Having done so, she concluded by strongly objecting to the editors' republishing the works of 'an old drinking mate'. My impression was that she disliked 'old [male] drinking mates' far more than she disliked the poetry.

The most welcome response to the book, for me, was not any review but a note from my old Lincoln friend, John Olsen. In it he congratulated me on my 'very nice gesture' in preserving Banning's verse, and ordered additional copies. Earlier we had corresponded about his (Olsen's) entry in the fourth edition of *The Australian Encyclopaedia*. His reply and the accompanying sketch are reproduced overleaf.

Myff Gollan, in her review quoted above, praised *There Was a Crooked Man* because its introductory essays helped 'record one of the lively intellectual groups which have always existed in Australia'. To expand such a record is one of the main purposes of these recollections of mine. Now, perhaps, is the time for me to pontificate on that group, the Sydney (Libertarian) Push.

'The Old Rectory' CLARENDON. SA 5157
22. 9. 81.

Dear Dick,
    your July letter at last to hand
in SA.
        Yes we will have a lunch, I'm at
present living here & wont be up to the
bitch goddess Sydney until the end of October
for a book opening.
                    Regarding my entry
in the encyclopedia its not bad for a
generality
                    best wishes
                        John

* I've landed in the wine country. (Olsen)

Illustrated note from John Olsen to Dick Appleton, 1981.

In my first chapter I listed what I saw as the three main strands of Sydney Libertarianism. The first strand saw sexual liberty as a necessary precondition for political liberty. It can still be argued that it is a precondition, but given the 'sexual permissiveness' common to most Western societies today, it would be hard to contend that it is a sufficient condition. Still, if one liberty is curtailed, any other liberty can as readily be constrained.

The second strand was 'permanent protest'. That, surely, is even more relevant in this electronically intrusive age than it was in the 1950s. History, and especially twentieth-century history, makes it evident that any revolutionary political change leads inevitably to the creation of a highly authoritarian state. Hence revolution can be realistically supported only if an existent state is so objectionably authoritarian that violence may result in lowering the temperature of whatever hell one resides in. But that a revolutionary heaven is a myth does not mean that permanent opposition to, or permanent protest against, an existent state is pointless. To those 1950s Libertarians who, because of my membership of the Labor Party, labelled me a 'meliorist', I would quote again Max Nomad (see chapter 16):

> [Radicals] can fight back. They can achieve a reduction in the temperature of the hell in which the majority of the human race is fated to live only by fighting for more and more, now, of the good things of life ...

The third strand was pluralism. Today this is a much misused term, applied to virtually every parliamentary capitalist democracy. But democracies are based on the fallacious ideology that societies, or rather their members, have some basic real interest in common, and that the state defends this 'real interest'. This may well be true sometimes, briefly, for some societies, but a person's real interest, all the time, is what he or she is interested in at that time. It is paternalistic and authoritarian for the state, which has its own interests, to tell us what our 'real interests' are or should be. Pluralism consists of the recognition of different and frequently conflicting interests, both *within* and *between* societies.

The use of logic and of Andersonian realism was another basic tenet of Sydney Libertarianism. It was not always strictly followed. One well-known Libertarian was Darcy Waters, who, because of his obsessive punting, was burdened with the affectionate nickname 'The Horse'. Once, at the Royal George Hotel, I heard him singing softly to himself. What he chose to sing was a then popular ditty of which some lines went:

> Love and marriage, love and marriage,
> Go together like a horse and carriage.
> And this I tell you, brother,
> You can't have one, you can't have none,
> You can't have one without the other.

Obviously, The Horse did not believe in the truth of what he was singing. And judging by my own experiences, related in a previous chapter, with a horse by the name of Ongie, the horse mentioned in the song would have detested being harnessed to a carriage almost as much as The Horse would have detested having his sex-life restricted to 'connubial bliss'. Still, in his singing, though only in his singing, Darcy was not obliged to follow the precepts of Andersonian realism. But usually, at least outside the racecourse, he did. Darcy is now dead and realism decidedly unwell. A little more realism, and a little more logic, might well serve to leaven the dough of contemporary social and political discourse.

26 The Last Word

Cessnock is an almost mineless coalmining town in the Hunter Valley of New South Wales, about an hour's drive north-west of the city of Newcastle. While coalmines are few, the town's coalminers are many — consequently they face daily long drives to their places of work. It was not always so. Near the site of each and every former mine there is still now or once was a pub. Around that hub of social intercourse there gathered, in the past, distinct groups — Scottish, Welsh, Cornish or English. While those comprising the older descendants of those groups now speak with Australian accents, to some extent they tend to keep to those same groups, relating to them rather than to the town as a whole.

In recent years the wine country adjacent to the town has seen a tourist omnibus grind into gear, pushing up house prices as those working in the vineyard tourist traps seek somewhere to live. A mini-invasion of retirees from the Central Coast has added to that price push. Like Barbara and me, they are economic refugees, but when we moved to Cessnock prices had not yet risen. Despite a fairly hefty mortgage still owing on our Petersham place, our equity in it was sufficient to buy a house outright, and also a second-hand car. On our first night there Beth, our still very young daughter, complained to me, 'Dad, I want to go home.' Not surprisingly, I felt much the same.

When first I tried to socialise with the locals I felt that I was inhabiting some sort of time-warp. To start with, the accent most heard other than an Australian one was Scottish. The values of most of those with whom I yarned were those of the Sydneysiders of the 1940s. At a pub in my early days in the town, the bloke behind the bar declaimed: 'I'm no racist, but I can't stand slopes or boongs.' Yet that same bloke, when questioned about any particular Chinese or Aboriginal who lived locally, would reply: 'Oh, he's all right. It's just all the others.' Wogs were tolerated, but definitely not as equals, and an Indian restaurant that existed for a time in Cessnock's main street had its windows smashed night by night even more frequently than did other nearby businesses.

During the late 1940s and the 1950s those electorates made up of Cessnock and nearby coalmining and industrial centres commonly allocated about sixty per cent of their votes to the Labor Party and thirty per cent to the Communist Party. The Tories rarely bothered nominating a candidate. This was one factor that influenced me to move there. What legacy I now see from Cessnock's radical past is dominated by the respectability of the former Communist Party members rather than by their revolutionary fervour.

One afternoon, though, two members of the by then fast-fading Push managed to savour, briefly, a cosmopolitan aura in the town of Cessnock. Jean Curthoys and Alan Olding were staying for a day or so with Barbara and me, and as Jean and Barbara did not feel like pubbing, Alan and I decided to have drinks at my local watering place. While we were there, the only drinkers in the pub at that time, a mini-bus pulled up outside and out jumped our Federal member of parliament. 'What are you doing,' I asked him, 'bussing in voters?' 'No,' he responded, looking rather strained, 'I have the entire Belgian Cabinet to entertain, and I've decided to show them what a typical Australian country pub is like.' (It must have been a cold winter in Brussels.) What Alan talked to the Belgians about I cannot be sure, but I did hear the word 'Darwin', and Alan, though a philosopher by profession, had an abiding interest in biology and evolution. As for me, I ended up alongside the Belgian Ambassador. For lack of anything more interesting to say, I mentioned the Spanish Lowlands. Until then the ambassador's eyes had been glazed, from boredom, I assume, but they then visibly brightened, and he responded, 'So you know something about my country!'

I didn't, really, and the conversation moved on to the alleged superiority of Belgian beer. I can only hope that the Belgian Cabinet subsequently made no policy decisions based on their experiences in a typical Australian country pub.

Before moving from Sydney I had assumed that I would have no problems in securing editorial work no matter where I lived. I was wrong. Two factors made me so. The first was that those publishers and publishers' editors who in the past had given me work had since been promoted, had retired, or had been inconsiderate enough to die. Their successors did not know me. The second was the nuisance factor: to be consistently a nuisance, proximity is essential. From Cessnock, of which most publishers had never heard, I could not goad them regularly enough for work so that they would give me some just to shut me up. Only one long-term contract came into being as a result of my plethora of self-promoting circular letters, and one short-term contract.

The short-term contract was to write articles for *The Penguin Australian Encyclopaedia* (Penguin, 1990), edited by Sarah Dawson. To the best of my memory, entries I contributed included biographies, articles on primary and secondary industries, towns, natural geographical features and some on historical subjects. My general guidelines were to be concise, but amusing — a task rather difficult when writing about, say, the wheat industry — and on one occasion Sarah, with some justification, chided me for being facetious.

The long-term contract was to plan, compile and write, for Cambridge University Press, *The Cambridge Dictionary of Australian Places* (casebound edition, 1992; paperback edition, 1993). On this book I toiled at the written contents for two years, while Barbara, who was then still working full-time as a registered nurse, put together the drafts of the necessary maps. It was just as well that she was still working: Cambridge had given us an advance that, at a severe pinch, might have provided me with food, as well as more essential commodities such as wine and cigarettes, for one year. When we signed the contract I anticipated finishing the book in that time, but we didn't.

The length limit agreed to for the book was two hundred and fifty thousand words, and this limit curbed my endeavours to make it interesting as well as informative. (Though when a local drinker asked me how many pages my book was to be and I replied that I didn't know how many pages, but it would be a quarter of a million words, he looked stunned and responded, 'But that's a life's work!') Despite space limitations I did let myself go a little on the entry on the Queensland town and shire by the name of Nebo. Under that heading I wrote:

> **NEBO**, Qld (*nee*-boh), a shire ... and town ... to the south-west of MACKAY. Both presumably take their name from Mount Nebo, the Biblical mountain from which Moses surveyed 'the whole land, from Gilead to Dan; the whole of Naphtali; the territory of Ephraim and Manasseh, and all Judah as far as the western sea; the Negeb and the plain; the valley of Jericho, city of palm trees, as far as Zoar' (*Deuteronomy* 34: 1–2). The view from Queensland's Nebo is less extensive, but the town of GLENDEN is within the shire boundaries.

Also, in the article about the term 'Outback' I was able to write:

> [A] geographically indeterminate term applied to isolated regions in Australia's interior. It is indeterminate because, in most parts of Australia, it is used to refer to some place farther west (or north, south or east) than the place where the discussion is taking place.

Some of the entries are of interest without any artifice on my part to make them so. Examples include Coonamble, the name of which

> is derived from *gunambil*, a Kamilaroi Aboriginal term meaning 'full of shit'. A meaning previously given, 'bullock camp', was presumably a bowdlerisation, but it also indicates that the name 'Coonamble' was bestowed only after British settlers, and their livestock, arrived.

Similarly, the name Trangie, 'probably arising from conversations with Europeans, may be derived from a Ngiyambaa term meaning 'anal intercourse' (*thaara* = 'copulate with'; *ngii* = 'arse').'

A rough translation of that name might well be 'Go fuck yourself'. And if so, this echoes my own response to some of the euphemisms and nanny-state interventions in twenty-first-century social relationships. To drink in any pub or club today gives one the impression of revisiting a rooming house of the 1950s: every available patch of formerly bare wall is plastered with 'Thou shalt not' commandments. Fortunately, alongside such warnings there are frequently messages containing quite contrary advice. Among the many admonitions there intrudes the ubiquitous 'We do not have promotions or advertising which: encourage excessive drinking; encourage rapid drinking; unfairly target men or women'. How does a pub fairly (as opposed to unfairly) target men or women? What other species other than men or women could it target? And how much is 'excessive' and how fast 'rapid'?

In an ideal world, such incitements to 'responsible drinking' would be replaced by the words of a song, said to be 'English traditional' and recorded by Ewan MacColl on a Larrikin Records LP released in 1976. The LP's title is *No Tyme Like the Present* and the song itself is simply called 'Drinking'. Some of its lines go:

> ... I'll drink ...
> Till the dukes and the lords
> Have to sort clean from dirt
> And the big Prince of Wales
> Has to wash his own shirt.

> *Chorus:*
> For I mean to get jollywell drunk, I do,
> I mean to get jollywell drunk, I do,
> As long as I'm 'ere
> I'll stick to me beer
> For I mean to get jollywell drunk, I do.

I'll drink till all wealth
Is shared out amongst men,
And I'll drink and I'll drink
Till it's shared out again.

Chorus.

In nineteenth-century England the ruling class drew a sharp line between what they saw as the 'deserving poor' and the 'undeserving poor'. Any singer of this song would definitely have been consigned to the latter category. The same sharp line is back with us again, with moralistic governments legislating to create two classes of the unemployed.

And then there is the smoking ban. Outside the local (Cessnock) hospital there is a sign that reads: 'Our buildings and grounds are smoke-free. Thank you for your cooperation.' Below that sign there is another, that reads 'Butts' (at least it does not read 'Smokers Please'), and below that again an ashtray that every day is well supplied with butts by obliging smokers, be they patients or visitors.

Drinking and smoking, of course, are activities that many regard as 'sinful'. Consequently politicians feel that they can pass stringent regulations regarding them without losing votes. (How many decades did it take before State governments were game to abolish the six o'clock closing of pubs that began during World War I?) Other activities that, like drinking and smoking, may be harmful, and may or may not also have beneficial effects, are rarely subjected to similar regulations.

Euphemisms and 'Thou shalt not' admonitions are, of course, not confined to hostelries and hospitals. The word 'gender', I was informed by those who taught me Latin and French at school, had nothing to do with sex. This was in response to lewd smirks by pubescent and inky-fingered schoolboys. Not so now, apparently: instead, 'gender' has largely replaced 'sex' in all discussions comparing male and female differences and the ensuing disputes. The word 'sex' is not banned, of course: to the contrary it can be used as a verb (nobody ever accuses the government of *gendering up* security advice); 'sexy' as an adjective is also popular, but only if it does not refer in any way to tits or bums, or, for that matter, to vaginas or penises.

Similarly words like 'short', 'tall', 'blind', 'deaf', 'cripple', 'mad' and 'half-wit' (or 'less than the full quid') have been inscribed on today's equivalent of the Papal Index. It has been found necessary to replace such words with much longer, and preferably meaningless, alternatives. But 'visually impaired as a bat' somehow lacks clout, and the only blind man I know personally insists on being called just that.

And finally, would the Orthodox churches please reclaim for their own exclusive use the word 'icon'.

In this litany of complaints about the nanny-state and the age of euphemisms I have, I suppose, nailed my colours to the mast. Though nails *do* rust. With this in mind it is probably appropriate for me to conclude with the last poem of any merit that I have written. Initially, for lack of a better title, I used the poem's first two words for that purpose, but after learning that Clive James had pronounced me dead I changed the title to that of this chapter, 'The Last Word'.[39]

> Coming home, or perhaps not,
> but to where age rots reason
> (age and wine),
> why does the world shrink
> to a treason of shadows?
>
> Is it true that once,
> in a less discordant world,
> words were well spent
> (Or were they squandered?)
> spelling out doubts in speculation?

Or were the doubts themselves
soft self-persuasion?
Or doesn't it matter now
what the delusion?

Words will be last to go
— long after reason.

One parting thought, though. After Barbara and I finished writing *The Cambridge Dictionary of Australian Places* I approached Ken Shadbolt, whom I had known when he was a young student but who was by then a New South Wales judge. The book, I thought, might have been of use to trial barristers. It wasn't, Ken told me, but after that the conversation got around to the subject of respectability and whether a judge needed to take care with what company he kept. 'Appo,' Ken announced, 'you are one of the most respectable people I know.'

Where had I gone wrong?

Notes

[1] Clive James, *As of This Writing: The Essential Essays, 1968–2002*, W.W. Norton & Company, New York, 2003, pp. 133–4.

[2] Quoted from John Anderson, 'Art and Morality', republished in D.Z. Phillips (ed.), *Education and Inquiry*, Basil Blackwell, Oxford, 1980.

[3] A.J. Baker, 'Libertarianism, Sydney', in Richard Appleton (ed.), *The Australian Encyclopaedia*, 1988 edn, vol. 5.

[4] D.J. Ivison, 'Futilitarianism — A Libertarian Dilemma?', in *Libertarian*, no. 3, January 1960.

[5] Sir Charles Belcher (1876–1970) was an eminent colonial judge, ornithologist and author.

[6] Harry Hooton, *It Is Great to Be Alive*, Century Art Group, 1962.

[7] Terence McMullen, 'An Anarchist Dictator', in Les Murray and Geoff Lehmann (eds), *Hermes 1962*, magazine of the University of Sydney.

[8] From Richard Appleton and Alex Galloway (eds), *There Was a Crooked Man*, Angus & Robertson, Sydney, 1987.

[9] From Lex Banning, *Apocalypse in Springtime*, Edwards and Shaw, Sydney, 1956.

[10] Isaac Deutscher, *The Prophet Armed*, Oxford University Press, 1970, pp. 299–314.

[11] The Red Dean, so called because of his pro-Soviet views, was Hewlett Johnson (1874–1966); the conference was held in April 1950.

[12] 'At the Sign of the Golden Cabbage' was published in *Quadrant*, no. 393 (vol. XLVII, no. 1), January–February 2003, p. 59.

[13] A.J. Baker, '1951: The first Libertarian Society, Libertarians and John Anderson', in *Heraclitus*, no. 89, July 2001.

[14] Anne Coombs, *Sex and Anarchy: The Life and Death of the Sydney Push*, Penguin, Melbourne, 1996, p. 40.

[15] Ibid., p. 48.

[16] Ibid., p. 302.

[17] *The European*, no. 14, April 1954, p. 57.

[18] Trevor Lucas performs on several LPs, some with the group The Fairport Convention. He died in 1989.

[19] The Vanity Fair, too, was used by some of the Push until about 1969. (Anne Coombs, op.cit., p. 234.)

[20] Anne Coombs, op cit., p. 143.

[21] John Penfold in *The Australian Highway*, journal of the Workers' Educational Association, winter 1965, pp. 30–31.

[22] Stephen Knight, ibid., pp. 31–2.

[23] Jenny Anderson, Graham Cullum and Kimon Lycos (eds), *Art & Reality: John Anderson on Literature and Aesthetics*, Hale & Iremonger, 1982.

[24] Kylie Tennant, *Evatt: Politics and Justice*, Angus & Robertson, 1970, p. 188.

[25] *Parliamentary Debates*, vol. 191, 23 April 1947, p. 1509.

[26] Ibid.

[27] From a series of interviews in 1987 with Eric Dark at his home, by Enid Schafer for the Blue Mountains City Library.

[28] At the 2008 NSW State Conference of the ALP, Richard Appleton was posthumously given a Life Membership Award for his contribution 'to the local branches and the Party at large'. Ross Free, by then a former Federal minister, officially supported the nomination.

[29] In 2007, Bob Debus gained preselection for the Federal seat of Macquarie, and upon winning the seat at that year's election was appointed Minister for Home Affairs by the new Rudd Labor government. He held the portfolio until 2009, when he resigned following his decision to retire at the end of his term.

[30] Anthony Barker, *George Robertson: A Publishing Life in Letters*, Angus & Robertson, 1982; University of Queensland Press, 1993, pp. 180–81.

[31] Quoted in Barker, ibid., p. 8.

[32] From 'The Hippopotamus' by T.S. Eliot, in *The Complete Poems and Plays of T.S. Eliot*, Faber and Faber, London, 1969; reprinted 1970 and 1973.

[33] For this indexing job, Fisher was awarded the inaugural Medal of the Australian Society of Indexers.

[34] A reference to a much-reported incident in 1986 when the former prime minister, then chairman of the Commonwealth Eminent Persons Group, appeared in the foyer of his Memphis hotel wearing only a towel and searching for his trousers, which had disappeared overnight.

[35] David J. Jones, in*Cite*, Library Association of Australia, 9 December 1988.

[36] *Age*, 27 June 1987.

[37] *Weekend Australian*, 16–17 May 1987.

[38] *Sydney Morning Herald*, 16 May 1987.

[39] The poem was published under the title 'Coming Home' in *Quadrant*, no. 357 (vol. XLIII, no. 6), June 1999, p. 19.

Index

There is no index entry for the author of this book. Aspects of his life are indexed directly under their own topics. The abbreviation RA = Richard Appleton ('Appo'). People who are identified in the text only by given names or nicknames are indexed under those given names or nicknames.

Page numbers in bold type, e.g. **158–70**, indicate the most detailed discussion of the topic. Bold numerals within square brackets, e.g. **[12]**, refer to the numbered photographs that appear between pages 148 and 149.